'Packed with memorable tales [and] scores of unfamiliar gems... enjoyably confirms the truth of its opening declaration that 'The past three centuries of British politics is, in no small part, a story of sippers, swiggers and bon viveurs''  *Spectator*

'A sobering and entertaining history of politics and alcohol'
*Daily Mail* Books of the Year

'Life in Westminster can be lonely, especially for those pols from farther afield, and Wright doesn't gloss over the fact that behind many diverting anecdotes lie crippling hangovers and destructive behaviour. Well researched and breezily told, Wright's book is an enjoyable romp through the properly lubricated halls of British political power'  *New Criterion*, Editors' choice

'A thoroughly enjoyable, comprehensive book' Harry Mount, *TLS*

'A fascinating account of politics and drink... informative and entertaining'  Alastair Campbell

'A fascinating read'  *Camden Review*

'A book that is essentially a history of political drinking... could turn out to be a wet weekend of nothing more than drunken anecdotes or a dry cautionary tale on the dangers of drinking. Wright... hits the sweet spot between the two brilliantly'
*Boney Abroad*

'A witty and well informed insight into one of Britain's longest standing political traditions'  *Chris Hallam's World View*

© Jeff Overs

Ben Wright has been a political correspondent for the BBC since 2008. He appears regularly on BBC News, and on BBC radio programmes including *Today* and the *World at One*. Ben has previously worked as a correspondent in Washington and Brussels. He lives in London.

# ORDER, ORDER!

## *The Rise and Fall of Political Drinking*

### Ben Wright

**Duckworth Overlook**

First published in 2016 by Duckwork Overlook

This edition first published in 2017

LONDON
30 Calvin Street, London E1 6NW
T: 020 7490 7300
E: info@duckworth-publishers.co.uk
www.ducknet.co.uk
For bulk and special sales please contact sales@duckworth-publishers.co.uk

9780715651858

1 3 5 7 9 10 8 6 4 2

**To Poppy**

'I have taken more out of alcohol than alcohol has taken out of me.'

Winston Churchill

# CONTENTS

# Contents

# Contents

# LIST OF ILLUSTRATIONS

# ILLUSTRATION CREDITS

# INTRODUCTION

In his memoir, Tony Blair confessed that his evenings in Downing Street were accompanied by a stiff G&T and half a bottle of wine. Although he thought, rightly, that his drinking was modest by historic standards, he nevertheless worried that it had become a 'prop'. He also knew that his own rise to the top of the Labour Party had happened because of the sudden and early death of his predecessor, John Smith, who had been a serious drinker.

It was claimed, too, that the fall of Mrs Thatcher at the hands of her own party could be attributed, at least in small part, to the fact that the Conservative MP running her re-election campaign was sozzled. Then there was the sad fate of Charles Kennedy, the talented and engaging leader of the Liberal Democrats, whose alcoholism had brought him down (and was to end his life).

It was all this that started me thinking about the role of alcohol in politics; and whether there was a story to be told about it. I soon discovered that there was. It is a story full of remarkable characters and extraordinary events. There is much that is amusing, but also much that is disturbing. As a political reporter working in Westminster, I knew that alcohol had long lubricated political life (including for journalists), but I wanted to explore how its role had changed over time. It soon became clear that Blair's concern about alcoholic over-indulgence would not have impressed the dedicated political drinkers of the past.

These have included Winston Churchill, of course, a whisky and soda always close at hand. And his wartime Minister of Labour, Ernest Bevin, who was said to use alcohol in the way a car uses petrol. Herbert Asquith's fondness for a drink earned him the soubriquet 'Squiff' and shortened his tenure in Downing Street at the start of the First World War. Several Prime Ministers drank more the longer they stayed in office. In fact, alcohol threads its way through the political past, bridging time and place.

When Labour MP Clare Short caused uproar in the House of Commons by accusing the Tory minister (and diarist) Alan Clark of having such slurred speech that he was clearly drunk in charge of a dispatch box, she was not the first politician to make this charge against a political rival. Two thousand years earlier, the Roman statesman Cicero launched a ferocious attack on his political enemy, Mark Antony, claiming that he had been incapacitated by drink at a meeting of the senate: 'At an assembly of the Roman people … when it would be disgraceful for a man even to burp – he was sick! And he filled his own lap and the whole tribunal with scraps of undigested food reeking of wine.'[1] Before Cicero's time, the Greeks believed wisdom flowed from wine and upper-class men would assemble in symposiums for drinking and discussion. Alcohol has lubricated politics ever since.

It is largely a British story that is told here, but alcohol is woven through the history of international politics too. Joseph Stalin flushed out traitors with vodka. Franklin Roosevelt's evening ritual was to mix martinis for friends on the Oval

Office desk. The two leaders carved up post-war Europe during alcohol-fuelled dinners with Churchill at Yalta. The disintegration of both Richard Nixon and Boris Yeltsin was largely down to drink. Whether in Britain or abroad, alcohol is a bridge between the politicians of the past and those of today. It enhances the exhilaration of political success and numbs its disappointments. It unknots in moderation and unbalances in excess.

For politicians under pressure and burdened by difficult choices, alcohol can be a seductive friend. Tony Blair was not the first political leader to agonise about its power and wonder whether the upsides outweighed the downsides. In the early years of the Mughal empire, alcohol was widely enjoyed by its Muslim rulers. Babur, the empire's founder, created a dynasty that stretched from Afghanistan to southern India. A warrior, poet and writer, he produced a remarkably candid and colourful autobiography that includes several paeans to the pleasures of alcohol and drinking parties. But in 1527, on the eve of a major battle for the future of India, Babur made a vow to give up drink, smashing all his goblets and destroying his stocks of wine, a decision he soon regretted. By February 1529 he was having second thoughts, writing in a letter:

> Through renouncement of wine bewildered am I;
> How to work know I not, so distracted am I;
> While others repent and make vow to abstain,
> I have vowed to abstain, and repentant am I.[2]

In part at least, it is through his soul-searching over alcohol that Babur is brought to life and becomes a person we can recognise half a millennium later. The hope is that this will also be the case with the people who appear in this book, revealing something of the personalities of politicians known otherwise only for their public lives and political actions.

Of course, this is an incomplete story. In giving attention to the political drinkers, it neglects both the teetotallers (except as noises off) and the moderate imbibers. This is like telling the story of motoring only through the antics of dangerous drivers, ignoring those who kept assiduously to the speed limits. Alcohol is a discriminating political lens, though not a distorting one. It is also a depressingly male story of chaps drinking with chaps. Apart from such rare exceptions as Margaret Thatcher, this glimpse into the drinking habits of politicians is a reminder of how far politics has been dominated by men. Yet when politicians fret about the drinking habits of the public, it is usually women – whether in Gin Lane or Binge-Drinking Britain – about whom they panic most.

There are politicians who drank with epic enthusiasm and are remembered for adding to the vitality and gaiety of parliamentary life. There are others, including some of the same ones, who drank too much and died too young. Some had a capacity for consuming large amounts of alcohol without any noticeable damage to their performance as politicians, while for others even a small amount produced unfortunate consequences for their behaviour. Some drinkers reached the political heights, while others are the forgotten casualties of Westminster life who turned to alcohol to relieve loneliness, boredom and frustration.

When Charles Kennedy died in June 2015, a searchlight was briefly cast across Westminster. Why did Kennedy drink? Was there something about politics that made its practitioners more susceptible to the bottle? Were the abundant bars of the Palace of Westminster somehow to blame? Did Kennedy's drink problem and our attitude to it mirror Britain's relationship with alcohol? In the days after his death such questions swilled around in the press.

When preparing this book, I had planned to write to Charles Kennedy to ask if I might talk to him. I wanted to ask him why he drank and whether the pressures of political life had pushed him towards the bottle. But I hesitated for months, wary of causing offence, and then it was too late. Yet the questions remain.

Simply telling a ribald story about the antics of drunken politicians, of which there are many examples in this book, would not be complete if it did not also recognise that alcohol has ruined the lives and families of many politicians, just as it has ruined the lives of others. While many can safely navigate their way through the bars, receptions and trays of free drinks, others clearly cannot. The enduringly seductive power of alcohol was memorably described in the celebrated 1902 lectures by the Harvard psychologist and philosopher, William James:

> The sway of alcohol over mankind is unquestionably due to its power to stimulate the mystical faculties of human nature, usually crushed to earth by the cold facts and dry criticisms of the sober hour. Sobriety diminishes, discriminates, and says no; drunkenness expands, unites, and says yes. It is in fact the great exciter of the Yes function in man. It brings its votary from the chill periphery of things to the radiant core. It makes him for the moment one with truth. Not through mere perversity do men run after it.[3]

Politicians have certainly run after it, as this book will show. Perhaps there is something about the activity of politics that has made alcohol particularly attractive to its practitioners. It breaks the ice, oils the wheels, enlivens conversation, perks one up, boosts one's confidence (even if falsely) and provides a shortcut to camaraderie. All this matters in politics. But it can also depress and deaden, leading to a dangerous dependency and making people a liability both to themselves and to others. Perhaps this, along with a growing concern for their livers, is one reason why today's politicians have started to sober up. Only Charles Kennedy knew why he drank and I never had the courage to ask him. But I hope this canter around political drinking might throw some light on why so many of us reach for a bottle, whether we are in politics or not.

# CHAPTER 1

## Government under the Influence

Before Twitter, television, universal suffrage and party discipline, Britain's leading politicians were free to drink with impunity. Spared the scrutiny of the press and the opprobrium of voters, government ministers could drift through their days in a state of inebriation. In Georgian Britain, politicians flaunted themselves in drunken revelry while bribing voters with alcohol. Political drinking today is very tame by comparison. Now a brawl in a parliamentary bar leads to tabloid scorn and resignation. Campaigning party leaders pose with pints for the cameras but their glass is merely a prop, a symbol that they have something in common with voters.

The past three centuries of British politics is, in no small part, a story of sippers, swiggers and bon viveurs; political sybarites who enjoyed the pleasing effects of a good drink. It is a story of political casualties too, such as the former Labour Foreign Secretary George Brown, who Harold Wilson thought brilliant in the job until four o'clock in the afternoon. It is also a story of change. In the 1970s, the drinks cabinet was still a crucial piece of Whitehall furniture and its spirits used to oil the cogs of government. But the days when senior politicians could drink themselves into oblivion while they held high office were coming to an end. Ministers became more wary about trying to do the job half-cut and they started to sober up. Today's most prominent politicians are practically teetotal compared to the dissolute rakes of the eighteenth century.

## Three-Bottle Men

There was a time when privileged young men dressed in bow ties and tails shamelessly paraded their wealth in rituals of frivolous debauchery. These men were members of secret dining societies and clubs such as White's and became the most prominent politicians in Britain. But the political ancestors of David Cameron and George Osborne felt no need to airbrush away their antics to placate the press or public opinion. In the eighteenth century, excessive drinking, gambling and carousing with cronies in Pall Mall clubs did not stop if a gentleman went into politics. As London's poor destroyed themselves with gin, the leading statesmen of Georgian England played their own part in this era of huge alcohol consumption.

One of the most extravagant politicians of the time was Sir Francis Dashwood, who became Chancellor of the Exchequer in 1762. A lecherous rake with a riotous private life, the aristocratic Dashwood founded the Society of Dilettanti in 1732 after spending time cavorting around Europe. The stated qualification to join Dashwood's new society was having been to Italy, but Horace Walpole, a Whig MP and son of the first Prime Minister, Sir Robert Walpole, said the real test was being drunk.[1] But it was for founding a hell-fire club in a ruined Cistercian abbey near his home in West Wycombe in Buckinghamshire that Dashwood is remembered. He had rented Medmenham Abbey since the 1740s and there, according to various accounts, he presided over an orgiastic, drunken, debauched cult dedicated to reviving the decadence of the original hell-fire clubs.

The Brotherhood of the Knights of St Francis met at Medmenham on Wednesdays and Saturdays between June and October. Because the Commons was in recess, this was handy for the many MPs who were members. Lord Sandwich, the First Lord of the Admiralty, was one of the 'brothers', as was Thomas Potter, the Paymaster General. Other MPs who went included Sir William Stanhope, John Tucker, Sir John Aubrey, John Martin, Richard Hopkins and John Wilkes.[2] The Earl of Bute was the only Prime Minister who is believed to have belonged to the Brotherhood.

The extent of their debauchery has long been disputed by historians. For instance, it is questionable whether the brothers actually did drink wine out of a human skull or administer the sacrament to a baboon. However, there is plenty of evidence that Sir Francis Dashwood and his friends enjoyed dressing up as monks and seducing the masked 'nuns', who may have included the wives and sisters of members as well as prostitutes recruited from London brothels. By flickering candlelight they frolicked in the caves that Dashwood had excavated, holding elaborate rituals and ceremonies fuelled by the contents of Medmenham Abbey's vast cellar. As one historian says: 'Grave statesmen would not have indulged in this outrageous behaviour without copious libations.' Horace Walpole wrote that 'Bacchus and Venus were the deities to whom they almost publicly sacrificed', and the cellar accounts of the club, some of which survive, suggest deep toping.[3] The brothers left gin drinking to the poor; claret and port were their drinks of choice, although the wine books also list calcavella, hock and Dorchester beer. When Sir Francis Dashwood died in 1781 there was £6,000 worth of wine in the abbey's cellar, the equivalent to £900,000 today.[4]

Artists such as Knapton and Hogarth portrayed Dashwood as a debauched drunkard, but that did not stop him being made Chancellor by the Earl of Bute. It was a dreadful choice and Dashwood survived only a year in the job. He presented the first Budget to follow the Seven Years' War but his confused statement was listened to with derision in the House of Commons. According to Horace Walpole, he 'performed so awkwardly, with so little intelligence or clearness, in so vulgar a tone and in such mean language, that he, who had been esteemed a plain country gentleman of good sense, said himself afterward: "People will point at me, and cry: There goes the worst Chancellor of the Exchequer that ever appeared!"'[5] His Budget also caused popular uproar because it put up taxes on cider, the staple drink of rural England.

By now, salacious stories about the revelry at West Wycombe were beginning to circulate and the fantasy world Dashwood had created quickly crumbled. But the hard drinking indulged in by Dashwood and the brothers was of its time. It was an age of indulgence, conversational conviviality and gout, in which government ministers thought nothing of drinking until dawn. Many were known as 'three-bottle men', a reference to how much booze they could consume in a single session. They led lives of reckless extravagance, none more so than Charles James Fox, the most prominent Whig of the late 1700s. His drunkenness was on such a scale that it was commented on in the press and caricatured in cartoons.[6] This at a time when Britain had lost its colony in North America and revolution in France was provoking political turmoil in Westminster.

For much of the eighteenth century the state had been good at raising taxes and borrowing money to fight wars but little else. But Parliament's importance had grown steadily and by the 1770s the words of MPs in the Commons were beginning to be relayed through the press to the public, with great orators like Fox and Edmund Burke the lead actors in the House of Commons theatre. In a letter written to his wife in January 1788, the MP Sir Gilbert Elliot captures the drinking habits of the late eighteenth century's star politicians:

> The men of all ages drink abominably. How the men of business and the great orators of the House of Commons, contrive to reconcile it with their public exertions I cannot conceive. Fox drinks what I should call a great deal, though he is not reckoned to do so by his companions, Sheridan excessively, and Grey more than any of them; but it is a much more gentleman-like way than our Scottish drunkards, and is always accompanied with clever lively conversations on subjects of importance. Pitt, I am told, drinks as much as anybody.[7]

But Fox did not care how his gambling, womanising and drinking was judged by people outside Westminster, and inside Parliament he was in good company. One of his great friends was the Whig playwright, theatre impresario and politician Richard Sheridan, another hearty drinker. His biographer, Thomas Moore, said that Sheridan drank for inspiration: 'If the thought (he would say) is slow to come, a glass of good wine encourages it, and when it does come, a glass of good wine rewards it.'[8]

Sheridan was a close adviser to the Prince of Wales and held a number of ministerial jobs. Another of his biographers, Oscar Sherwin, describes the drinks consumed by these colourful Cabinet ministers:

The business of Great Britain is transacted over oceans of liquor and continents of food … Fox champagne and burgundy; Sheridan, first claret, then port, latterly rack-punch, hot negus, brandy, and eventually back to port again. Wilkes alone drinks hock, and Burke, who begins with a modicum of claret, ends by copious draughts of hot water, though in earlier days he once assured the Speaker, 'I am not well. I eat too much, I drink too much, and I sleep very little.'[9]

To the Liberal MP and Cabinet minister George Trevelyan, looking back from the more puritanical Victorian period a hundred years later, it was a wonder that any of them could function properly in office:

A statesman of the Georgian era was sailing on a sea of claret from one comfortable official haven to another, at a period of life when a political apprentice in the reign of Victoria is not yet out of his indentures. No one can study the public or personal history of the eighteenth century without being impressed by the truly immense space which drinking occupied in the mental horizon of the young, and the consequences of drinking in that of the old.[10]

At this time, and into the nineteenth century, alcohol played a crucial role in parliamentary elections too. The eighteenth century saw party labels start to harden and constituency elections become much more vigorously fought. Of course, before the Reform Act of 1832 the electorate was tiny (and it remained only a little less so afterwards). There were different property requirements between voters in counties and boroughs; and the rotten and pocket boroughs returned MPs to Parliament despite having few or no electors, while seats were often passed from one member of a family to another. Voting was done in public and newer towns had no representation at all.

This ramshackle system was wide open to corruption and, irrespective of party label, it was beer that candidates used to bribe constituents. An example is the election of Jacob Houblon, a Tory MP for Colchester and a close relation of the first governor of the Bank of England. The *Daily Gazetteer* newspaper described his nomination on 14 September 1736: 'Most of the gentlemen within 15 or 20 miles of Mr Houblon's seat in Essex were present, and most of the common people within 4 or 5 miles were made so welcome that they lay in heaps round his house dead drunk.'

Even those ineligible to vote would have attended the public nomination ceremony, a riotous fixture of election-eering that survived until the late nineteenth century. Rival candidates were obliged to attend open-air meetings of their constituents and address the crowd, who often pelted their prospective MPs with mud, rotten food and dead animals. Their nominations would then be confirmed with a show of hands, after which there would be a formal poll limited to those allowed to vote. That process could grind on for ages and in 1785 the vote was restricted to a maximum of fifteen days. As Jon Lawrence writes, through these long elections 'beer would have flowed freely and even the humblest freeman voter would have been conscious of holding the fate of his master in his hand'.[11]

It proved a miserable experience for Richard Meyler, a young dandy with a huge inheritance to squander. He stood successfully for Winchester in 1812 but a letter to his lover reveals the alcohol-soaked ordeal of the campaign:

> I had not the smallest idea that it was necessary to kiss so many dirty ugly women and drink so much ale, rum and milk, grog, raisin and elder wine, with porter and cider, all in one day, otherwise I don't think I would have gone into Parliament; for I have been sick for a fortnight, and then, in this wretched state of stomach, one must get up, and make a speech to one's constituents, full of lies, about future protection, friendship and God knows what.[12]

Meyler was chums with Beau Brummell, but later denounced him after the famous fop failed to honour his gambling debts at White's. Despite the drinking misery he endured to win his seat, Meyler died young at twenty-six, falling off his horse during a hunt.

Not only were elections awash with drink but alehouses were used as candidates' headquarters and polling stations, providing a convenient way to top up wavering voters. In 1755 the artist and satirist William Hogarth published the first in a series of four paintings inspired by the infamous contest for the County of Oxford seat in the 1754 general election. The constituency had sent two Tories to Parliament in uncontested elections since 1710. But two years before the 1754 election the Duke of Marlborough (Blenheim Palace resident and vehement Whig) decided to fight the seat and field two candidates, one for the County and one for the City. There followed an epic campaign of bribery, inducements, meetings, dinners, feasts, fights and boozing. The press picked up on the raucous antics in Oxford and gave Hogarth the material for his series (which can be seen at Sir John Soane's Museum in London).

The first scene, 'An Election Entertainment', encapsulates the mood of bawdy, drunken corruption. The setting is a room within a pub in the aptly named Guzzletown. The pub has been hired by a candidate as his headquarters and at two chaotic tables voters are being bribed with money, oysters, plates of lobsters, chops and gallons of drink. Upturned bottles are strewn across the table, while a boy in the foreground pours brandy into a huge tub of punch. While a mob of rival supporters riot outside and a brick is thrown through the window, a decrepit-looking man who has fought with the gang is slumped on the floor drinking gin while his friend pours alcohol onto his wounded head. Around the table, gentlemen of refined appearance rub shoulders with the poor and old, tradesmen and clergymen, and many raise a grateful toast to the free drink.

In the second of the series, 'Canvassing for Votes', the setting is a village street containing three pubs, the Royal

Oak, the Crown and the Portobello. The inns are being hired by the parties and outside the Royal Oak the landlady counts her golden coins. In the middle of the road a young farmer is being courted by a Whig waiter from the Crown and the Tory innkeeper from the Royal Oak, both of whom drop money into his hands and thrust dinner invitations at him. After the bribery and blandishments of the campaign, the next two paintings in the series depict the poll and its aftermath as the conquering Tory candidate is paraded through the town in a chaotic, rowdy procession. Barrels of beer have been placed along the street in case anyone was sobering up, and one man has his head wedged in an upturned keg, slurping out the last drops. Hogarth's paintings capture both the principle-free corruption of the election candidates and the craven bribe-pocketing greed of voters. Above all, they demonstrate how central alcohol was to the theatre of Georgian elections.

Drink-sodden electioneering continued into the nineteenth century. When Mr Pickwick and his friends arrive in the fictitious constituency of Eatanswill they find a town punch-drunk with election fever. The competing parties – the Blues and the Buffs – have rival mobs of noisy supporters, and Charles Dickens describes the hullabaloo of a campaign full of frenzied skulduggery. The Blues and Buffs seem to have no political principles beyond opposing every-thing the other party supports. Newspapers, shops, pubs and the pews in church are divided between the two tribes. Mr Pickwick's first stop is the Town Arms Inn, where the Blue candidate Samuel Slumkey holds meetings every day. His agent, Mr Perker, tells Pickwick that the rival Buff campaign has locked thirty-three of its voters up in the White Hart pub. 'They keep 'em locked up there, till they want 'em. The effect of that is, you see, to prevent our getting at them,' Mr Perker explains. 'And even if we could, it would be of no use, for they keep them very drunk on purpose,' he says with a nod of admiration to his rival.[13]

Some voters are bribed with free parasols; others are dumped in a canal. But it is drink that dominates Mr Pickwick's account of the election. Free beer is poured down the throats of prospective supporters until they collapse. The barmaid at the Town Arms is bribed to spike the brandy of fourteen voters, sending them to sleep until after the poll. Surveying the scene as Eatanswill votes, Dickens' satire evokes the drunken exuberance of reform-era electioneering:

> During the whole time of the polling, the town was in a perpetual fever of excitement. Everything was conducted on the most liberal and delightful scale. Exciseable articles were remarkable cheap at all the public-houses; and spring vans paraded the streets for the accommodation of voters who were seized with any temporary dizziness in the head – an epidemic which prevailed among the electors, during the contest, to a most alarming extent, and under the influence of which they might frequently be seen lying on the pavements in a state of utter insensibility.[14]

The worst election abuses were outlawed in the 1832 Reform Act, which introduced a uniform property franchise in boroughs, created sixty-seven new constituencies and scrapped the 'rotten' seats. Subsequent reforms not only extended the franchise further but also started to clean up elections. The secret ballot was introduced in 1872 and the

1883 Corrupt Practices Act banned parliamentary candidates from treating voters to drinks at the bar in return for their vote. It also made it an offence for an elector to receive such a bribe.

Edwardian writers reported that free or heavily subsidised beer still sloshed around constituencies at election time and claimed that pub landlords bragged they could mobilise large blocs of votes.[15] But elections that doubled as riotous drunken carnivals had gone by the time of the First World War.

## Old Beaujolais

However, serious ministerial drinking continued into the twentieth century. When government was small and ministers had little to manage, then perhaps it did not matter greatly if they conducted their business through an alcoholic haze. It mattered more when, during the twentieth century, government vastly extended its responsibilities and ministers presided over huge departments. During the Second World War many government ministers ran their departments with a drink close to hand. Even leaving Churchill out of the picture, at least for the moment, other examples make the point. Perhaps the best is provided by Ernest Bevin, the second most important man in Churchill's wartime government, who as Minister of Labour had the job of mobilising Britain. In 1940 J.B. Priestley described Bevin as a 'powerful, thick-set, determined figure of a man, a fine lump of England which we all love; one of those men who stand up among the cowardices and treacheries and corruption of this recent world like an oak tree in a swamp'.[16] Before the war Bevin had been the leading trade union figure of his generation and after the war he was the driving force behind NATO, insisting that Britain should have the atomic bomb because he was not going to have the country 'barged about'.

One of the most formidable politicians of the twentieth century, Bevin had a gigantic ego and colossal stamina. He was also an epic drinker. As his biographer Alan Bullock wrote:

> When he was under pressure, Bevin drank a lot – whisky, champagne, brandy, whatever was to hand. He used alcohol, one of his secretaries said, like a car uses petrol, to keep himself going, and he and his doctor (who certainly watered his whisky) had a running fight on the subject, not least because the effect of drink was to make him truculent.[17]

Bevin's health eventually disintegrated and he died in 1951 aged seventy.

For the next forty years, it was common for government ministers to continue to drink heavily. But politicians grew increasingly prickly about any suggestion of over-indulgence. The libel lawyers were always ready to pounce, as they did in 1957 when the *Spectator* magazine published a mischievously comic account of the twenty-third annual congress of the Italian Socialist Party held in Venice. The gathering was attended by three prominent Labour Party politicians from Britain: the former health minister Aneurin Bevan, the party's general secretary Morgan Phillips and the future Cabinet minister and diarist Richard Crossman. The *Spectator* piece was written by a political journalist, Jenny

Nicholson, and headlined 'Death in Venice'. Nicholson said that during their occasional appearances, Bevan, Phillips and Crossman

> puzzled the Italians by their capacity to fill themselves like tanks with whisky and coffee, while they (because of their livers and also because they are abstemious by nature) were keeping going on mineral water and an occasional coffee. Although the Italians were never sure the British delegation was sober, they always attributed to them an immense political acumen.[18]

The article did not say the men were drunk, but that was the clear inference.

Within days of its appearance, the *Spectator* received a complaint of serious libel from the men's lawyers. After the complainants failed to agree an acceptable form of apology with the *Spectator*, the case went to court; and all three men swore on oath that they had been sober and denied the accusation of drunkenness. The jury took just twenty-eight minutes to agree with them. The judge, Lord Goddard, the Lord Chief Justice, awarded Crossman, Bevan and Phillips a hefty £2,500 each in damages from the *Spectator* – a huge sum at the time – plus the £4,000 costs of the two-day hearing.

The case has been argued about ever since. Were the three men drunk? Did they commit perjury in order to pocket a substantial sum of money? According to Richard Crossman's biographer, Anthony Howard, the Labour MP had never intended to go to court. In part this was because he had worked as a journalist himself, but mainly it was because the accusation of drunkenness against Morgan Phillips was entirely true.

Crossman would become famous for his political diaries, the first Cabinet minister to reveal what went on behind the scenes during his years in government. The Cabinet diaries were published after his death in the mid-1970s and provoked a huge controversy at the time. In his diary of earlier life on the backbenches, published in 1981, Crossman confirmed that Phillips had hit the bottle in Venice: 'He [Phillips] drank steadily ... with the result he got tiddly by mid-day and soaked by dinner-time.'[19]

The controversy continued long after the deaths of those involved. In April 1978, the *Spectator* published an article by Auberon Waugh claiming that Crossman had boasted at a *Private Eye* lunch that he and Bevan had been 'pissed as newts' in Venice. And in 2000, the journalist Geoffrey Wheatcroft said he had once heard Crossman say all three men had been toping heavily and at least one was blind drunk.[20] But Anthony Howard did not think 'pissed as newts' was a phrase Crossman would ever have used. Nor did the politician care much for whisky.[21]

What became laughingly known within the Labour Party as the 'Venetian blind' incident certainly illustrated the risks British libel law posed to journalists. But proving anyone was drunk on some occasion in the past is not easy and Jenny Nicholson could not convince the jury that her account was true. Her career in journalism was tarnished by the trial, even though it was subsequently shown that there was a large slug of accuracy in her story. What the *Spectator* trial had demonstrated was how sensitive senior politicians were now becoming about any public amusement at their tippling.

The post-war generation of politicians included other serious drinkers. A distinguished member of this generation was Anthony Crosland, raffish, clever and charismatic, whose book *The Future of Socialism,* published in 1956 (with its concluding call for more Liberty and Gaiety in Private Life, including 'more open-air cafes ... later closing hours for public houses'), became the bible of Labour modernisers.[22] As Education Secretary in the 1960s he promoted comprehensive schools; he was made Foreign Secretary by James Callaghan in 1976, but died suddenly a year later.

Crosland's enthusiastic enjoyment of alcohol had threatened to scupper his early career. In 1951 he received a letter from the historian A.J.P. Taylor, who was by then his brother-in-law. Taylor had been talking to the Tory MP Bob Boothby (the long-time lover of Harold Macmillan's wife Dorothy, and a man with his own colourful private life) and passed on what was being said in the Commons about the young Tony Crosland:

> You're extremely able; have a high reputation as an economist; and speak very well. You ought to be a junior minister by now; & would have been if it wasn't for drinking too much. I know on the very best authority that Attlee has said as much: he won't give you an appointment because he has seen you drunk too often in the smoking room. This is really deadly serious for you and your future ... It's the worst thing that can happen to an intellectual – I've seen it with one of my colleagues and it's a ruin. You can go to rot when you've had your career, but not when your career is beginning; and I do urge you most humbly to face this danger.[23]

Taylor recommended complete abstention, or at the very least that Crosland should limit his alcohol intake to beer. Crosland wrote back saying it was none of his business.

Labour lost office in 1951 and Crosland became bored with Westminster life. When Richard Crossman suggested he should not get so drunk when going into the House of Commons, Crosland replied: 'How else is one to endure being here?'[24] The Oxford economist never got his dream job of Chancellor of the Exchequer, but his enjoyment of the good life did not prevent a distinguished career in government. According to Alan Watkins, 'He drank a good deal, though not excessively by the standards of many politicians and journalists. He liked gin in the middle of the day and whisky in the evening. He enjoyed wine too, though made a fuss about not fussing.'[25] Like Harold Wilson, Crosland was in the habit of knocking back alcohol to relax him before facing MPs at the dispatch box. 'Crosland had cut down on drink by the time I got to know him but it's relative. He used to have three large G&Ts before answering questions in the House,' remembers his former adviser David Lipsey.[26]

The man who became Chancellor in 1967 instead of Crosland was Roy Jenkins, whose well-known fondness for claret was mocked by his friend and rival. One of Crosland's favourite quips was 'let's just have the carafe wine and leave the vintages to Roy'.[27] Jenkins' conspicuous enjoyment of the good life also irritated his HP sauce-eating neighbour next door at Number 10. According to Harold Wilson's press secretary, Joe Haines, the Prime Minister used to call Jenkins 'Old Beaujolais'.[28] Long after the pair had left office, Wilson quipped at a press conference that Roy Jenkins had been a good Chancellor until seven o'clock in the evening.[29] The implication was that after that he devoted himself to his club, Brooks's, dinner and drink. The charge is unfair. Roy Jenkins was an industrious Chancellor at a bleak economic moment, adroitly handling the balance of payments crisis and devaluation. As Home Secretary in the mid-1960s he had made a big impact through a range of liberalising measures and was regularly tipped as a future Prime Minister. But he was never quite in step with his party and in the early 1970s Labour's hostility towards deeper European integration drove him away, first to the European Commission and then towards the creation of a new political party, the SDP. He was an acclaimed writer of political biography, Chancellor of Oxford University and mentor to Tony Blair. It was on the morning after one of Blair's dinners with Jenkins that Alastair Campbell, Blair's director of communications, first registered that the new Labour leader had arrived at work with a hangover.[30]

Sir Menzies Campbell also recalled his enjoyment of Jenkins' hospitality: 'The empty magnums of what had gone before were on the sideboards. A certain amount of compare and contrast with the magnificent Pomerol and Margaux that had gone before. You always got very good drink and no shortage of it when you went to Roy's for lunch.'[31]

But Jenkins took indulgence in his stride. This is his own description of how he fortified himself at lunch before delivering his first Budget in March 1968 in the midst of economic crisis: 'Although I was determined to get through the afternoon's performance without the bogus prop of some specially prepared alcoholic concoction on the dispatch box, I drank a fair amount at lunch. The wine seemed to do my headache more good than the fresh air had done.'[32] Jenkins drank, but was never a drunk.

In fact he was one of the most rounded of post-war politicians. Like Denis Healey, Jenkins had a hinterland outside politics and was unapologetic about his enjoyment of expensively lubricated conviviality. As he got older his manner grew ever grander and *Private Eye* started calling him 'Smoothiechops'. Why did Jenkins' imbibing of claret become such a well-known element of his caricature? Perhaps because it symbolised the distance he had travelled from his Welsh mining roots. Jenkins had impeccable Labour ancestry. The son of a miner who became an MP, by the time he went up to Oxford the boy from Pontypool was already developing a taste for fine wine that aped the social habits of someone much richer. With a Labour leadership contest brewing in the 1970s, there is a story of Jenkins attempting to butter up his colleagues with beer. Jenkins' supporters told him it would be a good idea to pop into Annie's Bar and buy some of the old boys a pint. The grimy bar was not Jenkins' natural habitat, but in he breezed and treated the grateful backbenchers to a round of drinks. After putting his cash on the bar, Jenkins said, 'I'm terribly sorry not to join you, but I've got an important engagement,' and swept out again.

What made Jenkins attractive to some, but less so to others, was that he did not seem to care what others thought about his claret drinking. For him a vigorous social life, organised around good food and wine, along with an appreciation of books and culture, enhanced a politician's professional life rather than distracted from it. Significantly, even though Jenkins' drinking was far more generous than today's generation of government ministers, it does not seem to have harmed his ability to do the job. In fact he found it much harder to write books after an evening of imbibing than he did trudging through ministerial business. As the historian David Cannadine says, Jenkins insisted it was 'perfectly feasible to transact a morning's ministerial business with a mind-numbing and physiologically debilitating hangover'.[33]

Roy Jenkins and Tony Crosland were by no means the only Cabinet ministers in the 1960s and 70s who could have been seen strolling back to their offices through Westminster and Whitehall, well lubricated after a long lunch. Many leading politicians of the era kept the sommeliers busy, as the journalist Alan Watkins remembers:

A politician of the day – Anthony Crosland, Richard Crossman, Denis Healey, and Iain Macleod come to mind – would think nothing of enjoying a large aperitif beforehand, sharing a bottle of wine with the meal and having some brandy afterwards with his coffee. He would then go either to the House of Commons or to his department, where he would put in a long afternoon's work or, if he went to the House, even make a speech. Tomato juice and mineral water and much worse, the bringing along of press officers, came in during the 1980s, to the detriment of politics and journalism alike. Roy belonged to an earlier and better age.[34]

Perhaps the 1970s marked the final era of serious and routine ministerial drinking. According to the former Cabinet Secretary Robert Armstrong, a tumbler of something strong used to punctuate the political day: 'It would have been perfectly normal to have a drinks cupboard – with whisky, gin and sherry and glasses in it. And if the minister had a visitor before lunch or in the evening he would offer them a drink.'[35]

There were exceptions of course – like Tony Benn, who was famously teetotal. But in general government floated along on a sea of booze. David Lipsey, Crosland's special adviser in the 1970s, says drinking at work was routine: 'The amount of drinking would shock a modern politician. It was easier to drink a lot because there wasn't any 24-hour media. In those days if Crosland was on the TV twice a month we thought it was tremendously good going.'

In the early 1970s Victor Rothschild, head of the government's think tank, the Central Policy Review Staff, dreamed up a test called 'Are You Fit to Make Decisions After a Long Air Flight and Two Extra Gins?' He wanted to see whether ministers' powers of logical reasoning deteriorated under the pressures of their job. But every minister he asked refused to take the test.[36] Most probably felt that they could only make decisions after at least two gins.

It was a decade of strikes, high inflation, unemployment, pessimism and economic decline, and politicians were not the only ones drinking their way through it. As the historian Andy Beckett says, 'in the seventies, when booze pervaded British life, from City of London lunches to the onstage stumbles of bands like The Faces to the pissy terraces of football grounds, politicians almost certainly drank more than they do now.'[37] At the time senior ministers would think nothing of getting through a bottle of wine at lunchtime and tucking into the drinks cabinet in the evening. Civil servants would join them for a drink too if the minister offered, and Lord Armstrong believes alcohol could usefully lubricate the wheels of discussion: 'I remember many occasions when it's eased a relationship or particular occasion. I can think of relatively few occasions when I thought its effect was damaging on public life.'[38] But it is very difficult, if not impossible, precisely to measure the effect of drink on government decision making. There are certain jobs that clearly demand a clear head and a steady hand – bus drivers and heart surgeons for instance. They could not do their jobs to the same standard after a bottle of Burgundy and a noggin of brandy. But for three centuries, many government ministers ran their departments with a drink close to hand.

Of course, running the country is not like operating a lathe. Ministers do not sit at their desks pulling at a panel of policy levers, and there are armies of sober civil servants to supervise their actions. For most of the time, the daily life of a government minister is a relentless schedule of meetings, receptions and red boxes of policy papers to work through, along with questions in the House to prepare for and the legislation process to navigate. It is a slog, says Lord Armstrong, and drink has long provided a prop and an escape: 'The life of a minister is a grind. He has to combine running a department, running a constituency, being a member of the Cabinet if he's in it, maintaining some kind of social life. There are lots of things that are social or semi-social that you need to do so the pressures on a minister are very great. Every minister that I've ever seen has always found those pressures in the end very wearing and has been made very exhausted by them over time. When people get as stretched as that, one of the ways you can get relief or apparent relief is a drink. Or two drinks, or four drinks.'[39]

There is also the fact that in the 1970s the pressures on ministers were huge. With industrial unrest and relentless waves of economic crisis to contend with, perhaps it is no surprise that ministers sought some solace with a bottle. The Leader of the House of Commons in Jim Callaghan's government, Fred Peart, used to hold his morning conferences with the chief whip on the floor of his office with a bottle of sherry between them.[40]

### 'Tired and Emotional'

The name of one leading politician in particular of this post-war generation became synonymous with drink. It was a sleepy, work-worn Friday evening in November 1963 when the first Reuters report about the shooting in Dallas rattled out from the newsroom wire machines at 6.42 p.m. At the Dorchester Hotel on Park Lane, the tuxedoed talent from ITV and the BBC were gathering for the annual dinner of the Guild of Television Producers and Directors. In east London, the Deputy Leader of the Labour Party, George Brown, was attending a mayoral drinks reception at Shoreditch Town Hall.

That year had already been a rotten one for George Brown. In February, Harold Wilson had beaten him to the Labour leadership in a contest Tony Crosland described as a choice between a crook and a drunk. Wilson then denied the heavy-drinking Brown the job of Shadow Foreign Secretary, a snub that triggered a five-day disappearance by the party's volatile deputy leader. And so it was a bruised George Brown who helped himself to another gin and tonic on the evening of 22 November. Within an hour of the first report from Dallas, drinks had been downed at the Dorchester and stunned television news teams and schedulers were scrambling to cover the biggest breaking story of their lives.

It was Milton Schulman, assistant controller of programmes at the independent London television company Rediffusion, who told Brown that President Kennedy was dead. Brown had met Kennedy briefly three times since 1960, including a ten-minute encounter less than a month earlier. Schulman snapped Brown up for ITV's hastily arranged *This Week* special on the assassination and a car took him to the studios in Kingsway, central London. More drinks were poured for the guests, who included the historian Sir Denis Brogan and the actor Eli Wallach.

Brown was already showing signs of intoxication before they went on air, almost coming to blows with the American film star. In the studio, he angrily reprimanded Wallach for not having heard of the playwright Ted Willis. But it was Brown's drink-soaked, toe-curling sentimentality on camera that outraged viewers. He told the interviewer Kenneth Harris that he and the late President were great friends and implausibly claimed to be very close to the Kennedy family. With tears in his eyes Brown said: 'Jack Kennedy, who I liked a lot, who I was very near to ... I remember it's not many weeks ago I was over there with my daughter who lives in New York. We were walking across the garden, and she was talking to Jackie across the garden. One is terribly hurt by this loss ...'[41] In a performance that managed to be both weepy and aggressive, Brown slurred his way through the tribute. Watching at home, Richard Crossman was appalled at his colleague's antics, writing: 'At the first moment I saw that he was pissed and he was pretty awful.'[42]

The press condemnation took a couple of days to heat up. Brown was given a rollicking by Harold Wilson and had to apologise to the Parliamentary Labour Party. Some journalists were more forgiving, Anthony Sampson writing in the *Observer* that Brown's emotional performance was less of an outrage than the BBC's decision to carry on transmitting a light comedy show when even Moscow was broadcasting solemn music.[43]

Soon, though, letters of complaint started to arrive at George Brown's office. From St Anne's-on-Sea, a correspondent wrote: 'Dear Mr Brown, you have shown yourself unfit to govern yourself. How do you expect to govern others?' This florid reprimand came from a woman in Chester: 'Dear Sir, I have always thought of you as a small man, but after your disgusting performance in This Week last Friday I have altered my opinion. I now think you are a small drunken man.' And a letter from Renfrewshire read: 'You have appeared on canned television canned. On a solemn occasion you were as pissed as a coot. You are a disgrace to the nation.'[44] Brown wrote sorrowful letters of apology to them all.

Drink would sink Brown eventually, but not before Harold Wilson had put him in charge of economic planning and then appointed him Foreign Secretary. A year after his inebriated tribute to President Kennedy, Wilson decided to give Brown one of the biggest jobs in government. In October 1964 Brown became Secretary of State for Economic Affairs, a new ministry charged with modernising British industry. He also served as Wilson's deputy.

Brown was popular in the Labour Party and had indisputable proletarian credentials. The son of a Lambeth lorry driver, he grew up on the Peabody estate in Southwark and had a career as a fur salesman for John Lewis before becoming a trade union official and then an MP. A fiery public performer with a sharp mind, Brown could also be volatile and lachrymose when drunk. Not long into his new job he was pouring slugs of whisky into his morning tea and coffee and drinking heavily at lunchtime. Others in the government drank just as much, but the effect on Brown was ugly. Robert Armstrong was a civil servant in the Department of Economic Affairs at the time: 'He said and did things when under the influence of drink that he wouldn't have said if he hadn't had a drink. Quite a small amount would set him off. A single gin and tonic could make him paranoid about something – it sparked off his natural tendency to be suspicious and jealous of colleagues and sometimes to behave stupidly.'[45]

Although frequently drunk and rude to civil servants and secretaries, Brown did manage to oversee the publication of a national economic plan in September 1965, a plan that collapsed in the sterling crisis of 1966. But his behaviour shocked some of the journalists who encountered him. The renowned industrial reporter Geoffrey Goodman was sent to interview Brown on wages policy for the BBC, but when he got to the Treasury early in the evening he found the Secretary of State soused. 'He was absolutely pissed. It was at the peak of the incomes policy crisis. Discussions with the TUC were at crisis point. I got there at six in the evening and the private secretary said it's impossible. There he was at his desk, head in his hands on the desk. I said, George, we're going to do an interview, aren't we, and he shouted "fuck off!" I said the whole thing has been fixed, you can't say no. I went outside for five minutes. He went to the bathroom for twenty minutes and came out. In the end we did it, it was difficult but it was coherent. It was a hell of an experience.

He was completely pissed. Incomes policy was right at the centre of the government. And here was the number two in the government incapable.'[46]

But none of this prevented Brown's ascent to the job of his dreams. In August 1966 he became Foreign Secretary, a post that provided a constant supply of foreign dignitaries for him to insult. During a trip to Brussels, the Belgian government held a banquet for Brown and his party. Just as dinner was winding down Brown stood up, waved his arms, and said: 'While you have been wining and dining here tonight, who has been defending Europe? I'll tell you who's been defending Europe – the British Army. And where you may ask are the soldiers of the Belgian Army tonight? I'll tell you where the soldiers of the Belgian Army are. They're in the brothels of Brussels!'[47]

At a reception held in honour of the Turkish President at Hampton Court, Brown ignored the speech carefully crafted for him by officials and instead congratulated the Turkish President on being married to the 'most beautiful woman in the world'. The Foreign Secretary, who had been drinking at a Soviet Embassy party earlier in the evening, then started lashing out at the Church. When students from the Royal Ballet School began to dance, Brown said to an astonished President Sunay, 'You don't want to listen to this bullshit – let's go and have a drink.'[48]

But perhaps the most memorable George Brown drinking story of all comes from a trip to Brazil. The British delegation was invited to a diplomatic reception for some visiting dignitaries from Peru, held at the Brazilian President's Palace of the Dawn. Brown had already spent the early part of the evening drinking. The setting was sumptuous. According to someone who claimed to be there, Brown made a beeline for a 'gorgeously crimson-clad figure'. He asked the person to dance and received this reply: 'There are three reasons, Mr Brown, why I will not dance with you. The first, I fear, is that you've had a little too much to drink. The second is that this is not, as you seem to suppose, a waltz the orchestra is playing but the Peruvian national anthem, for which you should be standing to attention. And the third reason why we may not dance, Mr Brown, is that I am the Cardinal Archbishop of Lima.'

The one small caveat to this magnificent tale is that it is probably not true. There is no evidence in the Foreign Office archive that George Brown ever visited Brazil, or that he drunkenly propositioned the Archbishop of Lima.[49] But this apocryphal incident is entirely plausible because it fits so well with Brown's general behaviour.

This is why *Private Eye* put a photograph of Brown on the front cover in February 1967, standing alongside Harold Wilson and the French President Charles de Gaulle. A drunk-looking Brown is depicted singing the Hokey-Cokey, while Wilson says to the French President, 'George est un peu fatigué, Votre Majesté.'

The satirical magazine had another swipe at the Foreign Secretary when it imagined that the Foreign and Commonwealth Office had sent a dispatch to embassies abroad advising them how to deal with the foreign press. It listed six characteristics associated with George Brown – tired, overwrought, expansive, overworked, colourful and emotional. And so the phrase 'tired and emotional' was born, the universally understood political euphemism for being drunk.

According to fellow Cabinet member Denis Healey, Brown's frequent inebriation led to a dysfunctional decision-making process: 'I had to work with him because I was Defence Secretary at the time when he was Foreign Secretary and we arranged that we would meet once a week for an hour. I found I had to have the meetings before twelve in the morning, because otherwise there was the risk that George would be the worse for drink. It was a very, very serious problem with him.'[50]

Perhaps the Foreign Office did that to ministers then. As the historian Peter Paterson points out, all three Foreign Secretaries between 1964 and 1970 – Patrick Gordon Walker, Michael Stewart and George Brown – were convicted of drink driving after leaving office.

Brown had a regular habit of phoning Harold Wilson and threatening to resign when he was piqued by some perceived slight. He felt excluded from Wilson's inner sanctum and drink exacerbated his sense of grievance. Wilson, the technocratic Oxford economist, and Brother Brown, the working-class trade unionist, clashed quite easily but the Prime Minister was forbearing. When Brown fired off his resignation letters to Downing Street, Wilson would say 'file it with the others' and wait for his Foreign Secretary to simmer down and sober up.

Brown had been Deputy Prime Minister, Secretary of State for Economic Affairs during a serious balance of payments crisis, and Foreign Secretary at the time Britain was trying to join the European Common Market and the United States was stuck in the quagmire of Vietnam. These were important jobs and it was not just *Private Eye* that asked whether Brown's drinking damaged his ability to do them properly.

On 4 October 1967, the Labour-supporting *Daily Mirror*'s editorial read: 'The trouble with George Brown is not that he drinks too much but that he drinks at all.'[51] The newspaper said the Foreign Secretary had two personalities, Mr Brown the statesman and George the clown. When the BBC's Robin Day interviewed Brown at Labour's annual conference later that day, he quoted directly from the article. Brown tetchily acknowledged that times had changed: 'Nobody would pretend that Sir Winston Churchill didn't drink alcohol. It would be absurd to pretend. But there was then an unwritten rule that you didn't say it. Now today we are opening the whole lot up. I'm not pretending that I don't drink alcohol. I work jolly hard. I work very many hours every day. I don't do other things that people might frown upon. If we were living in a reasonable society I think the press and the radio and the television commentators would live by the rules we lived by yesterday. But if you want yourself a Foreign Secretary who doesn't do anything that's wrong I'm not the guy you want but I reckon the fellow you'll get won't be a very good Foreign Secretary.' Brown added with a theatrical flourish the famous quote by Stanley Baldwin: 'Power without responsibility has been the prerogative of the harlot through the ages.'[52]

In March 1968 the government was grappling with yet another economic nightmare, a crisis in the international gold markets. Late one Saturday night senior ministers were summoned to decide whether to have an emergency bank holiday on the Monday and close the London gold market. Nobody could track down the Foreign Secretary, so the Chancellor, Roy Jenkins, and Wilson made the call without him. When Brown discovered that he had not been consulted he erupted, phoning Number 10 at 1 a.m. and demanding a Cabinet meeting. The next morning he again rattled off a letter of resignation and this time Wilson accepted it, to the relief of many people in the government. In the view of Joe Haines: 'That was all drink, he ruined what might have been a good career through drink.'[53] Brown never held office again, and he resigned from the Labour Party in 1976 in protest against a government bill to strengthen trade union 'closed shops'. As he was leaving Parliament he fell over into the gutter beside his car, and the pictures were plastered over the next day's newspapers. They suggested drink; he blamed his bifocals. It was an ignominious end for a man whose prodigious talents had drowned in a bottle.

Brown's resignation prompted a warm tribute from *The Times*, which admired his stand against Labour's drift to the left and contrasted it with Harold Wilson's style of leadership. Describing Brown as one of the most patriotic Englishmen of his time, the newspaper's editorial concluded: 'When it comes to the heart of the matter, to the courage that supports a nation, Lord George-Brown drunk is a better man than the Prime Minister sober.'[54]

## A Rake's Progress

George Brown was not the last of the seriously embarrassing ministerial drinkers. The Conservative MP and minister Alan Clark, now remembered only for his racy diaries, would have fitted well into the age of the eighteenth-century rake. Unfortunately, his arrival in office coincided with the stricter disciplines of Thatcherism, even though the Lady herself was very partial to a glass of Bell's. Her press secretary Bernard Ingham says daytime ministerial drinking began to tail off in the early 1980s: 'Indulgence was out and earning your keep was in. The Thatcher idea of "apply yourself boy" was increasingly there and the 1970s was probably the last decade of the long liquid lunch.'[55] But Alan Clark clearly had not got the memo, and the castle-owning, car-collecting, woman-ising aristocrat lived a life reminiscent of those earlier rakes, Dashwood and Fox. Lord Armstrong says Clark's drinking was at odds with the time: 'We all had concerns about Alan Clark, who drank inside the office and outside it. His drinking was habitual and he didn't understand that you couldn't combine that with being a serious minister.'[56] Clark was maverick, charming and indiscreet. Charles Powell, Margaret Thatcher's private secretary, described him as 'the Lucifer of the Thatcher government; a brilliant, dark, quixotic, bawdy presence.'[57]

First elected to the House of Commons in 1974, Clark got monstrously drunk on his first day in Parliament.[58] After a decade of saying whatever he wanted and giving Conservative whips a headache with his frequently contro-versial off-message remarks, Clark was asked to join the government in June 1983 in the post of Parliamentary Under-Secretary of State at the Department of Employment. Clark was a good friend of Ian Gow, Margaret Thatcher's Parliamentary Private Secretary until 1983 and her eyes and ears in the Commons. As Gow, who was later killed by the IRA, briefed the Prime Minister over gossipy late-night whiskies in Number 10, Clark was recommended for promotion to the front bench.

And so it was that Alan Clark found himself standing at the Commons dispatch box on the evening of 19 July 1983 with the job of introducing a rather dry piece of government business. Clark's diary entry for the week is innocuously titled 'AC presents the Equal Opportunities Order to the House of Commons'. If that's all he had done, the moment would never have been remembered. But Clark had decided to go wine tasting with his friend Christopher Selmes, a financier who often spent Christmas with the Clarks at their chalet in Zermatt. Officials had written the statement Clark was due to deliver but he had barely glanced at it by the time he headed off to the event. The wine slipped down well, as the new minister recorded in his diary: 'We "tasted" first a bottle of '61 Palmer, then "for comparison" a bottle of '75 Palmer then, switching back to '61, a really delicious Pichon Longueville. By 9.40 I was muzzy ... the text was still virtually unmarked and unexercised.'[59]

Clark's diary deliciously captures the subsequent shambles. He is driven back to the House of Commons in his ministerial Austin Princess. Sitting on the back seat smoking a Havana cigar, he turns his attention to the statement and tries to read it using the tiny reading light in the car roof. The words are dreary Whitehall waffle and a muzzy Clark, vitalised by the vintages, has no patience with it. It is after ten o'clock when he stands up in the Chamber, which is surprisingly full for a late-evening session. Clark begins to read the statement.

The insouciant Eton- and Oxford-educated author of several acclaimed histories thought the words he had been asked to deliver to MPs were woeful:

As I started the sheer odiousness of the text sank in ... give a civil servant a good case and he'll wreck it with clichés, bad punctuation, double negatives and convoluted apology. Stir in a directive from the European

Court of Justice and you have a text which is impossible to read – never mind read *out*. I found myself dwelling on, implicitly, it could be said, sneering at, the more cumbrous and unintelligible passages.[60]

Drawling his way through the statement, Clark started to skip paragraphs, then pages. At one point the minister told MPs that he might have to rattle through certain passages 'at 78 rpm instead of 33' and his delivery accelerated. He was gabbling along when up shot the Labour MP for Birmingham Ladywood, Clare Short, on the benches opposite to make a point of order – 'dark-haired and serious with a lovely Brummie accent', Clark noted down later. Short said she had read that MPs were not allowed to accuse their colleagues of being drunk, but that she really believed the employment minister was incapable: 'It is disrespectful to the House and to the office that he holds that he should come here in this condition.'

The Commons erupted. 'Screams, yells, shouts of "Withdraw", counter-shouts. General uproar ... I sat, smiling weakly, my lips dry as sandpaper.'[61] Word of the kerfuffle quickly spread around the bars. The Chamber began to fill up and the Leader of the House, John Biffen, appeared in his seat. The Deputy Speaker, Ernie Armstrong, bellowed for the House to come to order and told Clare Short to withdraw her remark. Speakers stood up to criticise Clark and the chaos almost caused the government to lose the business in the House.

The journalist and former Conservative MP Matthew Parris remembered the night in his memoirs: 'I'm a little ashamed to say we all thought it was amazingly funny. Alan got away with it because he was handsome, charming and did subtly crawl to Mrs T – but in a way he was clever enough to disguise. In his place I would have sunk.'[62]

On the way home from the Commons, Clark's driver Joan asked what the row in the Chamber had been about.

'They were saying I was drunk,' said Clark. 'But I wasn't was I?'

'No minister, of course you weren't. I've never seen you drunk,' replied Joan.

'That's that then,' Clark wrote.

The following morning the minister issued a statement firmly denying drunkenness: 'Miss Short's allegation is completely baseless, as anyone who knows me would testify.'[63] Clark assured his boss Norman Tebbit that drink was not responsible for his peculiar performance at the dispatch box and his fledgling ministerial career survived, with Mrs Thatcher's affection for him proving crucial. Less favoured members of her government would have been axed. This was also a time before television cameras had been screwed into the wooden ceiling of the Commons chamber. Today a drunken dispatch box performance would instantly go viral on YouTube and mean curtains for a minister's career.

Alan Clark hated what he regarded as his sentence at the Department of Employment, spending most of his time trying to find ways to massage the rising unemployment figures in order to make them look more presentable. More to his taste were subsequent junior postings in trade and defence, where he stayed until he quit the Commons in 1992. His frank, funny and waspish diaries, with their lascivious tales of lust and longing, brought him huge notoriety and embellished the personality displayed at the dispatch box in the summer of 1983.

Clark was the last minister to be accused of being drunk in the House of Commons. In that one incident a reputation was born. But was he drunk? Years later, his wife Jane said: 'I never remember Al drunk.'[64] But while he could have been honing his statement into something readable, Clark was instead quaffing '61 Palmer. It did not make him incapably drunk, but the alcohol did remove a mental brake that other ministers would have been too nervous to release. In the *Sunday Times* at the end of the week, Hugo Young wrote a column headed 'Alas he was Sober' and then skewered Clark for being 'arrogant, facetious and brimming with self-amusement'.[65] Which is exactly what readers of his diaries came to relish about him.

## A Lost Leader

The late Labour leader John Smith was certainly a hearty social drinker. Older MPs smile warmly when they remember evenings sharing a whisky or three with the droll and loquacious Edinburgh lawyer in his Commons office behind the Speaker's chair. Smith's fatal heart attack in 1994 was as traumatic for Labour as Hugh Gaitskell's sudden death had been thirty years earlier. Both were much-liked party leaders who seemed poised to become Prime Minister at the time of their deaths. Instead, it was Tony Blair who walked into Number 10 three years after Smith died. In his memoir, Blair remembered his predecessor as a stupendous toper:

He could drink in a way I have never seen before or since. I don't mean he would ever be in drink when he needed to be sober – he was a complete professional

– but if there was an Olympic medal for drinking, John would have contended with such superiority that after a few rounds the rest of the field would have simply shaken their heads and banished themselves from the track.[66]

There had been one epic drinking session in Shanghai in the late 1980s, at the end of which Smith led the Chinese officials in an arm-linked rendition of 'Auld Lang Syne'. He relished camaraderie and late-night conversation, powered by tumblers of Scotch. Smith was a close friend of Blair's pupil master and mentor, Derry Irvine, Lord Chancellor in the Labour government and another hard-drinking Scot. According to Blair:

John would love to talk, reminisce, relax and wind down. Drink was a relaxant. In this regard, he was like Derry. They would never do it before a big occasion, but the two of them together betokened a monumental session that, if the time was free, could start at lunch time and go on well into the night.[67]

Blair stresses that drink never impaired Smith's performance the following morning and the lack of a hangover meant he had no reason to limit his drinking the night before. Derry Irvine seemed to have the same (Scottish?) facility. The overnight train that took Scottish Labour MPs back home on a Thursday night provided such a well-oiled experience that it became known as the Sleeper of Death.

In 1988 John Smith suffered a serious heart attack and began to work on his health, losing weight and pounding up Scottish mountains. But the boozy bonhomie did not stop, and Blair thought Smith was drinking more than was wise by the end of 1993. Despite his fragile health, Smith could not do without whisky-fuelled fellowship in the evenings. It made his life better. Whether it also contributed to his early death, depriving his party (and the country) of a putative Prime Minister, is something that can only be speculated about. What is the case is that, before Smith died, modernisers like Tony Blair and Gordon Brown were frustrated with the pace of change in the party and worried that Smith did not see the need for a sharper break with Labour's past. The opinion polls pointed to a Labour election win but it might not have been the Tory rout it eventually was. Despite years of strategy papers, the introduction of One Member One Vote and the incremental rebranding of the party, it was Blair's election as leader that convinced a swathe of swing voters that Labour really had changed. Blair's political ambition had been nurtured by one heavy-drinking Scot, and the premature death of Derry Irvine's whisky-supping friend presented Blair with his moment.

Smith was a political bon viveur, despite the harm it may have done to his health. He was a raconteur who drank socially for enjoyment and to the pleasure of others. Cast away on a desert island by the BBC, Smith chose to take a case of champagne as his luxury. It is interesting that booze has been the luxury pick of several prominent politicians. The Conservative MP and Secretary of State for Brexit David Davis wanted to take a wine cellar that never ran out. Norman Tebbit was more specific, requesting a drinking fountain with two taps – one gushing out claret and the other

Sancerre. Predictably, a case of Bordeaux wine was the choice of Roy Jenkins in 1989. His supply would have run dry by lunch on the second day, but Jenkins could have used the empty bottles to send out an urgent message for more.

# CHAPTER 2

## Parliament: Drinks on the House?

A warm breeze cushions the Commons terrace and wine flows beside the Thames. A contented, hazy stupor settles over Members of Parliament as they survey the shimmering river and order another round of drinks. It is the most exclusive members' club in London, but money will not get you in. No bar can match the gossipy, scheming, back-slapping, self-satisfied bonhomie. On a summer's evening such as this the terrace resembles the deck of a 1940s ocean liner, dwarfing the tourist boats chugging past. It is a pleasure that has been enjoyed by Members of Parliament since the new Palace opened in the middle of the nineteenth century. Victorian MPs looked back at the drinking antics of their eighteenth-century parliamentary ancestors with prissy disapproval. But they were hearty boozers themselves, as were generations of MPs to come. Parliament itself has been awash with drink for centuries. Its story is one of politically tribal bars that echo with the history of their parties.

For new MPs, the first day in Parliament feels like their first day at school. Separated from their families and yet to make friends, they are given a coat peg and a desk and try to find their way around. The neo-gothic gloom gives the place the feel of Hogwarts and our new MP spends their first days getting lost in a labyrinth of carpeted corridors that smell of school dinners. The aroma of sweating meats and boiled cabbage is the scented signpost to places in Parliament where they are likely to spend a great deal of time. These include the bars – not to be confused with the Bar of the House of Commons, a brass rail at the entrance to the Chamber where new MPs stand before they take their seat on the green benches for the first time.

As they inhale the history of the Chamber, pinching themselves on having made it there, our new MP might begin to plot their political ascent towards the front bench and, who knows, perhaps even to Number 10 itself. Such is the restless striving of many a Member of Parliament. Their parliamentary career is likely to be a rollercoaster of hope, exhilaration, recognition and fame, accompanied by troughs of boredom, loneliness, thwarted ambition and failure. Rab Butler talked about the 'patience of politics', the skill of riding out fluctuating political fortunes. And for centuries the places where politicians have gone to plot their careers, flatter political patrons, gossip with (and about) colleagues, mingle with the press and drown their disappointments are the watering holes of the Palace of Westminster. That is why they require their own place in this story. This chapter explores where politicians drink and what happens when they do.

For the backbench MP, the Houses of Parliament provide an agreeable life. As the former Conservative MP Julian Critchley described it, 'the place is kept uncomfortably warm; somewhere in the bowels is a boiler, taken from a battleship, and, while the House is sitting at least, the alcohol flows freely.'[1] This was not always so. Prior to 1773 Members of Parliament had to rely on the taverns of Westminster for their food and drink; it was not until the deputy doorkeeper, John Bellamy, was persuaded to set up his eighteenth-century snack bar that MPs could eat and drink on the premises. For sixty years Bellamy's provided politicians with their meat, bread, pies, cheese and wine, with a furnace of open fires and steaks spitting hot on the gridiron. William Pitt the Younger's dying words were said to have been 'Oh, for one of Bellamy's veal pies.' Bellamy himself was also a wine merchant, and his claret was priccy for the time at ten shillings a bottle.[2] Unfortunately, Bellamy's burnt to the ground in 1834 along with the rest of the old Palace, although a cafeteria of the same name was reborn in 1991 in Number 1 Parliament Street, a modern annexe to the Palace. It has since been converted into a crèche.

The new Houses of Parliament expanded the refreshment facilities for MPs, which have been renamed and relocated many times since. But their purpose has always been the same: to provide hungry and thirsty MPs with sustenance during their erratic working hours. Questions of access and pricing preoccupied the catering committee from the start. One visitor to the new Dining Room was the American novelist Nathaniel Hawthorne, who wrote of his experience in April 1856:

It was very much like the coffee-room of a club. The strict rule forbids the entrance of any but members of parliament; but it seems to be winked at, although there is another room, opening beyond this, where the law of exclusion is strictly enforced. (The dinner) was good – not remarkably so, but good enough – a soup, some turbot or salmon, some cutlets, and I know not what else; and a bottle of claret, a bottle of sherry, and a bottle of port.[3]

The port has dropped off today's menu, but otherwise Hawthorne's restaurant review would be echoed by many current MPs.

By the end of the nineteenth century Parliament's cellar was superb and alcohol was readily available. The centrepiece of the drinking apparatus were the Valentia Vats, a 1,000-gallon vat of Scotch whisky and a 300-gallon vat of Irish whisky. In his contemporary account of the Asquith parliament, Charles T. King describes the 'the great Valentia Vat, holding its hundreds of gallons of mellow whisky, the long catacombs of wine, the dining rooms with their flowers and palms', all presided over by the chairman of the Kitchen Committee, Colonel Lockwood MP.[4] During the great budget debate of 1909 Colonel Lockwood sustained the protagonists with his unceasing supplies of whisky; and King describes the House of Commons as 'about the easiest place I know of in which to drink wine'. The reason? A plentiful cellar with low prices:

If you have spent long hours indoors without a breath of fresh air and are jaded with much mental labour, and you find that wine is cheaper there than it is in the outside world, and that you can get a fairly sound claret for ten pence a bottle, the chances are that you will begin to experience the sort of reckless feeling that you really are able to afford half a bottle with your wing of chicken or your grilled sole.[5]

Such indulgence has been part of the parliamentary experience ever since, to the indignant consternation of those not elected to enjoy its subsidised delights. But they are delights that present dangers to the susceptible MP. Julian Critchley was warned by a Commons grandee that the two occupational hazards for MPs were alcohol and adultery. 'Obvious drunkenness is rare,' he wrote, 'but the MP who goes home sober is rarer still.'[6] Clement Attlee, who had been Labour's post-war Prime Minister, also knew that subsidised alcohol, late-night sittings, absent families, thwarted ambition and boredom could make a dangerous brew. His advice to the new Labour MP Roy Mason was simple: specialise in a subject and stay out of the bars.[7] But for decades before and since, many MPs have ignored his warning, preferring to drink their way through Westminster life in the convivial comfort of its numerous saloons.

## Licensing and Liquor

MPs drink differently from the rest of us. Not least because they imbibe in bars that operate without a licence and set their own opening hours. For many years Parliament's alcohol sales were thought to be illegal, a view tested in a court case in 1898 by a Mr Williamson against an employee of the Refreshment Department for supplying him with a brandy and soda. Although in that case the judge decided no offence had been committed, the legality of Parliament's bars remained murky until 1934, when A.P. Herbert laid an information against the Kitchen Committee of the House of Commons for selling alcohol without a licence. Herbert was a lawyer, wit and writer who became the independent

Member of Parliament for Oxford University the following year. His maiden speech was a passionate appeal for divorce law reform, a performance that met with Winston Churchill's witty approval: 'Call that a maiden speech? It was a brazen hussy of a speech. Never did such a painted lady of a speech parade itself before a modest Parliament.'[8]

Herbert wanted to test Parliament's exemption from its own complicated and restrictive licensing laws. If the public had rules to govern their drinking, then why not MPs? But in December 1934, Lord Hewart, the Lord Chief Justice, ruled that parliamentary privilege made the licensing laws redundant in Parliament, ensuring forever that its bars could serve liquor whenever they liked.

A further difference between public and parliamentary drinking is that MPs can never be described as being drunk. Parliamentary law, established in a formal ruling by the Committee of Privileges, is clear that no one may accuse MPs, individually or collectively, of being drunk within the precincts of Parliament. This judgment arose after a Member of Parliament was reported to the Committee of Privileges after saying at a public meeting in his constituency that some MPs were drunk at the end of the day's proceedings. Despite the undisputed truthfulness of his observation, the Committee ruled against him.[9] Alleging that an MP is drunk in the Chamber of the Commons will ignite uproar, as Clare Short discovered when she suggested Alan Clark was the worse for wear in 1983. When in 1947 a Labour MP, Garry Allingham, dared to suggest there was insobriety among Members, the House voted to expel him.

Then there is the perennial controversy over cost. The caricature of MPs draining bottles of subsidised champagne at the taxpayer's expense is one newspapers tirelessly propagate. In 2009 the *Daily Telegraph* exposed the way many MPs had been exploiting the old parliamentary expenses system for private gain, making small fortunes from playing the London property market with public money while furnishing their flats at John Lewis. There were claims for toilet seats, garlic presses, wisteria pruning, moat clearance and much else. Voters were furious and political careers were destroyed in the fallout. The focus on MPs' subsidised drinking therefore fits the picture, post-expenses scandal, of a self-serving political elite looking after its own interests and divorced from everyone else.

The reality, though, reveals a rather different picture, as a click through the many Freedom of Information responses and Commons Catering Committee reports show. All this can be found on the Houses of Parliament website. Taxpayers do subsidise its restaurants and bars by around £2.4 million a year, but that figure has dropped from £6 million since 2010.[10] Almost all the Commons facilities run at a loss, although the Strangers' Bar did manage to make a small profit in 2013/14 according to a Freedom of Information release in 2014. And its prices are about the same as those of the pubs around Westminster. The change, which started in 2010 in the wake of the expenses scandal, ended decades of cut-price boozing. Food remains less expensive than in nearby restaurants, but the parliamentary authorities say the subsidy is needed because of the irregular hours and unpredictability of Commons life. The House of Commons currently spends around £750,000 a year buying alcoholic beverages to sell to MPs, parliamentary staff and for sale at commercial functions. The Strangers' Bar has by far the biggest takings of any Commons watering hole: £202,575 in the financial year 2013/14.[11]

Here are some more facts to fill out the picture. In 2014 the House of Commons wine stock was valued at £41,077, and over the course of that year 4,350 bottles of House of Commons champagne were bought by Parliament for sale in the bars.[12] But it is the cheaper booze that sells. For example, between November 2012 and October 2013, the House of Commons bars served 15,075 pints of the guest ale, 9,504 pints of Becks, 9,484 bottles of Commons sauvignon blanc and 7,085 bottles of merlot.[13]

The prices charged have been creeping up in recent years, to the consternation of some MPs. In written evidence provided for a 2011 report on the catering and retail services in the House of Commons, the Administration Committee received some gems among MPs' submissions. The former Liberal Democrat MP Lorely Burt wrote that 'the Pugin Room has great and courteous service. However this little haven has now become a rare treat because of the hike in prices. One colleague said they had been charged £17 for 2 Chablis! That, with respect, is taking the Mickey.' Labour's Brian H. Donohoe was equally unimpressed: 'The prices in the facilities have got to Five Star Hotel levels. Two glasses of wine in the Pugin Room £14. Six cups of tea £10.50. I don't expect to pay that in my "Works Canteen".' And the Conservative MP Margot James, while seemingly content with the prices, did want better quality wine in the Strangers' Dining Room: 'Chardonnay is a very popular varietal and the only one available is a Chablis – which is a very flinty style of Chardonnay – and frankly at that price level really quite acidic! It would be nice to have another Chardonnay choice from a warmer climate capable of providing a slightly fuller bodied more rounded style of wine.'

As MPs wince at the cost and quality of the wines available today, they might be allowed a stab of nostalgia for the olfactory glories enjoyed by their parliamentary predecessors. The Commons wine cellar used to be famously good, carefully cultivated by the Tory grandees who presided over the Wine Committee. In June 1947 the *Manchester Guardian* reported that guidance was being provided to MPs to help them with their wine selections:

> The refreshment department of the House of Commons has taken in hand the delicate task of forming members' taste for wine. 'For the benefit of members who, due to the war years, are out of touch with recent vintages, the following notes are attached', says the House of Commons wine list. 'The wines of Burgundy in 1937 have, it seems, fulfilled their early promise and are now robust full-bodied wines. The following year was good but not exceptional. Burgundies of 1939 have a low degree. The Burgundies of 1940 have been destroyed but clarets of the same year have developed greatly in bottle. In terms of cash a bottle of 1941 Burgundy costs a Member of Parliament 23s. 6d. and a 1943 Burgundy 31s.'[14]

The vintage cellar survived the war but it did not survive Robert Maxwell, who was appointed chairman of the Kitchen Committee shortly after his election to Parliament in 1964. The bombastic swindler was given the job by Richard Crossman, the Labour Cabinet minister, who thought a successful stint in charge of the committee would persuade Harold Wilson to put Maxwell in charge of a government department. Fortunately he never did.

In his new role, Maxwell found that the cellar was full of wonderful wines from the turn of the century and decided that there was money to be made by selling them off, a move that instantly brought the loss-making department into profit. But as Maxwell drained the cellar in a grand sale he made sure to snap up some of the best bottles for himself at a bargain-basement price. As the former lobby correspondent Colin Brown says, 'everyone thought that it was brilliant because he'd made a profit but what they didn't realise was that he was ripping off their wine.'

Years later Brown and a party of political journalists were skiing in Austria when they were invited to see the wine cellar of a ritzy restaurant in St Christophe. A number of the dusty bottles bore a Robert Maxwell stamp. After his death Maxwell's cellar was itself sold off and the hotel had bought a slice of it. 'I'm absolutely certain that some of those bottles came from the House of Commons,' says Brown.[15]

For many years the sale of the Commons wine cellar was a subject guaranteed to produce red-faced fury in a certain sort of MP. But newer members have known nothing other than screw-top table wines and the days of a six-shilling glass of Chateau Latour have gone. So have some of the old bars, as the drinking has dwindled.

## The Smoking Room

The grand dame of Westminster watering holes has traditionally been the Smoking Room. It is the only bar reserved exclusively for Members of Parliament. The wood-panelled room is one of the finest in the Palace, with portraits of long-forgotten parliamentarians brooding over the sagging leather armchairs. For decades this is where Conservative MPs have come to drink, gossip, plot and play chess. Once the place would have been heaving either side of dinner, the air thick with cigar and cigarette smoke as Tory MPs guzzled their whisky, gin, brandy, wine and cocktails.

Journalist and former Conservative MP Michael Brown first discovered its clubby charms on his election to the Commons in 1979. On his first visit to the Smoking Room that summer he ended up chatting to Labour's Harold Wilson. Brown told the former Prime Minister that he was the new MP for Brigg and Scunthorpe. 'Wilson said, "I'll give you a tiny bit of advice lad, don't get up at the Parliamentary Labour Party too soon. Give it two or three years before you make an impact there." I said, I'm actually on the other side. "Tories won Scunthorpe?" exclaimed Wilson. "Have another drink lad." He got the barman round and had a large brandy. I was in seventh heaven.'[16]

Although the Smoking Room has traditionally been a Conservative drinking haunt, it has occasionally welcomed in other Labour grandees including Hugh Gaitskell and Richard Crossman. Aneurin Bevan used to have a corner in there too. The fiery left-winger from Tredegar, who was to be the midwife of the National Health Service, loved the London dinner party scene and had started to hobnob with the rich and fashionable during the 1930s. At one dinner hosted by the millionaire proprietor of the *Daily Express*, Lord Beaverbrook, the Conservative politician Brendan Bracken roared his disapproval at what he perceived to be

Bevan's drinking hypocrisy: 'You Bollinger Bolshevik, you ritzy Robespierre, you lounge-lizard Lenin. Look at you, swilling Max's champagne and calling yourself a socialist!'[17] But Nye Bevan saw no reason why the workers should not enjoy fine wines and champagne too, a crusade that took him into the citadel of Tory drinking.

For Michael Brown, drinks in the Smoking Room were a daily pleasure for eighteen years. He shared an office with Ian Gow, Margaret Thatcher's Parliamentary Private Secretary, whom he remembers buttering up Conservative backbenchers with drink: 'He regarded it as his job to lubricate a problem with alcohol. Ian would come back at five o'clock from a day in Number 10 and say in fruity tones, "Michael, we are now going to the Smoking Room where we will partake of a White Lady" [a cocktail of gin and lemon juice served in a martini glass]. The Smoking Room used to be full from six o'clock onwards. We'd go and get a cocktail first, then into the members' dining room, then into the House for the wind-ups at 9.30, then back into the Smoking Room until the early hours.'[18]

The Conservative MP David Davis describes the Smoking Room as once a barometer of his party's mood. He recalls the scene on the night of Nigel Lawson's resignation as Chancellor. 'It was a cross between a party and a pool of piranhas. Everyone was excited, gossiping, talking about their chances of promotion. I was dumbstruck. It was the Smoking Room mood, which used to be very important in the Tory party.'[19]

A week into his Commons career, the Tory MP Julian Critchley was sitting in the Smoking Room reading a book. A fellow MP came up to him and said: 'Young man, it does not do to appear clever: advancement in this man's party is due entirely to alcoholic stupidity.'[20]

Today it is rather different. The cigarettes and cigars have been extinguished in the Smoking Room and so has the bar's reputation for Tory toping and party intrigue. When I peered in on a recent evening, the armchairs sat empty. The clock ticked on but the likes of Churchill and Bevan were long gone. A silver trolley of freshly made blancmange was parked forlornly at the door, failing to entice anybody in.

The cost of staffing the bar is now greater than the takings. The place where Disraeli, Churchill and Thatcher used to fire up the troops is a room of ghosts. In 2011 the Administration Committee recommended that Smoking Room staff could be replaced by 'alcohol vending machines'.[21]

### The Terrace

There is another corner of the Palace where MPs can go and drink privately. The riverside terrace of the Houses of Parliament stretches along the southern side of the Palace, facing St Thomas' Hospital on the opposite side of the Thames. From Westminster Bridge there is a view of the roof of a pair of green and red candy-striped canvas marquees that were conspicuously not part of Charles Barry's original design. They provide a garish colour-coded contrast to the honeyed stone of the Palace. Red stripes for the Lords, green for the Commons. Inside, peers and MPs host receptions and lobbyists do their business, while bow-tied Commons catering staff proffer silver trays of wine glasses for the guests. The wine is free but ropey, and seems more so when there is rain running down the plastic windows.

But when it is not cold and wet, and especially on a balmy early summer evening, the uncovered areas of the terrace are a splendid place to drink. As with the rest of the parliamentary estate, access rules are strictly enforced. The colour of your pass controls your movements. Visitors may not enter the terrace unless they are with an MP (and then only in very restricted numbers) and only certain pass holders can sit on the terrace unaccompanied.

A drink on the terrace is what really impresses a visiting constituent. Parliament loves its hierarchies and its pleasures are carefully guarded. For MPs the terrace is a treasured place and the easterly end by Westminster Bridge is a spot reserved for them alone. A prominent sign warns the uninitiated that these wooden tables and chairs are 'Members Only'. It is not a particularly private area, though, and the buses and tourists passing over the bridge can gawp freely upon their elected representatives. But that has not inhibited MPs from enjoying themselves when out there.

Writing in 1872, Sir John Sinclair considered the dining rooms of Parliament 'very inferior to the Clubs'. He liked the terrace though: 'Close to the library is the newspaper-room, inside it the tea room, and down below is the smoking-room, from which in the summer evenings you can walk out on the broad terrace which overhangs the Thames, and which is a cool, cheerful, and animated spot – enlivened by the steamers, boats, and barges, which are continuously passing.'[22]

A century later the MP Gerry Fitt was one of those who particularly enjoyed the liquid delights of the terrace. Fitt was a founder and one-time leader of the Social Democratic and Labour Party. One of Northern Ireland's best-known politicians, he was a civil rights leader, a Catholic, a socialist and a nationalist. First elected to Westminster as the Republican Labour member for West Belfast in 1966, he ended his career in the House of Lords after moving his family to London following the burning down of his Belfast home by the IRA.

Fitt was gregarious, garrulous and a drinker. In Belfast bars he always faced the door, lifting his glass with his left hand so he could grip the concealed pistol in his coat with his right. But in Westminster Fitt could relax a little more. He is remembered for sitting on the terrace during summer evenings waving great glasses of gin and tonic at the passing boats crying, 'It's free! It's all free!'[23] And the former Principal Doorkeeper of the House of Lords, Michael Skelton, a close friend of Fitt's, remembers his generosity with the drink: 'The river police used to come in and pull in onto the terrace at the House of Lords and I used to help him pass drinks down to the police,' Skelton tells me. 'That is perfectly true.' Fitt's first drink of the day was usually a G&T with no ice or lemon. When Skelton asked him why, Fitt replied that the ice cubes banging together made his hangover much worse.[24]

Of course, not all Northern Ireland politicians followed Gerry Fitt's example. The Reverend Ian Paisley was a ferocious teetotaller. Before doing an interview at Stormont with the Press Association's political editor, Chris Moncrieff, Paisley once asked, 'Have you taken drink, Mr Moncrieff?' When the reporter admitted to having consumed two halves of Guinness, Paisley barked, 'That's two halves of draught Guinness too many for me,' and walked off. With typical understatement Paisley denounced Ireland's favourite drink as 'the Devil's buttermilk'.[25]

But in general, MPs are prone to wax lyrical about the delights of the terrace. The veteran Labour MP Paul Flynn nicely reflects this: 'There is a lovely ambience on the terrace on a summer evening, a bubbling contentment as the view of St Thomas's gets more lovely looking with every drink.'[26] It more than compensates for all those constituents with their incessant complaints and problems. There is a well-known tale of an MP in the early 1990s who went out onto the terrace one summer's evening after a few too many pink gins. The unnamed MP was carrying a stack of constituency correspondence, and he lobbed the lot into the Thames with a cry of 'Bollocks to the lot of you!', a gesture that sparked cross-party cheers.

### Strangers' Bar

There was a time when Labour's political opponents liked to smear the party by associating it with Soviet communism. The Strangers' Bar looks nothing like the Kremlin, but for many years that was the nickname of Labour's drinking domain. The party might have changed over the years, but this place has remained resolutely the same. It could even be described in Labour-speak as offering traditional values in a traditional setting, with 1970s décor, beer, dartboard, stumpy wooden tables, wood panelling and packets of pork scratchings.

While Conservative MPs enjoyed the clubland atmosphere of the Smoking Room, Labour preferred to sink pints in the comparatively pub-like surroundings of the Strangers' Bar, so called because that is how you will feel inside it if you are not an MP. 'Strangers' is the somewhat sniffy name

Parliament gives to the visiting public, a reminder that the Palace is for MPs, not those who elected them. If you are being entertained by a Labour MP there is a good chance that this is where you will be taken. The added bonus is that the MP has to buy the drinks. It says so on a wooden board above the bar. The rules are strictly followed. MPs and their staff can bring in three guests, but the MP must pay, or at least hand over the money.

For a now disappearing generation of Labour MPs, Strangers' was a haven, a place to drink in familiar surroundings. Bruce Grocott arrived in the Commons in 1976, and ended up as Prime Minister Blair's Parliamentary Private Secretary. Now a Labour peer, he explained to me over a pint in Strangers' that for MPs who had tipped up in Westminster from coalmines and factories, the bar was the nearest thing to reality in a very strange environment. 'People had come from very settled occupations, shift work in the mines or on car assembly works. It was a huge shock to the system turning up here.'[27] But in the Strangers' Bar they could sup the same Federation ales available in northern clubs and replicate the serious drinking habits of home. Bill Stone was one who tried to take away the pain in his lungs after years down the pits with a steady stream of pints. Once he overheard a couple of MPs sitting at the bar complaining with disdain that the Commons was 'full of cunts'. A couple of feet further along the bar a normally taciturn Labour MP from the north-east looked up from his beer and said firmly, 'There's plenty of cunts in t'country,' putting down his pint, 'and they deserve some representation.'[28]

According to Geoffrey Goodman, those Labour MPs who had grown up with the drinking cultures of their unions and working men's clubs continued to booze in the same way at Westminster.[29] It could get boisterous in there. Veteran Press Association reporter Chris Moncrieff remembers Strangers' as a sweaty spit-and-sawdust place, sticky with stale beer. Pints of Federation ale would slosh around and there would be occasional brawls between MPs. At one time there was even a little arrow nailed to the wall two inches from the floor with an accompanying inscription that said 'Way Out'. A policeman told Moncrieff it was to guide MPs crawling out on their hands and knees.[30]

Today the arrow has gone and Strangers' is more sedate. Dropping in late one afternoon I found three solitary Labour MPs nursing pints on their own. They were members of the old guard, overlooked and unknown outside their constituencies. It was livelier on a Thursday evening, with drinkers spanning the political spectrum from Labour's Tom Watson to the former Tory defence secretary Liam Fox. Milling around were several newspaper journalists mopping up the gossip. But the Strangers' Bar of the 1970s and 1980s has gone, as have the Labour MPs who worked down pits and toiled in factories before becoming politicians.

The demise of heavy industry has been matched by the rise of the professional politician. Today it is common for MPs of all stripes to be incubated in think tanks or serve political apprenticeships as ministerial special advisers before entering the Commons. To many new MPs the Houses of Parliament are a familiar place. The number of MPs with backgrounds as researchers or special advisers grew rapidly in the 1990s; by 2005 over 14 per cent described their background as 'politician/political organiser'.[31] While Labour MPs of the past propped each other up in Strangers', recreating the working men's clubs of their home towns in fraternal solidarity, that world has gone.

David Lipsey for one is not nostalgic for what has been lost. As a special adviser himself in the 1970s and later a journalist, he was not impressed by the calibre of the Strangers' regulars: 'They'd come down from the north for the week not always sure what their function in life was so they'd just inhabit the bars and drink Newcastle Brown Ale. They didn't have the constituency workload then and they weren't manoeuvring for their own interests because there was no way they could be a minister for anything ever.' Lipsey adds that in one sense the House of Commons has improved: 'You meet hardly any completely unemployable duds any more.'[32] Perhaps that is so, but there are also fewer MPs rooted in the lives of the working-class communities they represent. The changing character of the Strangers' Bar reflects that story.

### The Pugin Room

On a gloomy rain-lashed October evening I meet the veteran Conservative MP and historian Keith Simpson for a drink in the cosy gothic grandeur of the Pugin Room. This is where MPs bring guests to impress. It is all that the Strangers' Bar is not. The stone windows frame the view of boats passing by, and bow-tied waiters serve the drinks and bring nibbles in silver bowls. Over a glass of white wine and a gin and tonic (combined price £7.10) Simpson rattles off a list of post-war Commons drinking casualties. There was Horace King, Speaker of the House in the late 1960s and the first to come from the Labour benches. A clubbable chap with a soft spot for the limelight (he once agreed to turn on the Blackpool illuminations), King was a familiar figure in the bars. There was the former Conservative MP for High Peak, Spencer Le Marchant. Tall, grand, boisterous and loud, and a serious drinker, Le Marchant was the first MP the political journalist Simon Hoggart met, having been instructed by an editor to take him to Annie's Bar for a drink. The young Hoggart asked for a pint: 'It came in a pewter tankard, and when I took the first swig I almost choked – being Spencer he'd had it filled with claret.'[33] Even Margaret Thatcher mentioned Le Marchant's imbibing in her memoir, describing the whip as 'famous for his intake of champagne'.[34] After ten o'clock in the morning that was the only drink served in his office, poured into half-pint silver cups.

On one occasion Le Marchant almost pulled off a dazzling display of parliamentary pantomime. His idea, as recounted by Matthew Parris, was to organise an MPs' horse race, in which Members of Parliament would play the part of horses. Le Marchant had decided that Parris would be his horse, dressed up in the livery colours of his actual racehorse. Senior MPs also selected the services of more junior, sprightly colleagues to be their runners. The racecourse was to be the perimeter of the Smoking Room, around which coffee tables, chairs and sofas were to be lined up. The MPs would then leap from one piece of furniture to the next around ten circuits of the course. Everything was set and the Chairman of the Commons Catering Committee had even given his assent. Sadly, the London *Evening Standard* diary got wind of the plan and the government whips thought it wise to cancel the race.

Drink eventually killed Le Marchant. Matthew Parris remembers the now yellow-tinged MP trying to stay sober in his final days, drinking only water for dinner in the Members' Dining Room but ordering melon with port for dessert. 'Into the shallow depression left in the half-melon by the removal of the pips, they pour a couple of teaspoons of port. Spencer was desperately scrabbling in this depression with his pudding spoon, trying to recover the last drop.'[35]

As Keith Simpson mines his formidable memory for more names, the Pugin Room fills up with pre-dinner drinkers. The room is also the front line of a long-running territorial dispute between the Commons and Lords. Although technically in the Lords, it has been captured by the Commons. Its carpet, like everything else in the Lords, is red, but its occupants are those from the green end of Parliament. The room was given over by the Lords to the Commons in 1906 in return for the use of a committee room. But peers have long felt deprived of places to drink and want it back. According to the Conservative peer Lord Norton, it is a running sore between the two Houses and the Chairman of Committees has previously tried to persuade the Commons to return it, so far without success.[36]

## Annie's Bar

There is another drinking den, now defunct, that journalists and MPs of a riper age remember with affection. In popular folklore, Annie's Bar was the epicentre of political scheming and intrigue at Westminster. It was a place for politicians to drip poisonous gossip into the ears of story-hungry hacks and to hatch plots with parliamentary colleagues. This reputation was fortified when Annie's Bar had a starring role in a risible 1996 Channel 4 mini-series of the same name.

Like many Westminster bars, Annie's was moved around over the years. The original, named after a long-dead barmaid, was opened before the Second World War in a small room adjacent to the Members' Lobby. Annie sold drinks from a jug of ale and two bottles of whisky, one blended and one malt, to MPs as nerve-stiffeners before they stepped into the Chamber. But that bar was flattened when the Commons took a direct hit from the Luftwaffe. The rebuilt Chamber had no bar attached; Clement Attlee's teetotal chief whip, William Whiteley, did not want to encourage drunken fraternising between MPs and journalists. But the bar was reborn in 1968 by decree of the Commons Catering Committee chairman Robert Maxwell. Annie's was moved to a ground floor room beneath the tea room that had once been the office of the Victorian Irish nationalist Charles Stewart Parnell; it was opened by the then leader of the opposition, Ted Heath.

It then survived for thirty years at the heart of Westminster's political trade. The crucial difference between Annie's and other parliamentary bars was that journalists could buy the drinks. It put them on equal terms with the politicians. They could lubricate their sources without the power imbalance of other bars. With journalists buying the booze, the exchange of gossip could be more direct – and because the terms of discussion were the same as in the parliamentary lobby itself, nothing said or done could be reported, either in the press or to the party whips, without permission.

In the 1970s and 80s Annie's became, in the view of one Fleet Street veteran, an informal pillar of the constitution. During the dramas of Barbara Castle's effort to curb the trade unions, the miners' strikes and the three-day week, Annie's became the main marketplace for transactions between journalists and politicians. According to the journalist Ian Aitken, its heyday was during the 1974–9 Labour government: 'With no government majority, every Commons division became a cliffhanger which had to be monitored. The monitoring was most effectively done from Annie's, just one flight of stairs from the members' lobby. One could gauge the degree of crisis every night by how often the whips scuttled in and out in search of missing MPs.'[37]

Ian Hernon became a lobby journalist in 1978 and now writes for *Tribune*, the left-wing magazine first published in 1937. He says both journalists and politicians welcomed an off-the-record drinking den far from the prying eyes of party bosses. 'I realised it was a place where those on the way up briefly mixed shoulders with those on the way down, which made it all the more valuable as a source of contacts.' He remembers:

After 1979 people who had been Cabinet ministers and players on the world stage ten minutes earlier were drowning their sorrows, and sharing their wisdom, with members of the raw intake, and new junior ministers, who you just knew would eventually be given a place at the top table. However, no-hopers, some of whom deserved the tag and others who could fall back on pristine principle, remained the bulk of the MP customer base. I saw fights aplenty and was sucker-punched in the balls by a whip who wrongly assumed I was behind a drinking session which left half Labour's defence front bench legless before a crucial division. But above all it was a place where you could judge the mood with parties and governments.[38]

During Mrs Thatcher's reign, the discarded Conservative 'wets' washed up in Annie's to bemoan their plight to grateful journalists ready to loosen their tongues with drinks paid for on expenses. But it was not necessarily the best place to get a story. In Chris Moncrieff's view, Annie's obviousness and lack of privacy meant it was a hopeless place to get a scoop. 'Everyone saw you there. Despite all the intrigue around it Annie's just became a boozing bar full of north-east MPs. If you wanted to get a story privately that would be the last place you'd go.'[39]

And eventually both MPs and journalists stopped going. Not even the Channel 4 drama could arrest the bar's decline. In 1995 it moved again, to a sterile, windowless room below Central Lobby, and today all that remains is a nameless locked wooden door. During the Catering Committee's inquiry in 2002, the chairman warned the press gallery and MPs that they should 'use it or lose it'. By the end Annie's Bar was costing two and a half times as much to run as it took in sales, so it finally closed for good. Ian Hernon is one of a dwindling number of journalists who remember the old Annie's Bar and he despairs of the creeping modernisation that extinguished it. 'We call it vandalism,' he tells me, 'part of the anti-drink culture which has infected the parliamentary estate over the last fifteen years.'[40] Now only the bar's reputation lives on.

### Moncrieff's: The Press Bar

Named after the legendary Westminster journalist Chris Moncrieff, a reformed alcoholic who had not had a drink for twenty-five years, and opened by the teetotal former

Commons Speaker, Michael Martin, this is the bar where the press pack comes to drink. Or, more accurately, where they are supposed to. In fact this latest incarnation of Parliament's press bar is now open to all pass holders and is snubbed by most journalists. It may be due to its soulless atmosphere or its 7 p.m. closing time, but this is one of the most forlorn, underused bars in Parliament. Reached by a gloomy staircase lined with ancient political cartoons, Moncrieff's sits on top of the press gallery and the cramped warren of rooms that house Westminster's political reporters. It livens up only once a month for the press gallery lunch, when a prominent politician comes to entertain the journalists and their guests with some on-the-record anecdotes and a chummy post-pudding Q&A. This is now one of the few occasions when politicians and press might risk a modest glass of House of Commons claret with their lunchtime lamb. Otherwise, Moncrieff's is where the scribes downstairs nip up to grab a sandwich from the fridge.

But the press bar was not always so lifeless. In the days when Chris Moncrieff was the most influential political reporter in the land, it was a riotous drinking den. For many years it was run by a barman called Sam, who stored a cardboard cutout of Margaret Thatcher behind the bar and kept pace drink for drink with his patrons. Moncrieff remembers him getting so drunk he could not be bothered to work out the prices, so simply charged the same for everything, whether half a glass of lemonade or a double Scotch. Apparently the stocktake the next morning was completely accurate.

Even after the shutter had come down, the thirsty hacks found a way to carry on. 'Once we managed to get a straw through the grille and into an open bottle of whisky and drank the whole lot like that,' recalls Moncrieff. The police used to join the journalists in the evening too; Moncrieff remembers witnessing a Welsh officer being so drunk one St David's Day that he ate a bowl of daffodils.[41]

Another Welshman was a regular in the press bar. 'When Neil Kinnock was Leader of the Opposition he used to come up to the press bar and sing rugby songs and a huge amount of drink was taken,' remembers Colin Brown. 'There was one night that Kinnock was singing his head off, Welsh folk songs, when we got a message from the Speaker that we had to turn down the noise because we could be heard in the Chamber.'[42] After that Kinnock's people decided it was not prudent for someone who aspired to be Prime Minister to be seen singing beery renditions of 'Land of My Fathers' in the press bar and his trips upstairs ceased.

But drinking at Westminster continued, and Moncrieff believes booze was responsible for one of his best scoops and one of the oddest moments of Neil Kinnock's leadership. In June 1988, Labour's Shadow Defence Secretary Denzil Davies suddenly and sensationally resigned. In the early hours of the morning he phoned the Press Association's chief political reporter and launched a ferocious attack on his party leader. 'I am fed up with being humiliated by Mr Kinnock,' Davies said. 'He never consults me on anything. He goes on television and he talks about defence but he never talks to his defence spokesman. So frankly I do not think I have a job to do any more. I have resigned as of now. Maybe I will write to Kinnock in the morning.'

After Davies hung up, Chris Moncrieff filed the story to the Press Association and it was soon splashed on the front pages. Moncrieff was in no doubt Davies had been drinking, but the following day he was criticised for breaching an unwritten code of trust. 'I got told off by Tory MPs the next day for doing the story. They said he was plainly drunk and I should have shown more compassion. That's not my job. They thought it was like taking candy from kids.'[43] By the end of the 1980s the booze-soaked bonding that brought journalists and politicians together was beginning to dissolve.

## The Sports and Social Club

While the press bar no longer sways to harmonious renditions of 'Cwm Rhondda', drink-assisted parliamentary singing continues at the Thursday karaoke night at the Sports and Social Club – or 'Sports and Socialist', as some Tories call it. This is the most pub-like place in Parliament, a bar where researchers come to drink in the bowels of the Palace beside the bins. There are wooden boards etched with the names of parliamentary darts champions; cabinets of sporting silverware; a pool table and tables crammed with drinkers eyeing each other up. Andrew Marr describes the 'burly squalor' of the Sports and Social, a place frequented by policemen and the more desperate tabloid hacks.[44] In 2011, Black Rod decided the place had become too raucous and limited the number of guests pass holders could bring in. But it is still the liveliest drinking destination in the Palace of Westminster, popular with the people who work for MPs, whether researching their speeches and carrying their bags or cleaning the corridors and cooking their food.

After the 2015 general election the former First Minister of Scotland, Alex Salmond, said his advice to the new intake of MPs from the Scottish Nationalist Party would be 'make your voice heard, represent your constituents, and stay out of the Strangers' Bar'.[45] The 56-strong clan of SNP MPs, several still in their twenties and fresh from obliterating Labour in Scotland, heeded Salmond's words and colonised the Sports and Social instead. On a wet Wednesday evening in the beery scrum, a SNP MP told me this was now the tartan bar. He said the English weather forced them to drink here instead of on the windswept terrace.

### The Lords Bar

The teetotal Prime Minister Clement Attlee once compared the House of Lords to a glass of champagne that had stood for five days. The former Liberal leader Jeremy Thorpe was even more brutal, describing the Lords as 'proof of life after death'.[46] Their Lordships have always had a bar of their own in which to contemplate the wonders of democracy, and today it is a shiny little nook beside the Lords cafeteria, which excels in traditional school puddings like spotted dick and custard. Hereditary peers have been largely phased out, although (for reasons that nobody can quite remember) when one dies their numbers are replenished by election among those remaining. According to Michael Skelton, former Principal Doorkeeper in the Lords, the hereditary peers used to be the big drinkers: 'If you're a hereditary you're there because it's a club. You arrive, check your email and go straight to the bar.'[47] But the bar is sparsely attended these days. With its high pine tables it feels like a compact All Bar One, which is perhaps why it is rarely busy. In the view of experienced Commons researcher Sadie Smith, young parliamentary assistants now avoid the place because the bright lights make everyone look unattractive. She also remembers a false door by the bar that people used to lean on before falling straight through into the adjourning Churchill Dining Room. Like the Chamber it serves, the Lords Bar is of uncertain purpose.[48]

However, alcohol has certainly kept aged peers well oiled in the past. The Conservative leader of the House of Lords during the coalition government, Lord Strathclyde, is a believer in what he calls the 'corruption of good catering', although he is too self-deprecating to claim the phrase as his own. It may have been minted by a Rothschild, he muses. But the idea behind it is that, if you look after someone well, entertain them with fine food and drink, then the appreciative recipient will feel obliged to return the favour. We meet for morning coffee in the sun-dappled tea room of the House of Lords in early spring. Thomas Galloway Dunlop du Roy de Blicquy Galbraith, 2nd Baron Strathclyde (Tom to his chums) joined the House of Lords in 1986 and was immediately made a Conservative whip by Margaret Thatcher. He remained on the front bench for the next twenty-five years, serving six Tory leaders including three Prime Ministers. The jovial millionaire peer is one of the most affable yet shrewd people in Parliament. From 1994 until 1997 he was the Conservative chief whip and readily dispensed a generous tumbler in his office to move business along.

'Already there was a good bar, largely whisky,' he tells me. 'The great thing about whisky is it doesn't need mixers. G&T is such a bore. Lemon, tonic water and god knows what else. But whisky is very good and the Famous Grouse was a wonderful oil. People were offered a glass of whisky to help them relax and make them be a little more helpful than they might have been. It helped create a camaraderie. I did find if you offered people a drink they felt more willing to help than perhaps if you hadn't,' he says with a grin, adding: 'There was certainly a time in the 1990s where alcohol proved a good lubricant to help manage the backbenchers of the Conservative Party in the House of Lords, and that made a difference. People liked it and they appreciated it.'[49]

But those were the wilderness years for the Conservative Party. Once back in power, Lord Strathclyde insists, tea and biscuits trumped whisky and brandy when he had the job of corralling Tory peers through the government voting lobby.

Their lordships, or at least some of them, are perhaps more likely to have studied the ancient civilisations of Greece and Rome than are their elected colleagues down the corridor. Certainly peers are expected to bring historical perspective and mature wisdom to Parliament. It is not impossible, therefore, as they enjoy a glass of Bordeaux with their grouse in the Peers' Dining Room, that the Greek symposium might come to mind. The word means 'drinking together' and describes a male, upper-class evening of gossip, poetry reading, political discussion and rumination. It was also the setting for young teenage males to be initiated into the social and political life of Athens, often with the guide of an older male lover. That aspect of the symposium may not have a modern echo, but the drinking certainly does. Then, as now, wine was used to stimulate a lively conviviality conducive to political reflection.

## The Commons Chamber

With so many bars for Members of Parliament to imbibe in, and with so much time to kill between votes, it is no surprise that history records many instances of drunkenness seeping into the Chamber itself. Popping into the reporters' gallery on 19 December 1666, the diarist Samuel Pepys witnessed the antics of a couple of well-refreshed MPs. Pepys was not amused:

> Sir Allen Brodericke and Sir Allen Apsley did come drunk the other day into the House, and did both speak for half an hour together, and could not be either laughed, or pulled, or bid to sit down and hold their peace, to the great contempt of the King's servants and cause; which I am grieved at with all my heart.[50]

Two centuries later, the novelist Anthony Trollope (who also stood for Parliament) described the drunken demise of the villainous financier and Member of Parliament Augustus Melmotte. His inebriated performance in the House of Commons preceded the swindler's suicide:

> Melmotte was persistent, and determined not to be put down. At last no one else would speak, and the House was about to negative the motion without division – when Melmotte was again on his legs, still persisting. The Speaker scowled at him and leaned back in his chair. Melmotte standing erect, turning his head round from one side of the House to another, as though determined that all should see his audacity, propping himself with his knees against the seat before him, remained for half a minute perfectly silent. He was drunk, – but better able than most drunken men to steady himself, and showing in his face none of those outward signs of

intoxication by which drunkenness is generally made apparent. But he had forgotten in his audacity that words are needed for the making of a speech, and now he had not a word at his command. He stumbled forward, recovered himself, then looked once more round the House with a glance of anger, and after that toppled headlong over the shoulders of Mr. Beauchamp Beauclerk, who was sitting in front of him.[51]

And the drunken antics of nineteenth-century MPs were not confined to fiction. In the early years of the century, the Tory gent and ally of Pitt the Younger, George Rose, caused outrage in the Commons when he turned up in the Chamber drunk and asked the Speaker to perform a comic song. According to an excitable account from 1902, it was the 'greatest astonishment ever created in the House of Commons' and MPs were 'paralysed with astonishment'.[52] Ordered to stand at the Bar of the Commons and apologise, the MP refused and was carted off to the room known as the lock-up to sleep off the booze. The next day, sober, he begged the Speaker's pardon and was discharged from custody on the condition that he paid a hefty fine.

George Rose was a gregarious chap and a founding member of the Ministers' Fish Dinner, an annual knees-up which took place shortly before the parliamentary summer recess. Fried whitebait from the Thames was very popular at the time and the dinners took place at a tavern in Greenwich, with invitations to Cabinet ministers dispatched in their ministerial boxes.

The parliamentary sketch writers peering down on proceedings pray for such a performance, but now usually have to quarry their reports from more arid and predictable material. Most MPs are not dazzling orators and some are so dire they can rapidly empty the Chamber. But there are notable exceptions. One of the most captivating speakers in nineteenth-century politics was the Irish playwright, barrister and politician Richard Laylor Sheil. He made a name for himself by writing witty sketches of contemporaries in London legal life and politics for the *New Monthly Magazine*. One sketch from 1829 describes the ordeal of watching another Irish politician, John Leslie Foster, make a speech in the Commons. For the MPs there, drink was the only way to endure it.

Sheil was in the gallery of the Commons watching a debate on the Catholic question. The Chamber was full when John Leslie Foster stood up to speak. 'In an instance the House was cleared,' writes Sheil. 'The rush to the door leading to the tavern upstairs, where the Members find a refuge from the soporific powers of their brother legislators, was tremendous.' Whatever their views on Ireland, all MPs agreed that Foster was agony to listen to. Sheil followed the hundreds of MPs out to Bellamy's where they tucked into dinner and wine:

Half an hour passed away, toothpicks and claret were now beginning to appear, and the business of mastication being concluded, that of digestion had commenced ...
At the end of a long corridor, which opened from the room where diners were assembled, there stood a waiter whose office it was to inform an interrogator what gentleman was speaking below stairs. Nearly opposite the door sat two English county Members. They had

just disposed of a bottle each and just as the last glass was emptied, one of them called out to the annunciator at the end of the passage for the intelligence; 'Mr. Foster on his legs' was the formidable answer. 'Waiter, bring another bottle', was the immediate effect of this information, which was followed by a similar injunction from every table in the room. For two hours this went on and more bottles were ordered, until 'Mr Plunket on his legs' was heard from the end of the passage and 'the whole convocation of compotators rose together and returned to the House'.[53]

It would be nice, but inaccurate, to be able to say that there are no comparable instances today.

At this period, speaking in the House of Commons and taking part in debates was a minority interest for MPs. The majority did not say a recorded word throughout their parliamentary careers. But between 1820 and 1828, there was a 20 per cent increase in the number of MPs who got a mention in Hansard.[54] After the 1832 Reform Act, that trend accelerated. Press coverage of proceedings increased massively and Victorian politicians began to find fame among a growing electorate. But one constant was the conviviality to be found by MPs in Parliament's bars. The Victorian MP and writer Justin McCarthy recalled that in the Commons chamber in the early 1850s,

there hardly ever took place a night's debate then and for many Sessions after during which some members did not make it evident by the manner of their speeches that they had been stimulating their nerves and screwing up their courage a good deal too much at the expense of the bottle or the decanter ... In the former days it might be said without exaggeration that hardly a night passed without giving the public some exhibition of a drunken member amusing his audience by trying to take part in a debate.[55]

Similar behaviour was evident a century later, when the Commons assembled for one of its most critical moments: a two-day debate on the failure of British forces to stop Germany's invasion of Norway in April 1940. In his biography of Winston Churchill, Roy Jenkins describes a boozy Commons chamber during the 'inquest on Norway' debate that followed on 7 and 8 May 1940. As Churchill was wrapping up his crucial swashbuckling speech just after 10 p.m. on 8 May, Jenkins writes, 'There developed one of those scenes of faintly hysterical disorder with which the House of Commons has long been inclined to accompany its most serious decisions. It began with a few allegedly intoxicated Scottish Labour members but was quickly reinforced by at least equally inebriated responses from the other side.'[56] At what would turn out to be a decisive juncture in British history, alcohol fumes filled the Commons air. By this time, the Prime Minister Neville Chamberlain was clinging on to office. A confidence vote followed and the Conservative government's majority was cut to eighty-one, shattering Chamberlain's authority. Two days later Hitler invaded France and the Low Countries; and the military architect of the Norway debacle, Winston Churchill, was asked to lead a new government.

A vivid glimpse of the drinking culture in Parliament at this time is provided by Fenner Brockway, a radical

Labour MP and prominent anti-colonial campaigner who was a boy when Gladstone ran the country, and who died during Thatcher's third term at Number 10. Writing in 1942, during a twenty-year break from the Commons, Brockway said the typical parliamentary existence could easily destroy unwitting, under-occupied MPs:

> More and more of such members settled down to an existence of inertia. They descended after a question time to one of the lounges and smoked, gossiped, drank, according to their tastes, or slept until the division bell rang ... Automatic machines would have filled the part just as efficiently. The inevitable deterioration of their existence was hastened by the ease with which drink could be obtained.[57]

Brockway remembered one Cabinet minister winding up a late debate who could stand 'only with difficulty'. The shocked, disapproving MP left the chamber, saying to a colleague, 'a workman would be sacked if he were found drunk at his bench.'

Despairing about the drudgery of parliamentary life, Brockway was rare in breaking the *omerta* around drink:

> I know it is the habit of Members of Parliament, and even of ex-Members of Parliament, to be silent on this matter. I am writing of it, not because I am unconscious of human frailty in myself, but because the drunkenness which occurs at the House of Commons is only a reflection of the futile, wasted existence which large numbers of MPs are encouraged to live by the procedure of Parliament.[58]

Late-night sittings continued to be the norm as the century progressed, with alcohol always a heavy presence at that hour. The political journalist and essayist Henry Fairlie describes the atmosphere of the 1960s, when MPs would return to the Commons from dinner 'a little flushed with food and certainly noisier than at any other time of the day' to hear the closing front bench speeches. 'The House of Commons at this hour is a superb political animal,' he writes.[59] But the Speaker at the time, Dr Horace King, struggled with alcohol and was once too drunk to ascend the few steps to his chair. Sir Robin Maxwell-Hyslop remembered the incident:

> Horace came in at 9.25, and he had two goes at getting up into his chair ... and the second time he fell to the right across the Clerks' Table with his wig 45 degrees to the left and Bob Mellish (the government chief whip) called out 'You're a disgrace, Horace, and I'll have you out of that chair within three months.' Horace turned round so abruptly that his wig was then 45 degrees out the other way, and he gave a brilliant riposte: 'How can you get me out of the chair, Bob, when I can't get myself in to it?'[60]

Horace King was the 151st Speaker but the stress of the job was too much for him and the drink ensured he was shuffled out of the Speaker's chair in 1970.

On the evening of 28 March 1979, the Callaghan government lost its Devolution Bill and faced a vote of no confidence, which it then lost. But the Commons catering staff had gone on strike. As the journalist Frank Johnson remembered, this might have been the first time ever that a government had lost a vote of confidence with everyone sober. Watching from the press gallery were gasping reporters:

> All evening we waited for the answer to the question: Would we get a drink? ... There were hopes that on humanitarian grounds the unions would allow essential supplies of alcohol to reach the press gallery. As the night wore on, passers-by were confronted with that most frightening spectacle: a sober mob of journalists.[61]

As a minister for health in the mid-1970s, David Owen testifies that it was possible to talk complete rubbish in the wind-up debates after dinner. 'At least a third of the House of Commons were pissed. There's no question about it. It was quite respectable to be the worse for wear by 10 o'clock.'[62] A qualified doctor, Owen told me about the time he was called to help an MP who had collapsed in the Chamber:

'We got the person out and into a small room off the lobby. We put him down and I examined him and I told the policeman we should just leave him there for a while. I checked him every half an hour. The truth was that the person was blind drunk. That was the diagnosis. No heart attack. Completely and utterly plastered in the Chamber. That is a classic example and it wasn't the only case of someone being seriously ill from drink.'[63]

Into the 1980s, and Michael Brown describes a typical evening in the Chamber: 'The benches on both sides were full and you could smell the fumes, that's why it was so boisterous.'[64] Brown remembers the Labour MP for Dearne Valley, Edwin Wainwright, a former miner, getting sloshed in the Strangers' Bar one night before the 1983 election. The Labour whips decided it was best to pack him off home in a taxi. Thinking he had gone, they then turned in horror to see Wainwright's name on the monitor that showed who was speaking in the Commons chamber. According to Brown, the MP babbled away incoherently for some time, leaving the Hansard writers unable to record anything more detailed than 'Mr Wainwright made a number of observations.'[65] In those days television cameras were not present to record the inebriated ramblings of Members of Parliament. Their arrival probably did much to dissuade half-cut politicians from taking their unsteady place on the green benches, or at least from trying to speak.

But not all Commons debates are now duller. For example, the video record contains a particularly entertaining performance by the well-lunched Conservative giant Nicholas Soames, grandson of Winston Churchill and close chum of Prince Charles. One afternoon in April 1998 he pitched up at a debate on the Money Resolution in the Regional Development Agencies Bill, not the most exciting of legislative moments. During a lengthy, florid and wandering intervention, Soames was repeatedly steered back to the subject by the Speaker, Betty Boothroyd. Onlookers suspected Soames had been drinking, an accusation he denied. 'My lunches consist of bananas, still water, preserved apricots and bats' droppings,' he said, soberly.[66] But the aristocratic Soames also understands the relationship between class and drink. In the Commons Chamber and restaurants he used to hail John Prescott, Labour's former Deputy Prime Minister and one-time ship's steward, with the cry: 'A whisky and soda for me, Giovanni, and a gin and tonic for my friend!' The first time it happened Prescott shouted back: 'At least I'm here because of my brains, not my father's balls.'[67]

There is, though, one occasion when an MP is allowed to drink alcohol in the Commons chamber, a ritual that started in the Victorian era. On Budget Day the Chancellor of the Exchequer can tinker with alcohol duty while sipping from a glass of their favourite tipple. In 1853 William Gladstone gave the longest Budget speech in history (four hours and forty-five minutes) and fortified himself throughout with a hideous concoction of sherry and beaten egg. His great rival, Benjamin Disraeli, delivered the shortest Budget address (a mere forty-five minutes) while drinking brandy and water. Into the 1980s, Chancellors kept up the habit. Geoffrey Howe opted for a gin and tonic. His successor Nigel Lawson took a whisky and soda into the Chamber for his first Budget in 1984; and Kenneth Clarke confidently quaffed a glass of whisky. But then the showmanship abruptly stopped. Gordon Brown ploughed through his many Budgets with only a mineral water at hand. Alistair Darling and George Osborne followed this example. As dry Budgets become the norm, it will be a brave Chancellor who revives the ritual.

In fact all government ministers now sit through Commons debates with nothing more than water for sustenance. Some, I am told, add a splash of elderflower cordial to perk it up. But of course we can't be sure it is just water. John Biffen was a sharp, well-liked Conservative Cabinet minister and thinker who served in Margaret Thatcher's first two governments. As Chief Secretary to the Treasury from 1979 to 1981, Biffen found plain water 'inappropriate as a companion' through speeches and debates. He later revealed that his Parliamentary Private Secretary used to nip out of the Commons chamber while he was chained to the front bench and fill a carafe with weak vodka and tonic. It looked like sparkling water, so nobody knew.[68]

Biffen's career hit the rocks in 1986 when he dared suggest in a television interview that Mrs Thatcher might not be Prime Minister for the whole of the following parliament. The Downing Street press secretary, Bernard Ingham, briefed journalists that Biffen was 'semi-detached'. The soon to be ex-minister stoically excused Ingham for being 'the sewer, not the sewage'. Speaking in 2004, Biffen said a career in the Cabinet was comparable to being a football manager, both being short-lived experiences. 'You can't complain about being scratched if you work in a menagerie,' he mused.[69] This is a good description of the parliamentary zoo, where exotic high-flyers rub along with the grey and overlooked, the two species occasionally meeting while they queue for drinks at the bar.

# CHAPTER 3

## Drying Out

The story so far has been one in which a drinking culture played a central role in political life. As the street lights sparked up along Whitehall, ministers would fling open the drinks cabinet while Members of Parliament poured into the bars. In the latter part of the twentieth century, this began to change. It is not that politicians stopped drinking, or that there were no longer any celebrated political drunks, but there was a marked change in the culture and conduct of politics that had its impact on political drinking. Politics started drying out. This chapter explores how it happened, even while alcohol continued to exact its political casualties.

After Labour's landslide election win in 1997, the new government ministers were shown to their offices. Harriet Harman remembers her arrival at what was then the Department of Social Security: 'I couldn't believe it. You got a red box, a driver, a private office and a drinks cabinet! Wine, spirits, everything.' Perhaps typifying the newness of New Labour, Harman did not see the need to get the drinks out. 'The fog of drink never helped me understand what people were trying to tell me or explain to them what I was trying to do,' she tells me.[1]

While there certainly were members of that government who liked a drink, Robin Cook and the former Lord Chancellor Derry Irvine notable among them, with Mo Mowlam always ready to kick her shoes off and sink a few with the boys, the Labour governments of Blair and Brown generally marked a shift in the character of ministerial drinking, away from whisky and wine to still and sparkling water. Peter Mandelson's cocktail party preference for a canarino (hot water with a twist of lemon peel) symbolised the new sobriety.

Why the change? Perhaps a growing awareness of the damage drink can do is part of the answer. Governments that now spend so much time fretting about the number of units of alcohol that people are drinking are expected to set an example. There is also the relentless pace of modern government. Twenty-four-hour news means that political storms flare up and die down much faster than they did even twenty years ago and ministers are now expected to be ever-ready with a response. The television cameras would easily spot the glassy-eyed flush and slurred speech of a minister who had enjoyed an excessively liquid lunch.

The mood in Parliament itself has been changing too. Previous generations of backbench MPs routinely passed the time in the bars, waiting for late-night votes that often dragged into the early hours. But in 2002, MPs approved government plans to change the working hours of Parliament. The House of Commons now rarely sits beyond 7 p.m. and that has had a major impact on the Commons, including its late-night drinking culture. The place has undoubtedly sobered up. The arrival of many more women has been another significant factor. Labour's introduction of some women-only shortlists doubled the number of women MPs after the 1997 general election. There is a story, which may or may not be true, of a Tory MP from the shires surveying the Labour benches after that election and exclaiming: 'Who are all these people? They look like a lot of bloody constituents!' Before 1987 women had never made up more than 5 per cent of MPs, but after the 2010 election the figure rose to 22 per cent. It seems likely that the arrival of so many more women played a significant role in diluting the male drinking culture of Westminster.

However, the drinking habits of backbench Members of Parliament still continued to hit the headlines. There were brawls, missed votes and deaths that shocked the world beyond Westminster. Over the years there have been several MPs who drank too much and died too young because of alcohol. In fact one of the first such casualties of the New Labour years was a woman. Fiona Jones died from liver failure in January 2007 at the age of forty-nine. Ten years earlier she had been swept into Parliament as the new Labour MP for Newark in the party's landslide election win. She did not drink much before heading to Westminster. But once there, the bars were a place to nullify the pain of being away from the family home, and of the tedium and bullying she encountered. According to her husband Chris, Jones found the travelling tough and she was subjected to sexual harassment by an unnamed Cabinet minister.

Adding to her woes were questions surrounding the use of election expenses in her constituency. In February 1999 Jones and her agent were tried for expenses fraud and found guilty. When she overturned the ruling and went back to the Commons, many fellow MPs wanted nothing to do with her and she started drinking heavily. She eventually lost her seat in 2001 and failed to find another job. 'At home she drank vodka to hide the smell from the children but down there she drank whisky because nobody cared if she drank,' said Chris Jones a few weeks after his wife's death.[2] In his view, his wife's spiral into alcoholism 'can be traced directly back to her experiences at Westminster'. She did not go to Alcoholics Anonymous because she feared being recognised and by the end there was nothing her family could do to stop the disintegration. It is her husband's judgment that the fact nobody cared is most damning of all. As long as she turned up to vote when ordered, party managers did not care about her slide into alcohol addiction.

Party whips notice when their MPs don't turn up to vote. It is what sent the Conservative whip Derek Conway knocking on Iain Mills' door at the Dolphin Square apartment block in Pimlico (where many MPs keep a London flat) in January 1997. For eighteen years Mills had been a quiet, unassuming backbencher for a Midlands seat. He was found dead on his bed surrounded by gin bottles, his body undiscovered for two days. The inquest into his death concluded that Mills was five times over the legal driving limit when he died. After the inquest, Conway said the whips' office had known he was drinking, although they had no idea how much: 'We were encouraging Iain to try and get a grip on the things that were of concern to him.' But Mills died as he had existed in the Commons. Alone, only noticed when he failed to show up for a vote. In this same period another MP destroyed by drink was Jamie Cann, the Labour MP for Ipswich, who was found guilty of drink driving in 1998 and died of liver disease in 2001.

In his study of the political species, Jeremy Paxman noticed what a solitary existence is revealed in the pages of many political diaries. 'Whether they be snobs on the make or hair-shirted evangelists, the striking impression in many cases is how utterly lonely they seem,' he wrote.[3] Some Prime Ministers have displayed a rather weary disdain for the backbench drones who file through their respective voting lobbies day after day. Harold Macmillan once said that the only quality needed to be an MP was the ability to write a good letter. Winston Churchill was pitying: 'The earnest party man becomes a silent drudge, tramping at intervals through the lobbies to record his vote and wondering why he comes to Westminster at all.' In 1882, Gilbert and Sullivan famously captured the experience and set it to song in their comic opera *Iolanthe*:

> When in that House MPs divide
> If they've a brain and cerebellum too,
> They have to leave that brain outside,
> And vote as their leaders tell 'em to.[4]

There are many satisfactions in being a Member of Parliament, but there are also many frustrations and disappointments. Roy Jenkins took a dim view of life on the backbenches, without a real job to do:

> Being a full-time back-bench MP is not in my view a satisfactory occupation. The time can obviously be filled in, but not with work of sufficient intellectual stimulus ... Excessive attendance at the House of Commons, with the too many hours spent hanging around in tearoom or smoking room which this implies, either atrophies the brain or obsesses it with the minutiae of political gossip and intrigue.[5]

Both the growth of constituency work and the development of select committees have altered the picture somewhat since Jenkins wrote that, but there is still much about the life of a Member of Parliament that sends them in search of diversions and distractions. And drink has remained a crutch for many.

### Kennedy's Curse

In July 2002 the then Liberal Democrat leader, Charles Kennedy, was interviewed by Jeremy Paxman on the BBC's *Newsnight* programme. It was an echo of Robin Day's interrogation of George Brown thirty-five years earlier but Paxman was blunter, telling Kennedy that every politician he had spoken to in preparing for the interview had said the same: 'You're interviewing Charles Kennedy? I hope he's sober.' The Lib Dem leader brushed off this suggestion of heavy drinking as Westminster tittle-tattle, a slur that should not be taken seriously. Paxman then asked Kennedy directly how much he drank and got a twinkly, knowing reply: 'Moderately and socially, as you well know,' he said with a grin.

But if Kennedy had hoped this conspiratorial reminder of shared past pleasures was going to shake Paxman off, he was wrong. There followed a question about whether Kennedy drank privately and alone, 'a bottle of whisky late at night?' Instantly, Kennedy's face burned with anger and indignation. He snapped back: 'No, I do not, no.' It was the first time the Westminster whispers and rumours about the Liberal Democrat leader's drink problem had been put to him publicly and directly. Three and a half years later – after more denials, cancelled press conferences, missed appearances in Parliament and a sweaty speech at the party conference – Kennedy admitted he struggled with alcohol, but only after ITN had discovered that he was receiving treatment. In a statement at the party's headquarters on Thursday 5 January 2006, he said: 'Over the past eighteen months I've been coming to terms with and seeking to cope with a drink problem, and I've come to learn through that process that a drink problem is a serious problem indeed. It's serious for yourself and it's serious for those around you. I've sought professional help and I believe today that this issue is essentially resolved.'

In an appeal to party members, Kennedy announced a leadership contest in which he would stand, but senior Liberal Democrats told him he could not continue. They refused to be dependent on his dependency any longer. His public candour and promise to change was too late and on Saturday 7 January Kennedy resigned the leadership of the Liberal Democrats. He may have been given a final chance if the Lib Dems had been doing better in the polls at the time. Despite their popular opposition to the Iraq war and a tally of sixty-two seats in the 2005 election, many in the party were frustrated by a sense of inertia and drift. And senior figures had heard pledges of sobriety from their leader several times before.

Charles Kennedy plunged into politics in 1983 at the age of twenty-three, at which time he was the youngest MP in the Commons. He thought he had little chance of winning Ross, Cromarty and Skye for the SDP when his fledgling academic career was swapped for Westminster. Becoming president of the Liberal Democrats in 1990, his affable informality made him a popular figure, regularly appearing on television shows, and in 1999 he became party leader at the age of thirty-nine.

According to one biographer, he was suffering from a drink problem even before that. His close personal assistant for many years, the late Anna Werrin, told the *Times* journalist Greg Hurst that symptoms of his alcoholism were 'seen by party members' before the leadership contest. The source was not whisky, as Paxman presumed, but gin and wine. Anna Werrin told Hurst: 'He drank in private, by and large, and drank more than he ought.'[6] The first time Sir Menzies Campbell became aware of the problem was in October 2001, when Campbell and Kennedy met with Yasser Arafat in London. On the way to Arafat's hotel, Kennedy's hands shook as he tried to drink from a can of Lilt. At the hotel, Kennedy asked the Palestinian leader one question before sitting through the rest of the meeting in silence. 'Was Charles the worse for drink? Was he sick? I had no way of knowing since I had never seen Charles behave like that before but I presumed it was drink,' said Campbell, who complained to the party's chief whip.[7] But it was only when Campbell became the Liberal Democrats' Deputy Leader in February 2003 that he was taken into the confidence of those closest to Kennedy and the seriousness of the drink problem was spelt out. In June that year, Kennedy was too incapacitated to sit in the House of Commons chamber and hear Gordon Brown's announcement on whether Britain would join the euro. His failure to appear was not explained.

That summer, shortly before the parliamentary recess, Kennedy decided that he would hold a press conference explaining that he was temporarily stepping down as leader to have treatment. But while Campbell was travelling down to London by train, Kennedy changed his mind and cancelled the confessional. This prompted Campbell and others to talk to their leader candidly for the first time and tell him the problem had to be tackled. They received an assurance from Kennedy that it would be. But Budget Day in 2004 brought the biggest crisis yet. Just before Prime Minister's Questions, Anna Werrin told Campbell that the party leader was unable to appear because of a stomach upset. Campbell went up to Kennedy's office and asked to see him, but Werrin said he couldn't: 'He's very sick. He's in a bad way. It's better if you don't.'[8] Vince Cable had to give the Lib Dem Budget response and Westminster buzzed with gossip about whether booze was to blame for Kennedy's absence.

A week later Kennedy sweated his way through the leader's speech at the party's spring conference and again senior figures confronted him about the drinking. This time they were blunter, telling him that if he continued to drink he could not remain as party leader. Again, there was a promise to seek treatment. But the bouts of drinking did not stop and the effects of a heavy night might have been the cause of a confused press conference performance during the 2005 election. A new baby and sleepless nights were blamed for Kennedy's mangled explanation of the party's flagship tax plan. Through the autumn of 2005, his support both among new MPs and the party grandees flaked away and by the new year he was faced with mass revolt. What had been a private issue for Kennedy, his family and a small circle of confidants in the party was finally in public view.

Did reporters in Westminster collude in covering up Charles Kennedy's drink problem? The rumours were fiercely denied, and the issue was effectively hidden by Kennedy's discreet inner circle, but journalists knew the truth. Kennedy was very adept at concealing his drinking bouts, and for five years affection for him personally and loyalty to his leadership kept a lid on the problem. But by 2006 his colleagues had lost patience with the pattern of remorse and remission and the cover-up collapsed.

Why did Kennedy sometimes drink so much that he could not do the job? Three and a half years before Kennedy's death, Sir Menzies Campbell, the abstemious ex-Olympian who became Lib Dem leader after Kennedy, told me Commons life contributed to it: 'In Charles's case, in the first instance it was loneliness – dispatched into Westminster as a 23-year-old. It can be a very lonely place. Then stress and strain – having to assume greater responsibilities perhaps than he expected at an earlier stage. And maybe he just liked it, who knows.'[9] Only Charles Kennedy really knew, and he never returned to the chat shows to talk about it. He did not need to top himself up with alcohol during the day like Churchill, nor did his drinking flick a switch that made him volatile and embarrassing like George Brown. But his evenings of heavy private drinking could make the following day a write-off.

In the years before his death Kennedy's drinking was treated as a bit of a public joke, just as George Brown's had been forty years before. In December 2008, for instance, Kennedy appeared – as he often did – on the BBC's *Have I Got News For You* show. Jeremy Clarkson introduced his guest with a gag about his alcoholism: 'On Paul Merton's team tonight is a man who, after confessing to a drink problem, reported that four party officials cornered him in his private office – although later it transpired that there were only two of them: Charles Kennedy!' Merton's team-mate gamely fixed a half smile while the studio audience whooped and clapped.

Kennedy died at his home in Fort William on 1 June 2015. Several days later his family released a statement saying he had died of a major haemorrhage that was a consequence of his battle with alcoholism. 'Ultimately this was an illness Charles could not conquer despite all the efforts he and others made,' they said. A close friend of Kennedy's, Celia Munro, and her late husband John Farquhar Munro were among those who had tried to help. 'Alcoholism is a fearful, fearful thing. One can only assume that in the end he still couldn't reach the help he needed. I spoke to him very explicitly about it on many occasions. It was hard, like having your own child in front of you, and trying to reason with them. We sat many times with him. He had so many tragedies thrown at him,' Munro said, referring to the recent deaths of Kennedy's mother and father and the paralysis of his brother following a fall.[10]

Friends of Kennedy insisted it was not the loss of his seat in the SNP clean sweep of Scotland that precipitated his decline. He was looking forward to the future, as his close friend Alastair Campbell wrote in a tribute hours after Kennedy's death: 'Despite the occasional blip when the drink interfered, he was a terrific communicator and a fine orator. He spoke fluent human, because he had humanity in every vein and every cell.' A former alcoholic himself, Campbell said he and Kennedy frequently swapped coded text messages of support. If Kennedy wrote 'health remains fine' it meant a day off the bottle.

Of course Kennedy knew he had a serious drink problem.

Other people close to him complained about coy references to 'demons' in the tributes and obituaries that followed his death. Alcoholism, they insisted, was an illness and should be described as such.

Would Charles Kennedy have been a better leader sober? He might have had a sharper interest in policy detail and been less lackadaisical, a common complaint among critics in the party. But in electoral terms he was the Liberal Democrats' most successful leader, taking the party to its highest number of seats in 2005. What Kennedy did so well was to connect quite naturally with the electorate. With his merry face and sense of mischief, he was the party leader most voters said they would choose to have a pint with. His fatal flaw was that he could not control his own drinking and so became the most recent senior politician to be undone by alcohol.

## Reckless Drinking

Of course alcohol can produce very different effects on people. While some struggle on the edge of alcoholism, others can happily confine their consumption to a glass or two of wine at night. In some it produces behaviour that is embarrassing and aggressive, while in others it nourishes a gentle bonhomie. Most varieties of drinker were out in force on the House of Commons terrace in July 2010, on the night of the newly formed coalition government's first Budget vote, when the Second Reading of the Finance Bill was approved with a three-line whip. While they waited for the session to wind up, MPs did what they have always done to kill the time and headed to the bars for a drink. It was a balmy summer evening and the terrace overlooking the Thames was soon heaving.

For the newly elected, this late-night sitting was a novelty. Veterans could observe the collective slide into intoxication and took it steady. In the Commons chamber, the few MPs not guzzling the booze were giving their views on a Finance Bill that would bring in the biggest spending cuts and tax rises for a generation. It was a Budget that defined the government's decision to try and repair Britain's finances with a programme of austerity. But spending restraint was not in evidence the night MPs gathered for the vote. It was claimed that the Commons bar took some £5,000 during the evening as MPs splashed out on Pimm's, wine, beer and champagne.

Despite knocking back the drinks in the soft evening air, most managed to follow their whips' instructions and duly walked through the correct voting lobby at 2.07 a.m. All, that is, except the new Conservative member for Rochester and Strood, Mark Reckless. An MP for just two months, Reckless was legless; staggering around the terrace before reportedly falling to the floor. The former banker was bundled into a taxi and sent home, missing the vote. A remorseful Reckless told one newspaper he felt very embarrassed. 'It was a mistake I will not be repeating. I don't know what came over me. It was a long day and I'd had a very early breakfast meeting. I don't know what happened. I don't remember falling over.'[11] In an interview with BBC Radio Kent, Reckless said he remembered someone asking him to vote but not thinking it was appropriate to do so given his inebriation. 'I don't plan to drink at Westminster again,' promised the contrite MP, who later went teetotal and defected to UKIP before losing his seat in 2015.[12]

Mark Reckless was caught out. He had drunk too much to function and chose not to walk through the voting lobbies. But it is certain that many of the MPs voting either for or against the Finance Bill that warm July night would also have been over the legal limit to drive a car. If they were pilots, they would not have been allowed to fly. If they were surgeons attempting to operate, they would have been struck off. Yet MPs consider it quite normal to vote on legislation after a session in the bar. The Labour MP Paul Flynn has recommended that MPs be breathalysed before entering the Commons chamber. In his view being drunk in charge of a legislature is as dangerous as being drunk in charge of a lathe.[13]

But of course, even if every MP voted while sober, the results would be pretty much the same. For backbench MPs hoping for advancement (and that is most of them) it is a lesson quickly learnt that they are in Parliament to support the position taken by their own party's front bench. Every MP receives a weekly whip telling them how to vote, with each vote underlined. A one-line whip means they can turn up if they would like to; a three-line whip means compulsory attendance on pain of penalty. It is therefore an illusion to believe that MPs cast their votes after carefully weighing up the arguments in the House of Commons. Most debates in Parliament are not debates in the normal sense of the term. They are usually a thinly attended chance for MPs with an interest in the subject to recite their familiar views, or to catch the eye of their party, their constituency and the media.

Of course there are exceptions, and some MPs (often dubbed 'mavericks') make a point of being unbiddable. In recent years rebelliousness and independence have increased;

and the debates and subsequent votes on the invasion of Iraq, raising tuition fees and House of Lords reform have sparked fierce argument and significant backbench rebellions. However, the free thinkers remain a small minority in their parties. Most MPs are content to be herded through the division lobbies by their whips, voting on legislation they are unlikely to have read. It does not matter to the party whips whether their MPs are drunk or sober so long as they can clock up the numbers. Hence, in July 2010 the government was going to get its Finance Bill through the Commons whether MPs had spent the evening carousing on the terrace or reading in the library.

### Punches and Politics

One alcohol-fuelled incident stood out during the 2010–15 parliament and was destined to have far-reaching repercussions. On 22 February 2012, in the Strangers' Bar of the Commons, the Labour MP Eric Joyce headbutted the Conservative MP Stuart Andrew, punched a Labour colleague, Phil Wilson, and assaulted a couple of visiting Tory councillors. This ensured that the former army major made the headlines when he was arrested and charged with assault. Witnesses described scenes from a Wild West saloon as Joyce erupted and tables were upturned. He punched and headbutted his way through four people before eventually being restrained by police while shouting 'You can't touch me, I'm an MP!'

A few weeks later I sat in the press seats of Westminster Magistrates' Court as the crumpled-looking 51-year-old was given a £3,000 fine and banned from bars for three months after admitting to the assaults. He was lucky to escape a prison sentence. As he faced the cameras outside the court, Joyce apologised to everyone involved and said the incident had caused him 'considerable personal shame'. Expelled from the Labour Party, he announced that he would not be seeking re-election in 2015.

We met eight months later under the fig trees of Portcullis House, the modern building across from the Commons where many MPs have their offices. 'It was the final headbutt that did for me,' said Joyce, a burly, genial man with swept-back straw-coloured hair. He resembled a retired middleweight boxer. On the night of the fight he had been drinking House of Commons sauvignon blanc. The Falkirk MP said he was 'sufficiently loosened up' by the time a group of Conservatives began to rile him. 'One of them was being lippy and I do remember a Tory MP put his arm around me from behind like a bear hug and picked me up. And from that point it was game on really and I just whacked everybody.' He was eventually restrained by police, handcuffed and taken to Belgravia police station to calm down and sober up, before being charged with three counts of common assault.

Eric Joyce had become MP for Falkirk in December 2000 after winning a by-election. His 21-year career in the armed forces and his authorship of an article branding the army 'snobbish and rife with sexism and racism' made him a prominent and intriguing new MP, a favourite of BBC guest bookers. He stayed largely on message and was rewarded with a job as parliamentary aide to the then Defence Secretary, Bob Ainsworth. It was a job he quit in September 2009 after criticising the purpose of Britain's military campaign in Afghanistan.

Joyce's career, like that of many MPs, was static. He was not poised for promotion to Ed Miliband's front bench team. But nor had his prospects been fatally destroyed by scandal. And at least he was known to Westminster's journalists, unlike the many MPs who toil away in backbench obscurity and will never be ministers or invited to opine on *Newsnight*. There is no job description for MPs and each one has to work out for themselves what they are in Westminster for. Is it to be a diligent constituency MP and vote loyally for their party? Is their driving ambition to get a front bench job and the chance of becoming a minister? Some find their job satisfaction in scrutinising the work of government in a select committee. In practice many MPs follow a number of different paths during their Westminster careers.

Eric Joyce was clear about what he wanted. 'What's the point of being in politics if you're not a minister?' he said, as I fished around for reasons why he had cracked. 'I had no background in politics and just assumed, because I was so fantastic, that progression through the ministerial ranks would be fairly straightforward. But by 2005 there was a new government and I still wasn't in it.' After his brief stint as a Parliamentary Private Secretary, Joyce began to drink. Considering his political career to be a futile failure, he found consolation at the bottom of a glass. He said he hardly drank before arriving in the Commons. 'Was it a response to political failure? Absolutely, unquestionably. Most nights I'd have several glasses of wine, routinely, without thinking about it. It anaesthetised the experience of being here.' But the alcohol, mixed with a volatile temperament, made him prone to a fight. 'I'd been in lots of brawls,' Joyce chuckled.[14]

Four months after we met, Eric Joyce was again being pinned to the ground by police. On the evening of 14 March 2013, the Falkirk MP was arrested outside the Sports and Social Club bar, which was hosting a karaoke evening. Reports varied about the cause of the rumpus, but it may have had something to do with Joyce wanting to take a glass outside. At around 11 p.m., after a wrestle with police officers that was captured on the camera phones of other drinkers, he was once again hauled off to Belgravia police station and held there for twenty hours.

The parliamentary authorities called time on Joyce's drinking and banned him from buying alcohol anywhere within the Palace of Westminster. But the Crown Prosecution Service spared him another trip to court, deciding there was not enough evidence to bring charges. There were, prosecutors said, 'multiple inconsistencies' in the statements taken from witnesses at the Sports and Social. Two days after the fracas, Joyce posted a lengthy blog, denying he had been drunk or that he had ever been an alcoholic. 'I do not go into bars, nor drink in my office,' he wrote. The press again pilloried Parliament's drinking culture.

The impact of the Strangers' Bar brawl was felt far beyond Phil Wilson's chin. It is not fanciful to suggest that, if Eric Joyce had not seen red after too much drink on that February evening, then Jeremy Corbyn may not have become Labour's leader three and a half years later. How so? The chain of events goes like this. After Joyce was convicted of assault, he resigned from the Labour Party and said he would not stand for re-election in 2015. That opened up a vacancy in his Falkirk constituency. The Unite trade union wanted to ensure their chosen candidate was selected and was accused of signing up members to the local Labour Party branch without their knowledge with the aim of rigging the contest. Unite strongly denied doing anything wrong and the police found no evidence. But Falkirk became synonymous with a Labour variety of Tammany Hall politics.

The furore over trade union influence within the party prompted then leader Ed Miliband to radically change the rules for selecting Labour leaders. His aim was to broaden the membership base of the party, and appear to diminish trade union influence. The old electoral college system that gave MPs a third of the overall vote was ditched in favour of giving every Labour Party member one equal vote. And a new category of membership allowed people to become party 'affiliates' for just £3. So the influence of MPs was diluted while opening up the contest to non-party members.

After Miliband resigned, the contest to replace him saw more than 100,000 people sign up, 88,000 of whom voted for the veteran left-wing outsider Jeremy Corbyn. The majority of full members voted for him too, but the rule change undoubtedly made it easier for Corbyn to transform the contest, hoovering up support from enthusiastic new recruits. Labour MPs, the vast majority of whom emphatically did not want Corbyn to become leader, had no power to stop him. So the remarkable rise of Jeremy Corbyn had its roots in the events in the Strangers' Bar. His capture of the Labour Party and the surge in membership that took him there began with a drunken headbutt.

Eric Joyce was not the first MP to realise that life in the Commons was not what they had dreamed of. Elected because of their party badge, and rarely because of their personalities, new MPs confront a world in which their lives are governed by whips, they have very little power of their own, and there is none of the pastoral care or career development common in other walks of life. A long way from home, in a London flat, with time on their hands, MPs are prey to a multitude of temptations. The policemen on the doors might nod in deference, but the truth of a new MP's existence can be very different.

The journalist and former Conservative MP Matthew Parris describes the feeling of being a fraud:

> It breeds an internal cynicism and an imperceptibly opening up gap between your public life and your private, internal life ... The gap between these worlds becomes, for some, almost unbridgeable ... it is not surprising that MPs learn to despise, if not themselves, then the thing they are pretending to be. It is not surprising that they sometimes try to escape this, sometimes in a manner which to the rest of us looks desperate. Being an MP feeds your vanity and starves your self-respect.[15]

Some try to fill the gap with assorted diversions, which often get them into trouble. And as Eric Joyce and others have discovered, a readily available river of anaesthetising drink runs through Parliament from which to sip.

In 2014 drunken antics in the Strangers' Bar made headlines again, with the trial and subsequent acquittal of the Conservative MP Nigel Evans, who was also a deputy Speaker. The jury unanimously found Evans not guilty of all the sex offence charges brought against him. But the court heard how alcohol featured in every allegation against him, and Evans' defence barrister said the MP's 'drunken overfa-miliarity' with young male researchers was not disputed.

One Labour MP elected in 2010 told me about his vow not to drink at Westminster, wary of putting even a first foot on that particular ladder. Chatting to me over tea in the Strangers' Bar one afternoon, he described the pressures on politicians and how he had to wrestle with himself when it came to drink: 'Here I want to be seen as someone who's respected. I'm an ambassador of the people I represent. Once I have one or two pints I want more. It would be easy for me to slip into a drinking culture that wasn't in my own best interests. To me it's important I keep in the right place when I'm down here. I've thought about it greatly. I'll have soft drinks in here but at home I'll have a proper drink. It's something which, in a public position like an MP, you've got to give thought to. And I love drinking. I love a drink. I had to make a decision personally and stick by it. You've no idea how difficult it is when you come in here and fellow MPs are having one or two beers. And I say no. It's really difficult for me. There's a lot of pressure on people. It's easy to be lonely here. It's sink or swim. Survival of the fittest. If you've got problems and you're struggling there are not many people here to help you. And I've seen one or two people turn to heavy drinking. And that's in the main because it's lonely. Long hours, away from your family. People start off with a few drinks then have a few more and have a few more.'[16] In 2015 this MP returned to his small London flat to find a fellow member splayed out on the communal hallway floor, too drunk to move.

It is a culture the Conservative MP Sarah Wollaston was shocked to see when she arrived at Westminster in

2010. A former GP with no background in party politics, she created a stir when she said, at a fringe meeting of the Conservative Party conference in October 2011: 'Who would go to see a surgeon who had just drunk a bottle of wine at lunchtime? But we fully accept that MPs are perfectly capable of performing as MPs, despite some of them drinking really quite heavily.'[17]

Remembering what it used to be like, older MPs and journalists tend to roll their eyes in disbelief at such remarks. To them, the Palace of Westminster feels like a temperance bar in comparison with days gone by. If you spend a few hours watching MPs go about their business in the fig tree filled atrium of Portcullis House, the scene will be one of snatched cappuccinos and bottles of mineral water being glugged by MPs while they meet a ceaseless stream of visitors, mostly constituents or lobbyists. There will also be journalists trying to grab a word. Like the MPs, they generally no longer drink on the job either. The journalistic days of Lunchtime O'Booze are gone. Both MPs and journalists are now too busy writing, meeting, tweeting and blogging. The pace at which politics is now conducted is too unforgiving to permit an afternoon clouded by drink.

A big change has been in the relationship of MPs with their constituencies. When Roy Jenkins became an MP in 1950, he would visit his Birmingham constituency once a month and 'hardly ever raised constituency issues in the House of Commons'. For many years MPs did not even have to pen their own letters to constituents. The Liberal Democrat MP Sir Menzies Campbell remembers when the House of Commons Stationery Department used to provide a handy printed letter for MPs. 'It said, "I have taken up the matter you raise with me with the authorities and I enclose a copy of their letter." And that's what people used to sign. The idea of being a good constituency MP is a modern idea,' he tells me.[18]

An MP's constituency role has been transformed in recent years, with MPs doing much more and voters in turn expecting much more. By seven o'clock most evenings, the parliamentary restaurants and bars are quiet. Many MPs are tucked away in their offices desperately trying to catch up with their constituency correspondence. This has certainly contributed to the decline of political drinking, along with the changed hours, although seasoned *Guardian* journalist Michael White thinks several other factors have been at work: 'A desire to live longer, a desire to become a junior minister, a desire to be loyal to the party when the press persecuted dissent, all these things contributed. Family friendly hours was only part of it.'[19] The antics of MPs such as Mark Reckless and Eric Joyce are notable precisely because they are now rare, an echo from another age.

Labour's former Deputy Leader, Harriet Harman, has no nostalgia for the days when alcohol dominated the culture of Parliament and the bars groaned with MPs waiting around to vote in the early hours of the morning. I met Harman in her office with its wraparound view of Parliament Square, just days after Jeremy Corbyn had become Labour's new leader. She recalled how the male-dominated bars were a very uncomfortable place for women to be, particularly in the early years of her career: 'To be a young woman, to be on your own, in the middle of a whole load of men with drink flowing, it was a bit ambiguous. When you've got a meeting at least there's a sense of formality. But when you have a drinking culture it's an uncomfortable crossover between the social and the political.'

Harman is certain that her reluctance to be part of the drinking scene held her back at the beginning of her parliamentary career and defined how Westminster viewed her: 'Because I had young children and had a constituency close to the Commons I would go home. And if you weren't part of that drinking culture you were regarded as un-clubbable. That's what they used to say about me and it was reported by political journalists as fact. I was un-clubbable. What it meant was I wasn't hanging around in the bars drinking. Even if I hadn't had children I wouldn't have been comfortable doing it. There was no right way to behave. Either drinking tonic water or leaning on the bar, both would receive disapproval. If you weren't part of it you were snooty, unfriendly and not teamly.'

I asked if she thought this shaped the way the press presented her for the rest of her career. 'All the way through. I've never been unfriendly. I'm a total social animal. But the construct was a male drinking construct and there was no place for a woman in it. For decades I was apprehensive about going into Strangers' Bar. Which is why the arrival of a hundred women in 1997 was such an important change. Suddenly there was a critical mass.'[20]

Being absent from the bars meant political networks and relationships were being formed without you. When I asked Harman if this harmed her progress up the greasy pole, her reply was emphatic: 'Yes, definitely. You were seen as setting yourself apart and looking snooty. The one woman who did join in was Mo Mowlam. She became one of the boys in a way I never was.'

Harman insists Parliament must be the place of serious deliberation, not inebriation. 'I know everyone's against the professionalisation of politics but it's a workplace not a club.' Then why not just close down all the bars and sweep the whole culture away? Suddenly Harman becomes more guarded. 'It was what it was. We're in a different time now and it's not a defining part of the culture in the way it was. I'll leave it to other people whether they want to ban it or not,' she says wearily.[21]

While the bars are still places into which politicians and their staff drift at the end of the day for a pint or glass of Chardonnay, they are not the nurseries of political careers they used to be. Tony Blair and Gordon Brown did not build their reputations propping up Westminster bars; and the near-teetotal Jeremy Corbyn certainly did not. Nor did David Cameron and George Osborne. But perhaps they dipped in enough not to seem aloof. When the political bottle spun Theresa May's way in the frenzied aftermath of the EU referendum in the summer of 2016, she launched her Conservative party leadership campaign against a wall of books in the library of the Royal United Services Institute. There she made a point of defining herself against the clubby bonhomie of Westminster, a shrewd move after the referendum revolt. 'I know I'm not a showy politician,' she said. 'I don't tour the television studios, I don't gossip about people over lunch. I don't go drinking in Parliament's bars. I don't often wear my heart on my sleeve. I just get on with the job in front of me.'[22] In the political turmoil of the moment, Theresa May's serious clear-headedness was suddenly a very appealing prospect for Tory MPs, who swept the former Home Secretary into Number 10.

### Nick Clegg Splits a Bottle

Few modern politicians in Britain can have experienced the exhilarating high of political success followed by its cruel puncture as sharply as Nick Clegg. Taking over the leadership of the Liberal Democrats after Charles Kennedy's resignation, Clegg dazzled during the television debates of the 2010 general election and a fleeting phenomenon dubbed 'Cleggmania' was hatched by the press. In the end, the Liberal Democrats won five fewer seats than they had in 2005, but in the first hung parliament since 1974 the party suddenly held the keys to power. To the surprise of most Westminster pundits, Clegg welded his party to the Conservatives to form a coalition government in which he became Deputy Prime Minister. Suddenly, the Liberal Democrat leader was sauntering up Downing Street, had armed police drivers to ferry him around and occupied a huge Whitehall office. Along with David Cameron, George Osborne and the Liberal Democrat Chief Secretary to the Treasury, Danny Alexander, the four men formed the so-called 'quad' of key ministers that steered the government's decisions from Budgets to foreign policy.

It was the coalition's early decision to raise the level of university tuition fees that burst the bubble for Nick Clegg, breaking a pledge the party had made before the election to abolish student fees. The compromises required when in a coalition government with the Conservatives dismayed many who had voted Liberal Democrat and the party's support collapsed during its five years in power. At the 2015 general election Liberal Democrat MPs were scythed down, leaving just eight in the House of Commons, including Clegg.

I meet Clegg, now a backbench MP, in his parliamentary office on a gloomy November afternoon. He is typically ebullient and breezy, and as always seems to me one of the most likable and unaffected politicians in Westminster. As I probe his drinking habits, Clegg is apologetic that he does not have any stories of whisky-swilling desperation to share. Even in his most miserably pressured moments alcohol has never provided a crutch: 'My abiding sin was to have a few fags in the evening when I got back home, which I've now stopped. But it wasn't drink, no, and I certainly never got that impression for David, George or Danny either.' Such men mark a generational shift in government, ministers who would not dream of having a tumbler of whisky at five in the afternoon. Nor did Nick Clegg spend his early years in Parliament greasing political contacts in the House of Commons bars. 'I don't even know where these bars are!' he laughs.

However, alcohol did play a role in keeping coalition relations smooth. A few times a year, the quad would meet for dinner. Sometimes these were convivial affairs; at other times the backdrop to tough negotiation. They were often held in David Cameron's Downing Street flat and civil servants and special advisers were not invited. It was just the four people at the heart of the coalition, thrashing out policy issues and priorities over food and wine. Clegg is emphatic that no decisions were ever made while they were drunk, but the bottle of wine on the table was a useful lubricant. 'We would have eaten our feta cheese and fettuccini anyway but of course the alcohol helped, definitely, of course it did,' he tells me. 'It was very, very middle class. Classic wine drinking and we shared a bottle.' Just as the ancient Greek symposium was loosened up with a little libation, so the relationships underpinning the coalition were oiled with the help of a glass or two. However, this was tame stuff compared with the serious ministerial drinking of the past. Even though the economic problems faced by the coalition government were no less daunting than those faced by Wilson, Heath and Callaghan, the role played by alcohol in responding to them was much diminished. Instead, ministers jog, the Prime Minister setting an example by running around St James's Park with a personal trainer (and often with a photographer in tow).

Surely a Whitehall of ministerial sobriety is a good development? Having been an adviser to the Labour governments of the 1970s, David Lipsey is not so sure: 'Drink stopped the manic compulsion to do something every single day. A lot of what goes wrong now is due to ministers being too sober and too energetic and thinking up wheezes that they'd forget about if only they had a couple of large drinks.'[23] I put it to Nick Clegg that many of the big, memorable political characters of the past – like Ernest Bevin or Roy Jenkins – were also serious drinkers. Is there something about the new abstemiousness that makes for duller politicians? Clegg does not think a reluctance to booze is the explanation, but does accept that modern politicians are a blander bunch: 'There's clearly a trend to more identikit, pasteurised politicians. Partly because if you're not you get so mashed up by parts of the more censorious press we have.'[24]

## Boris

But there are still politicians who seem to float in a different orbit, and who are spared the sort of judgmental scrutiny applied to their colleagues, perhaps because they refuse to conform to the sanitised sameness of so many others in political life. One has his office on the opposite side of Portcullis House to Nick Clegg's; and when I visit him one evening there are bottles of House of Commons whisky and champagne laid out awaiting his signature, their destination possibly the raffle of a Home Counties Conservative Association. Also piled on the table are copies of the biography he has written of his political hero, Winston Churchill.

'I have seen distinguished members of the present Cabinet very far gone,' Boris Johnson says sheepishly, 'but in a lucid sort of F.E. Smith way,' he adds, referring to the rakish, witty and hard-drinking Conservative politician who blazed his way through British politics in the early years of the twentieth century. Lord Birkenhead, as he became, was one of Churchill's closest friends and served as Lord Chancellor and Secretary of State for India before dying of liver cirrhosis in 1930. Johnson, still Mayor of London as well as Conservative MP for Uxbridge and South Ruislip when we met, has a deep admiration for the formidable political drinkers of the past and values the fortifying power of alcohol himself. But drink, he tells me, is a 'treacherous friend' for a politician. It can encourage and embolden, while making the merry-go-round of dinners and rubber-chicken functions more bearable. There is usually a pint before dinner, then several glasses of red and white placed on the table: 'Two glasses is OK. Three you're starting to feel a bit prolix. And you notice the audience starting to look at each other.'

A politician has to be careful. 'The crucial thing about using alcohol at political engagements is you have to know exactly how much to have. It starts well, there's a terrific élan, but then after a while what happens with alcohol if you're not careful, two things. Your words start to slur and then you find yourself speaking very fast for no particular reason and then you suddenly start slowing down for no particular reason. And then you become somehow disembodied and you're spectating at this event. And then a blackness, a morbidity descends. And then you become sort of bitter,' Johnson says, trailing off.

A former journalist, Johnson believes booze at lunchtime used to help enormously to make the words flow: 'I certainly find that if I've drunk a bottle of wine at lunchtime I can write a piece unbelievably fast and it'll be as good as anything else. I can do 1,000 words in forty-five minutes and it will be fine. But if I've done it at dinner, no good.' Johnson is unabashed about his fondness for drink. 'Sometimes I drink a prodigious amount but I also go days without drinking at all. I haven't been drunk for a very long time.'

But what about coping with the stress of running London? Does that mean you drink more? 'No, not really. Sometimes a cup of tea's pretty good, you know. Sorry, I don't want to ruin your thesis!' he laughs.

But the sacramental aspect of shared drinking, its signal that a relationship has become closer and less formal, is alcohol's real importance to politicians, believes Johnson. 'Oh yes, alcohol's crucial, absolutely crucial. You always slightly worry about people who don't drink.' So has it helped lubricate any particular decisions, I ask.

The Mayor pauses for a very long time. 'I'd better be careful here,' he groans, rubbing his mop of hair, agonising whether to spill some secrets. 'I can't tell you for security reasons, I'm sorry ...'

Johnson grins. The silence is getting awkward, so I suggest some foreign examples might be easier. 'Yes!' he booms. 'My God, in China, it's absolutely true that we did a large number of deals there that resulted in huge investments in London – Battersea, Greenwich and elsewhere. In China they have this system when they have very serious toasts after every course. Loads of courses, nineteen of them. Huge tureens of Margaux wine. By the end we were pretty fluent.'

I end by asking Johnson about his hero Winston Churchill. He is in no doubt that Britain's wartime Prime Minister benefited from his gargantuan consumption of alcohol. 'God yes, absolutely. Churchill was very clever at making it work for him. His consumption was formidable but he could use it as fuel. He could keep producing and performing. It's the high-density lipoproteins. That's what you need to focus on. That's what alcohol gives you,' he says with the serious tone of a family GP. We swap stories about Churchill's prodigious wartime drinking, recounting his arrival at Casablanca at six in the morning, having flown around the world, and asking for a tumbler of white wine. Could anyone do that today, I wonder?

'The trouble is the 24-hour news cycle is so demanding. You'd have to be propped up and shoved out in front of the cameras the whole time as soon as something happened. I can't see it somehow.'[25] Eight months later, Boris Johnson was haring around the world himself as Foreign Secretary in Theresa May's new government, a chance to deploy his skills at drink-assisted diplomacy.

# CHAPTER 4

## Prime Ministers: Tipplers at Number 10

The portraits that line Downing Street's Grand Staircase can be seen as a story of prime ministerial imbibing through the ages. From the bewigged Sir Robert Walpole to the photograph of Cameron, it is a gallery of whisky sippers, wine buffs and beer drinkers. For three centuries Prime Ministers have turned to the Downing Street drinks cabinet for consolation and inspiration; to fire them up and to calm them down.

Pitt the Younger's heavy port drinking was done on doctor's orders, but it destroyed his health. Asquith's intake of wine earned him the sobriquet 'Squiff' and stained his reputation. Harold Wilson sought brandy to steady his nerves before he faced the Commons chamber; and a Bell's whisky helped Margaret Thatcher wind down when she slipped off her heels at the end of the day. Churchill drank in quantities unmatched by any other Prime Minister, although his whisky was watered down more than legend suggests.

Harold Macmillan, the last Prime Minister to be a habitué of Pall Mall clubland, enjoyed a tipple himself and was relaxed about the habits of others. On 25 April 1962, Macmillan's diary records that one of his junior ministers, Denzil Freeth, was arrested for being drunk in the Strand. 'The Chief Whip agrees with the poor man that he should resign,' he writes. 'I am very much against this – assuming that this is the only charge. There are worse things that can happen. There is nothing unmanly about being drunk, and very good precedents among my great predecessors.' Macmillan then adds, with a twinkle, 'in the street is perhaps a pity.'[1]

Not every Prime Minister sought solace in a bottle and some avoided alcohol altogether. Although by no means teetotal David Lloyd George had an appetite for women rather than wine. The diffident and modest Clement Attlee led a serious government with suitable sobriety and did not reach for drink to ease the strains of office. Playing the piano rather than pulling out a cork was Edward Heath's means of escape. James Callaghan resolved not to touch a drop once he got to Downing Street because he did not want alcohol to impair his judgment. But the focus here is obviously on those Prime Ministers who did turn to alcohol, some much more than others. And this invites an immediate question: what did drink do to their judgment?

There is no evidence of significant political decisions being taken by a Prime Minister who was obviously the worse for drink, but alcohol regularly sloshes around in the background. It perks Prime Ministers up, relaxes them, makes the grind and pressures of power more bearable and has effects on their behaviour. Their use of alcohol is a window into their characters; and into the political story of their times.

### Walpole's Wine

Britain's first Prime Minister, Robert Walpole, clocked up twenty years in the job. It remains an unmatched record. The aristocratic Whig dominated politics in the first decades of the eighteenth century, an era that required Walpole to juggle the demands of the King and Parliament using a combination of political cunning and corruption. Entering the House of Commons in 1701, Walpole soon saw that lavish entertaining was an essential ingredient of a successful political career. So he used his first government job to help stock up his cellar.

Walpole was made a member of the Admiralty Board, which advised Prince George on naval issues. It was not a particularly demanding role and Walpole spotted a chance to get his hands on forbidden French wine and champagne. Imports were banned because of Britain's war with France, but Walpole and the Secretary of the Admiralty, Josiah Burchett, came up with a ruse to smuggle booze in with the help of the navy. Ships (presumably with the compliance of their crews) picked up wine from Holland, hid it among the rigging and then floated it up the Thames on an Admiralty barge to the waiting Walpole. Other customs-dodging smugglers would have faced punishment and prison. Walpole, however, began to build up one of the finest wine collections in politics.

After Britain made peace with France in 1713, the wine started to flow in lawfully. Remarkably, some of Walpole's wine receipts have survived the centuries and provide a snapshot of the tastes and consumption of this discerning drinker. In 1733 he spent £1,118 with the wine merchant James Bennett – a huge sum for the time, equivalent to around £200,000 in 2014 prices.

As the historian J.H. Plumb reveals, Walpole's consumption was prodigious. He had a love of white Lisbon and in the first six months of 1733 bought 111 half-dozen bottles, far more than any other wine. It was more expensive than port and cost Walpole twenty-four shillings a dozen, ready-bottled. He also bought huge quantities of champagne and Rhenish from the Rhine. As for reds, it is clear he preferred claret to port and bought it by the cask. In 1732 and 1733 (the years for which complete bills exist) he bought four hogsheads of Chateau Margaux (£45 each) and a hogshead of Lafite every three months. The claret was usually bottled at Walpole's cellar by his merchant.

Twice a year, the Prime Minister entertained close friends at the Walpole family home at Houghton in Norfolk. They were lavish affairs. In July 1731, the political writer Lord Hervey wrote this description to Frederick, Prince of Wales:

> Our company at Houghton swelled at last into so numerous a body that we used to sit down to dinner a little snug party of thirty odd, up to the chin in beef, venison, geese, turkeys, etc; and generally over the chin in claret, strong beer and punch. We had lords spiritual and temporal, besides commoners, parsons and freeholders innumerable.[2]

In the intimate, aristocratic political world of the time, Walpole dominated the scene like nobody before and his wine bills give an insight into early eighteenth-century drinking habits. As much business as possible was done around the dinner table. As Plumb puts it, 'it was not an abstemious age'.[3]

### Pitt's Port

Bookending the eighteenth century was Britain's second longest serving Prime Minister and one of the heaviest drinkers to occupy Number 10. William Pitt the Younger was just forty-six when he died, probably from gastric ulceration brought about by years of overwork, pressure, recurrent illness and excessive drinking. By the end of his life there is little doubt that Pitt was an alcoholic, dependent on the port he had been reared on in his youth.

The precociously brilliant Pitt, the son of the Earl of Chatham, inherited his father's political skills but also his fragile constitution. He was often unwell as a child and developed gout when he started his studies at Cambridge at the age of fourteen. Unlikely remedies were prescribed. The Chatham family doctor, Anthony Addington, recommended that Pitt should follow a special diet, take regular horse rides and knock back a daily dose of port wine. As Pitt's biographer William Hague says, that dose has been variously recollected down the generations as a 'bottle a day' or 'liberal potations'.[4] At the time, alcohol was thought to be a good way of dispelling toxins from the body and Pitt's health did begin to improve. So, given the green light to guzzle large amounts of port by his doctor, Pitt drank heavily and regularly for the rest of his life.

The port Pitt drank differed from that consumed today. It could be white, red or rosé; and port was the name given to the region it was produced in, the Douro Valley, rather than a single variety of wine. All were sweet and fortified with brandy but, at around 14 per cent, eighteenth-century port was weaker than its modern namesake. The bottles that contained it were also smaller and thicker than modern wine bottles. Pitt was known as a 'three-bottle man', but it is unlikely he regularly drank that much at a single sitting. As William Hague concludes, 'Three bottles of port in Pitt's day would be roughly equivalent to one and two thirds of a bottle of strong wine today. This is still a large amount of alcohol to consume, but not an unimaginable one.'[5]

Indeed, it is perhaps more imaginable than Hague's own much-mocked claim, made as Conservative Party leader, that he could polish off fourteen pints of beer a day as a teenager while working for Hague's Soft Drinks, his father's Yorkshire delivery firm. And while beer drinking has become a way for modern politicians to signal their similarity to ordinary voters, port drinking in the eighteenth century was a way for the political elite to share the habits of the developing middle class. At the start of the century, Walpole had filled his cellar with claret. But by the end of the century, Pitt's chosen beverage was judged more masculine and patriotic than the weaker, pricier wines from France. Port drinking was a mark of middle-ranking Englishmen. Indeed, as Charles Ludington says: 'By the 1780s, port was the preferred wine of the most politically and socially elite men in England.'[6]

Pitt took his seat in the House of Commons in 1781 and his political ascent was astonishing. A year later, at the age of twenty-three, he was Chancellor of the Exchequer. By twenty-four he was Prime Minister, still the youngest ever to this day. His first ministry lasted for seventeen years and oversaw union with Ireland, brought in Britain's first ever income tax and gradually increased Westminster's grip over Britain's fledgling empire. Politics was everything to Pitt, and after the outbreak of war with Napoleon the pressures on the Prime Minister increased. So did his drinking.

Pitt had always been a heavy drinker and it had not gone unnoticed. In 1788 the Declaratory Act – which aimed to establish a permanent military force in India, paid for by the East India Company – went through the Commons. In the debate, Pitt was too ill to respond to a speech by his great rival, Charles James Fox. Pitt had been drinking heavily the night before and various accounts suggest he was suffering from a severe hangover. On another occasion Pitt was called away from dinner to answer an unexpected political attack by opponents in the Commons. It was clear he was under the influence of wine and it alarmed his friends. In fact, one of the clerks of the House was made sick by the sight of it and developed a violent headache. 'An excellent arrangement,' remarked Pitt; 'I have the wine and he has the headache.'[7] Shortly after the outbreak of war in February 1793, Pitt and his loyal friend and political fixer, Henry Dundas, entered the Commons clearly the worse for wear, leading to the memorable lines in an opposition newspaper:

I cannot see the Speaker, Hal, can you?
What! Cannot see the Speaker, I see two![8]

As other Prime Ministers have done, Pitt used drink to cope with the demands of the job. Although he first developed the habit of heavy drinking on the advice of his doctor, he also seems to have drunk more when under strain. Pitt was a workaholic who wanted to be involved in all areas of government and by the late 1790s the pressure was taking its toll. According to one historian, 'His consumption of alcohol increased; his optimism drained away when problems defied rapid solution.'[9] After a bout of illness in 1802, one of Pitt's friends, Earl Camden, wrote: 'He has recovered his appetite, and his strength is returning, but I observe no difference in his diet and he drank at least two bottles of port after dinner and supper last night.'[10]

The war with France dragged on longer than Pitt had expected. When he returned to Downing Street for his short second (and last) ministry, drink had become a crutch for the dutiful but exhausted and prematurely aged Prime Minister. In 1804 the army general William Napier noted that Pitt had become dependent on drinking alcohol in private: 'Mr Pitt used to come home to dinner rather exhausted, and seemed to require wine, port, of which he generally drank a bottle, or nearly so, in a rapid succession of glasses; but when he recovered his strength from this stimulant he ceased to drink.'[11]

Pitt was dead less than two years later. Decades of excessive port drinking had poisoned his body and William Hague is in no doubt that by the end of his days he was an alcoholic.[12] But Pitt's niece Lady Hester Stanhope thought the life Pitt led would have broken even the strongest character:

Oh doctor, what a life was his! Roused from sleep with a dispatch from Lord Melville; then down to Windsor; then, if he had an hour to spare, trying to swallow something; Mr Adams with a paper, Mr Long with another, then Mr Rose, then with a little bottle of cordial confection in his pocket off to the House until three or four in the morning; then home to a hot supper for two or three hours more, to talk over what was to be done the next day: – and wine, and wine. Scarcely up next morning when 'rat-a-tat' twenty or thirty people one after another, and the horses walking before the door from two till sunset, waiting for him. It was enough to kill a man – it was murder.[13]

For the next hundred years no Prime Minister comes close to matching Pitt's alcohol consumption. With his taste for large quantities of strong dark port, he was also a drinker of his time.

## Squiffy Asquith

The decision to go to war against Germany in 1914 was perhaps the most significant and far-reaching taken by any British Prime Minister in the twentieth century. Sixty-two-year-old Herbert Henry Asquith had been in Number 10 for six years by the time war broke out and his Liberal government had already ensured it would leave a big political footprint on Britain. The 1909 'People's Budget' increased several direct taxes on the wealthy and triggered a constitutional showdown with peers. The government's fight with the House of Lords culminated in the Parliament Act of 1911, which stopped peers from interfering with financial bills. In the same year a radical new national insurance scheme was introduced, the foundation stone of the welfare state.

So who was this man? The clever second son of a chapel-going Yorkshire family, Asquith dazzled at Oxford and practised as a lawyer before going into Parliament. He was known to be a bit scruffy but had a sharp and tidy mind. As Prime Minister he was an effective chairman of Cabinet who could be rather reserved with colleagues. But after his second marriage in 1894 to the extravagant socialite Margot Tennant,

Asquith loosened up and started enjoying the fizz of London society and country house weekends. One biographer says that although Margot introduced her husband to the habit of after-dinner brandy, he 'already fancied himself as a connoisseur of clarets and champagne'.[14]

The pre-war diaries and private correspondence of Asquith's colleagues contain references to his fondness for drink.[15] But by 1911 the effects of his drinking were becoming more obvious. One evening during the committee stage of the Parliament Bill, the Prime Minister appeared to be drunk on the government's front bench. In a letter to his wife on 22 April 1911, Winston Churchill wrote:

> On Thursday night the PM was very bad: & I squirmed with embarrassment. He could hardly speak: & many people noticed his condition. He continues most friendly & benevolent, & entrusts me with everything after dinner. Up till that time he is at his best – but thereafter! It is an awful pity & only the persistent freemasonry of the House of Commons prevents a scandal. I like the old boy and admire both his intellect and character. But what risks to run ... The next day he was serene efficient undisturbed.[16]

It wasn't the only time Asquith was seen in the Commons obviously the worse for drink. The MP Arthur Lee (who later gave his Chequers country mansion to the nation for the use of future Prime Ministers) provides this sketch of the well-oiled Asquith appearing opposite him on the government front bench during the committee stage of the controversial Welsh Church Bill:

The two Ministers on duty were Herbert Samuel and Rufus Isaacs, and at about ten o'clock Asquith, having returned from dinner, very flushed and unsteady of gait, plumped himself down between them on the bench and promptly went to sleep. Whereupon Balfour, who had been cynically surveying the scene, turned to me and murmured 'I am getting uneasy about this Bill and don't like at all the idea of the fate of the Church being left in the hands of two Jews who are entirely sober and of one Christian who is very patently drunk!'[17]

In April 1911 Asquith was diagnosed with hypertension and his doctor ordered him to slash his alcohol intake. It is claimed that the Prime Minister then moderated his drinking, pouring his energies instead into hundreds of love letters to Venetia Stanley, one of the clever and attractive young women to whom he unburdened himself throughout his life.

There is no sense that Asquith drank because he was depressed. In fact the golf club-swinging, bridge-playing Prime Minister had a sunny, optimistic outlook and it seems he drank because it made the dinner table more convivial. But it may have been a response to pressure too. As the historian Colin Clifford says, 'Asquith was never an alcoholic – his alcohol consumption was far less than Churchill's was when he was Prime Minister – and excessive drinking was as a result of too much wine and brandy at the dinner table to alleviate the strain of having to cope with one crisis after another.'[18]

As Britain approached one of the biggest crises of its history, critics inside and outside Parliament were beginning to notice and mock Asquith's drinking. According to the

*Oxford English Dictionary*, 'squiffy' has been used as a slang word for drunk since the mid-nineteenth century, but Asquith's drinking may have revived its use. Behind his back he was nicknamed 'Squiff', and in London's music halls the wartime Prime Minister was laughed at every night in George Robey's Bing Boys revue when it came to this verse of his popular song:

> Mr Asquith says in a manner sweet and calm,
> 'Well, another little drink wouldn't do us any harm.'[19]

None of Asquith's biographers conclude that the Prime Minister's imbibing impaired his judgment at this critical time. As Churchill remarked after the war, Asquith's mind 'opened and shut smoothly and exactly, like the breech of a gun'.[20] And in September 1916, with the war bogged down in the graveyard of the Somme, Sir Douglas Haig wrote to his wife after receiving the Prime Minister at his headquarters for dinner that Asquith's 'legs were unsteady but his head quite clear … indeed he was quite charming and alert in mind'.[21] Roy Jenkins, another claret-loving liberal, wrote in his sympathetic biography of Asquith that 'no one has ever suggested that his mind lost its precision or that there was any faltering in his command over what he did or did not want to say.'[22]

But in 1916 the war was going badly on all fronts and by the end of November there were 415,000 British casualties from the battles of the Somme. Compared with the ferocious energy of the man masterminding the munitions effort, David Lloyd George, Asquith's reputation as a rather mellow inebriate was now causing him political harm. Churchill complained to his brother in May 1916 that 'Asquith reigns sodden, supine, supreme.' The claret-quaffing bonhomie of the years before 1914 jarred with the grim misery of war. Lytton Strachey described meeting Asquith at a party, in a letter from May 1916:

> He seemed much larger than he did when I last saw him (just two years ago) – a fleshy, sanguine, wine-bibbing medieval-Abbot of a personage – a gluttonous, lecherous, cynical old fellow – I've never seen anyone so obviously enjoying life … One looks at him and thinks of the war … On the whole, one wants to stick a dagger in his ribs … and then, as well, one can't help liking him – I suppose because he does enjoy himself so much.[23]

Asquith's fondness for drink was also at odds with the drive for national sobriety being pioneered by Lloyd George. So concerned was Lloyd George with drunkenness among munitions workers that in a speech on 28 February 1915, he explicitly linked the problems of armaments production with those of drink: 'Drink is doing us more damage in the War than all the German submarines put together.'[24] Alcohol consumption was reduced after the creation of the Central Control Board later in the year and Lloyd George tried to persuade government ministers to set an example by giving up booze for the duration of the war. But the 'King's Pledge' scheme was a flop; only Kitchener and the King himself seem to have kept their promise of abstinence. According to Roy Jenkins, 'Asquith, like Churchill, took not the slightest notice of the gesture, and even Lloyd George, who was a very light drinker, with skilful opportunism regarded himself as exempt from his own scheme.'[25] It cannot have escaped the notice of workers being told to cut their drinking that the man leading Britain's war effort refused to do the same.

By the autumn of 1916 Asquith's drinking and clear enjoyment of life were viewed as frivolous by critics who encouraged the impression that he was an out-of-touch toper. Lord Northcliffe's newspapers increased the pressure on the beleaguered Prime Minister, blaming him for the war's mistakes. In December the Unionist leader Andrew Bonar Law pulled his support for Asquith and it fell to Lloyd George to assemble a new War Cabinet; there was no place for Asquith, who resigned on 5 December. If the war had been going better, if Asquith had risen to the demands of wartime leadership with more confidence, his drinking might not have mattered. But in the search for scapegoats it was a stain on his character that harmed his authority, contributing to the fall of a man of whom it had been said (by Bonar Law to the chief whip in December 1911), 'Asquith drunk can make a better speech than any of us, sober.'

## Winston Churchill

And so to Downing Street's champion drinker. While Asquith's intake was mocked and judged indecent during the First World War, the brandy-loving, champagne-swigging, whisky-sipping exploits of Britain's Second World War Prime Minister have been affectionately celebrated as evidence of the great man's exceptional character and physical stamina. Not only could he lead the nation in a victorious fight against Germany, the story goes, but he could do so with a daily alcohol intake that would make even the captain of a rugby team wilt. The reputation for alcoholic excess seems to have obsessed and irritated even his teetotal enemy. Hitler variously described Churchill as an 'insane drunkard', 'whisky-happy' and a 'garrulous drunkard'.[26]

It was a reputation that Churchill himself was happy to embellish, firing off a number of memorable bon mots that are among the most famous drink-related anecdotes ever uttered. 'I have taken more out of alcohol than alcohol has taken out of me,' Churchill mused one night at Chequers during the war.[27] Then there is his famous encounter in 1946 with the pugnacious Labour MP Bessie Braddock, who accused the former Prime Minister of being drunk as he was leaving the House of Commons. To which Churchill replied: 'Bessie, you're ugly. But tomorrow I shall be sober.'[28]

It was not the pressures of war that drove Churchill to drink. He had been absorbing huge quantities of alcohol for decades. When, as a young journalist, he sailed to South Africa to cover the Boer War in 1899, along with his pith helmet Churchill packed eighteen bottles of Scotch whisky and almost forty bottles of wine bought from wine merchant Randolph Payne in Pall Mall.[29] By the mid-1930s he was drinking very heavily; when the newspaper proprietor Lord Rothermere offered him a bet that he could give up alcohol for 1936, Churchill refused the wager saying that 'life would not be worth living'.[30]

The diaries and memoirs of people who knew and worked with Churchill through the war are peppered with accounts of his alcohol consumption. They have led some historians to conclude that Churchill was an alcoholic, while others have judged that his booze-soaked reputation is wildly overstated. So who is right? Here is one of the fullest descriptions of a day observing Churchill drinking that I have found. It is by General Sir Ian Jacob, who worked in the military wing of the War Cabinet secretariat during the war:

> He drank a great deal. At breakfast he had coffee and often orange juice, although I have seen him drink white wine for breakfast on occasion. During the morning he would often have a glass of iced soda-water by him which he sipped from time to time. He didn't drink cocktails or sherry, but drank a good deal at lunch, often champagne followed by brandy. He didn't have tea, but about tea-time or later, according to when he had his sleep, he would start drinking iced whisky and soda. He probably had two or three glasses, not very strong, before dinner, and then at dinner he always had champagne, followed by several doses of brandy. Then during the late evening and night he had more whisky and soda.
>
> He had obviously been accustomed to this kind of routine for years, and yet he was never the worse for drink in my experience, and, as far as I could see, he never felt the slightest ill-effects in the morning. This was the more peculiar in that he took no exercise at all …
>
> It is not for me to explain this phenomenon, but it is obvious that his body must have been capable of disposing of alcohol and its waste products with unusual efficiency.[31]

Here we have evidence of Churchill's extraordinary consumption – including sometimes wine for breakfast

– but also proof that he used plenty of soda water to dilute the whisky that he supped during the day. 'It was really mouthwash,' Churchill's private secretary Sir Jock Colville told the historian Martin Gilbert.[32] Churchill's post-war valet Norman McGowan said the first whisky and soda would be ordered about an hour after breakfast: 'For the rest of the day the tumbler was never empty, but he drank very slowly, absent-mindedly sipping it from time to time and making each glass last about two hours. It was literally drowned in soda at the outset and as ice cubes had to be in it, which melted long before he had finished, the drink was a very innocuous one.'[33] Another of Churchill's biographers, Roy Jenkins, describes his subject as a 'sipper not a guzzler', who had a metabolism that could cope with large quantities of alcohol. Churchill, Jenkins says, 'did not drink as much as he was commonly thought to do, although this is not incompatible with him being a fairly heavy and consistent imbiber'.[34]

During the war, Churchill spent a huge amount of time travelling abroad. Colville records the dinner on the third night of his voyage across the Atlantic to the Quebec conference in September 1944; on that occasion the Prime Minister managed to get through 'oysters, consommé, turbot, roast turkey, ice with cantaloupe melon, Stilton cheese and a great variety of fruit, petit fours etc, the whole washed down by champagne (Mumm 1929) and a very remarkable Liebfraumilch, followed by some 1870 brandy'.[35]

Churchill's talent for absorbing huge quantities of booze while apparently remaining sober came into its own at the big wartime summits. Secret intelligence files released in 2013 give an account of an epic drinking session between

Churchill and Stalin at the Kremlin in August 1942. Sir Alexander Cadogan, Permanent Under-Secretary at the Foreign Office, described the scene at one in the morning when he was summoned to join the two leaders:

> There I found Winston and Stalin, and Molotov who had joined them, sitting with a heavily laden board between them: Food of all kinds crowned by a suckling pig, and innumerable bottles. What Stalin made me drink seemed pretty savage: Winston, who by that time was complaining of a slight headache, seemed wisely to be confining himself to a comparatively innocuous effervescent Caucasian red wine. Everything seemed to be as merry as a marriage-bell.

Even though he held that there was nothing more awful than a Kremlin banquet, Cadogan thought the boozy atmosphere fostered frank questions and candid answers. 'Conditions have been established in which messages exchanged between the two will mean twice as much, or more, than they did before,' he concluded approvingly.[36]

The same diplomat noted that at the Yalta conference in February 1945 the Prime Minister seemed well, 'though drinking buckets of Caucasian champagne which would undermine the health of any ordinary man'.[37] As the future of post-war Europe was carved up over the dinner table, discussions between Churchill, Stalin and Roosevelt were lubricated by a succession of Russian toasts. But while Churchill knocked them back, the American President was careful not to down each drink and Stalin was seen surreptitiously weakening his vodka with water.[38]

What effect did this heavy drinking have on Churchill? Most contemporary accounts support Roy Jenkins' view that alcohol energised and exhilarated the Prime Minister rather than addled him. But it might also have been used to calm his depressive, sometimes manic temperament. The author Michael Dobbs has written extensively about Churchill and believes the drinking was a form of self-medication: 'It was enjoyable for him but it evened out a lot of the highs and lows he suffered from including his black dogs,' the melancholic slumps that descended regularly throughout Churchill's life.[39] David Owen agrees that despite the copious quantities Churchill drank it did not appear to do him much harm, but believes it was nevertheless a dependency.[40]

On only a handful of occasions do Churchill's contemporaries say that drink had a detrimental effect on his behaviour. On 6 July 1944, for instance, Field Marshal Lord Alanbrooke, one of Churchill's closest advisers, wrote in his diary:

> At 10pm we had a frightful meeting with Winston which lasted till 2am!! It was quite the worst we have had with him. He was very tired as a result of his speech in the Commons concerning flying bombs, he had tried to recuperate with drink. As a result he was in a maudlin, bad tempered, drunken mood, ready to take offence at anything, suspicious of everybody, and in a highly vindictive mood against the Americans. In fact so vindictive that his whole outlook on strategy was warped.

But this is one of the very few suggestions of inebriation. 'Personally, throughout the time I knew him I never saw him the worse for drink,' remembered John Peck, one of Churchill's private secretaries. 'The glass of weak whisky, like the cigars, was more a symbol than anything else, and one glass lasted him for hours.'[41]

So, other than watered-down Johnnie Walker Black Label whisky, what did Churchill like to drink? His preferences have been well chronicled by Cita Stelzer, and it is clear that he had no taste for beer or cocktails. For instance, when Churchill finally arrived at Quebec for his meeting with Roosevelt he turned down the offer of a second mint julep, the bourbon-based cocktail from Kentucky.[42] A mint julep, while refreshing, is not a Churchillian drink. Champagne, however, he drank with delight, and it was served from the beginning to the end of dinner. In 1898 Churchill wrote: 'A single glass of champagne imparts a feeling of exhilaration. The nerves are braced: the imagination is agreeably stirred; the wits become more nimble.'[43]

Churchill was a champagne connoisseur and his favourite was Pol Roger, either the 1921 or the 1928 vintage. In 1947 he told Odette Pol Roger, the grande dame of the champagne family, that '44 Avenue de Champagne, Epernay, is the world's most drinkable address'; doubtless flattered, but canny, Odette sent him a case of the 1928 vintage every year on his birthday until supplies ran dry in 1953.[44] After the war Churchill told Herbert Asquith's daughter, Violet Bonham Carter, that he had 'some relations' with the Veuve Clicquot during the First World War but that it was not a patch on the Pol Roger.[45] The company has made the most of its Churchill association, and in 1975 began naming its cuvée after him. Churchill enjoyed noggins of old brandy too, which helped to loosen up late-night conversation.

For most of his life Churchill survived on a drip feed of alcohol, supping steadily throughout the day and late into the night. His tumblers of whisky would have looked pretty transparent and were kept so with regular squirts of soda water. A glass of wine in bed for breakfast while he worked away on his papers was not a daily habit. But his intake of alcohol seems astonishing by today's standards, particularly at a time of such colossal national crisis. And that raises a question: if Churchill had to lead Britain today in a fight for survival, would his drinking be tolerated by a more intrusive and censorious press? Probably not. There would be outrage in the political blogs at the leaked reports from Downing Street of his heavy champagne and brandy drinking. Following up the internet rumours on television, Andrew Marr might quiz Churchill on whether his borderline alcoholism made him unfit for office: 'Prime Minister, people say you're frequently depressed and have to guzzle lashings of champagne to function. Are those reports right?'

Second World War Churchill would probably just stub his cigar out on Marr's sofa and walk off the set. A contemporary Churchill, if such a figure could be imagined, would be expected to weave his way around the question, make a non-denial denial and reassure anxious viewers that he was completely focused on the job. Instead, while Churchill led the fight to save civilisation, his appetite for alcohol was an accepted part of his complex, emotional and remarkable character. And since Churchill used alcohol to manage his moods and keep his mind sharp, it might even be concluded that drink played a small part in the Allied victory.

## Wilson: Brandy takes the Strain

When 58-year-old Harold Wilson re-entered Downing Street in May 1974, he was a wearier, slower figure than the energetic young Yorkshireman who first became Prime Minister in 1964. In that first term he was the intellectually agile face of modern, meritocratic Sixties Britain, a grammar school boy who looked and sounded like the people who voted for him. Wilson worked hard at presenting himself as a man of industry, aspiration and simple tastes. And drink was part of that pitch. 'I don't do much socialising and my tastes are simple,' he declared before that first election. 'If I had the choice between smoked salmon and tinned salmon I'd have it tinned. With vinegar. I prefer beer to champagne and if I get the chance to go home I have a North Country high tea – without wine.'[46]

It was a compelling contrivance. In public Wilson drank beer and puffed a pipe. In private he smoked cigars and drank more spirits than his image suggested.[47] The new satirists soon cottoned on to the artifice, but for much of the 1960s Wilson and his government had energy and vigour, despite the backdrop of growing economic crisis.

Wilson had not expected to win the first election of 1974 and retirement from front-line politics was already on his mind. The people who worked with him in Downing Street were very conscious of how he had changed, and one big difference was his intake of alcohol. Wilson had always enjoyed a drink and was pleased that he knew the difference between hock and burgundy, although 'he is good at drinking either,' Richard Crossman said later.[48] But as early as 1964, it was becoming a necessary prop and his intake of whisky and brandy increased. In the view of one of Wilson's biographers, 'an occasional stimulant had become a need'.[49]

Wilson once said to an official: 'I don't drink too much because I am like a man who is always driving.'[50] By 1974 he had been at the wheel of the Labour Party for eleven years and clocked up five and a half as Prime Minister; and by this time brandy had become a crutch to keep him on the road. Wilson had become more nervous about Prime Minister's Question Time and habitually knocked back brandy before facing the Commons. His press secretary, Joe Haines, remembers the need for nerve-calming doses before the then twice-weekly Commons interrogation: 'He always used to throw down a brandy at 3.10. And then it got to two brandies. He went in one day and the questions dragged on until 3.40. He came out and people flooded into the room and a private secretary said he'd done well. I told him his voice was slurred and that he couldn't drink two brandies and perform.'[51] Once the gruelling ordeal was over he would drink more brandy to recover.

Wilson was not alone in finding PMQs a nerve-shredding experience. Harold Macmillan was sometimes physically sick before walking into the Chamber, and Tony Blair described his weekly joust with MPs as 'the most nerve-racking, discombobulating, nail-biting, bowel-moving, terror-inspiring, courage draining experience' of his Prime Ministerial life.[52] But while Wilson drained a couple of glasses of brandy, Blair took a sleep-inducing melatonin pill the night before and ate a banana before going into the Commons. The same stress, different drugs.

It was not an easy time to be Prime Minister. In 1975 inflation hit 27 per cent, productivity was low, unemployment was rising, industrial relations were fractious and violence had broken out in Northern Ireland. To add to Wilson's worries, the Labour Party (and the Cabinet) were split on the question of Britain's future in Europe; and, on top of everything else, the Prime Minister believed there was a conspiracy – involving foreign intelligence agencies and possibly MI5 – to bring down the government. Downing Street was tense and dysfunctional, with Wilson's press secretary Joe Haines in bitter conflict with Number 10's political secretary, Marcia Falkender. It was a toxic feud that continued long after they both left Downing Street. For years, Falkender had been Wilson's most important and loyal political ally, but now her strident and angry presence was putting further strain on the Prime Minister, although he never stopped trusting her judgment.[53] Bernard Donoughue, Wilson's main policy adviser, says the Marcia Falkender situation was another trigger for Wilson to drink: 'I observed, and others working in Number 10 remarked, that whenever he'd had a difficult telephone call from his political secretary, when he put the phone down he immediately went to the cupboard and took out the brandy bottle.'[54] But Wilson stayed loyal to Falkender, misting out the problems with alcohol rather than taking them on.

Difficult meetings were preceded by brandy and civil servants disapprovingly noted Wilson's habit of sipping from a glass during ministerial discussions. He once told Barbara Castle that brandy was the only thing keeping him going, and by the time of his resignation only alcohol was making the job tolerable. In his diary entry for 3 July 1974, Donoughue writes: 'The PM ... went to lunch with the press and apparently was the worse for drink. This was embarrassingly obvious when the Cabinet committee on Energy met in the late afternoon. He rambled and ministers looked embarrassed.'[55] Joe Haines is blunt: 'It was only the drink then that sustained him in the last year or eighteen months.'[56]

For a time Wilson decided he needed to lose weight and stopped drinking brandy. Instead he started drinking five pints of beer a day. As Philip Ziegler says: 'On no one day was the input dangerous, but over the years the accumulated damage to his health must have been considerable.'[57] Efforts to persuade the press that all was well and to keep the Prime Minister's drinking secret were not successful, as Michael White noticed on the one occasion he visited Wilson at Number 10: 'The only time I went to his rooms he was there alone with a bottle of Perrier water conspicuously on the table. Young though I was, I realised that a man displaying Perrier water is sending out false signals.'[58] As Britain staggered through these turbulent, anxious years, the now baggy-eyed Prime Minister found consolation at the bottom of a bottle.

But as with Churchill, the people who worked with Wilson deny he was ever drunk or that the alcohol damaged his judgment. 'If he was taking big decisions over incomes policy, the referendum, the economy, on Britain's membership of the EU, that didn't seem to produce the kind of stress that led to him drinking,' says Bernard Donoughue. 'The normal routine of policy choices which he was well accustomed to, which he rather enjoyed, didn't seem to stress him in the same way.'[59]

If that is the case, why was Wilson clutching a brandy bottle for support by the time he left Downing Street? Joe

Haines believes that Wilson knew his formidable mental powers were starting to misfire. Statistics could not be rattled off with the same quick precision and his appetite for the contents of a red box was shrinking along with his concentration. According to Haines, Wilson drank more because he knew his mind was beginning to deteriorate: 'Drinking didn't influence his thinking. His thinking influenced his drinking.'[60] Twelve years after the cheerily dynamic Harold Wilson first walked into Number 10, a less sober and more world-weary Wilson surprised almost everyone by suddenly resigning in March 1976.

## Thatcher: Winding down with Whisky

When a frail and confused Margaret Thatcher is filmed recalling snippets of her premiership, and conversations with her late husband Denis, through the fog of dementia, a chunky tumbler of whisky is often seen in her hand. Thatcher's enjoyment of a stiff drink is a small detail the creators of *The Iron Lady*, the 2011 feature film about Britain's first female Prime Minister, got spot on. While she wrestled with the trade unions, crushed the wets in her Cabinet, sent a modern Armada to win back the Falklands and brushed herself down after the Brighton bomb, a constant, comforting companion for Margaret Thatcher during her eleven years in Number 10 was a glass of whisky. It was savoured when Downing Street was winding down for the evening and the Prime Minister was ready to relax.

Relaxing was something Thatcher did not do very easily, remembers her Cabinet Secretary Lord Armstrong: 'She liked a glass of whisky at six or seven o'clock and that very often turned into two glasses of whisky. It relaxed her at a time of day when she was beginning to feel frayed and it took her through the evening. She didn't need the stimulus but it just relaxed her a little bit and that was useful. I never in the least felt I needed to say, PM, you've had enough.'[61]

And there is no evidence that she supped too much. But the unscrewing of a Bell's whisky bottle marked the transition from the formal working day to an evening of red box reading and letter writing. Her pugnacious press secretary, Bernard Ingham, says the whisky was a useful lubricant: 'We used to gather at about six in the evening in her room before she went off to dinner or to the House to tell her what was going on over a Bell's – which she ruined with soda. And that I think certainly oiled the wheels of government. If you gather in a room with the Prime Minister who is having a drink it's a more relaxed atmosphere and people relax at the end of the day and tell it as it is. She wasn't exactly the most relaxed animal I've met in politics and to that extent it was beneficial.'[62]

Before she became Prime Minister, whisky was actually written into Margaret Thatcher's diet. In 2010, details of her 1979 pre-election weight loss plan were released. The protein-packed regime revolved around eggs (twenty-eight a week), steak, grapefruit and salad and was typed up on a piece of yellowing paper found inside her 1979 pocket diary. At the bottom of the two-week diet plan the note reads: 'Whisky may be taken on days when meat is eaten otherwise NO ALCOHOL'[63]

In December that year, the new Prime Minister made her first official visit to the United States. After meeting President Carter, Thatcher hosted a lunch at the British Embassy in

Washington and her whisky drinking was approvingly noted by the ambassador, Sir Nicholas Henderson, in his diary entry for the day:

> Mrs T took a glass of whisky. She had another during lunch as well as half a glass of red wine. I have noticed that whisky seems to be her favourite tipple and, as Peter Carrington (the Foreign Secretary) said to me later in New York, 'Thank God she likes the stuff.' She is disciplined without being puritanical, at least so far as the small pleasures of life are concerned.[64]

As a young Conservative MP, Michael Brown was regularly scooped up during late-night sittings by Ian Gow and taken to the Prime Minister's Commons office for a gossip over a glass of whisky. Brown remembers Gow's rather mean measures being topped up by Thatcher, her shoes slipped off and her legs tucked up on the sofa. 'Thatcher was never drunk but she was very happy to have a decent slug of whisky,' says Brown. 'She understood the role alcohol had in oiling the wheels.'[65] There were often House of Commons whisky bottles in the outer office awaiting the Thatcher signature, a tradition she started.

The journalist Petronella Wyatt said her father, Woodrow, was besotted with Thatcher in part because of her ability to drink with the blokes. 'She was regarded by my father as an honorary man ... It was spirits all the way – no nonsense about wine – stuff like scotch and gin.'[66]

Thatcher's drinking was routine and controlled. But at times of high stress she seems to have imbibed more, just as other people tend to do. During the Falklands war, for instance, Thatcher drank whisky while she waited anxiously for news from the South Atlantic. Late at night the Prime Minister and her close assistant Cynthia Crawford would sit on the floor of the master bedroom in the flat above Number 10 and listen to the latest updates on the BBC World Service. They used to have a whisky and soda to calm their nerves, because as Thatcher explained to her companion: 'You can't drink gin and tonic in the middle of the night, dear. You must have a whisky and soda because it will give you energy.'[67]

The former chemistry student knew when she wanted alcohol to calm her and when she wanted it to give her confidence. Lord Armstrong agrees that those tense weeks in 1982 saw the Prime Minister drink more than usual: 'I certainly remember times during the Falklands affair, waiting for news to come in and another drink would be had and that relieved the tension.'[68]

Margaret Roberts came from a teetotal, Methodist background. But then she married Denis Thatcher, the gin and golf loving businessman whose love of drink became part of his popular persona. It was satirised with extraordinary accuracy in the 'Dear Bill' letters in *Private Eye*, an imagined correspondence between the Prime Minister's husband and a golf partner called Bill. The first letter appeared on 15 May 1979 and read:

Dear Bill,
So sorry I couldn't make it on Tuesday ... M. insisted I turn up for some kind of State Opening of Parliament or other. I had assumed now the election was over I would be excused this kind of thing, but oh no. I had

just carried my spare clubs out to the jalopy when heigh ho! – up goes a window and M. is giving my marching orders. It's off to Moss Bros. for the full kit, and at that moment, I don't mind telling you, I couldn't help thinking pretty enviously of you, Monty and the Major enjoying a few pre-match snifters at the 19th without a care in the world.[69]

Snifters; part of Denis Thatcher's unique drinking lexicon. Bernard Ingham spent many long flights sitting next to the Prime Minister's husband and can still rattle off the list: 'I was able to compile Denis Thatcher's tally of drinks in ascending order of alcoholic potency on account of sitting next to him on countless flights. Broadly speaking it went like this: An opener (the first one), a brightener, a lifter, a tincture, a large gin and tonic without the tonic, a snifter, a snort, a snorter and a snorterino – which more or less emptied the bottle in one go. Denis certainly enjoyed himself.'[70]

On one occasion the Thatchers were catching an early morning flight to India. The stewardess asked them what they wanted to drink and Denis requested a large gin and tonic. Shocked, the Prime Minister said, 'Denis, it's not even breakfast time!' To which Denis replied: 'It's lunchtime where we're going and I always like to arrive prepared.'[71] Denis Thatcher used to boast that he and his friends could 'drink enough to sink a battleship' and turned down ice in his liquor because he thought it diluted the alcohol.[72] He used to say 'my glass isn't working' when the drink ran dry.

Carol Thatcher recalls a charity lunch at which Denis was asked how he spent his time as the Prime Minister's consort. Instead of affecting an interest in charitable good causes,

Denis declared: 'Well, when I'm not completely pissed I like to play a lot of golf.'[73] At a function in the shires, a Tory lady took Denis aside and discreetly sympathised: 'Mr Thatcher, I understand you have a drink problem.' Denis waved his glass and said: 'Yes, Madam, I have. There is never enough of it.'[74] Chris Moncrieff remembers a boozy Number 10 reception for Westminster journalists at which the Prime Minister's husband regaled the hacks with advice about what to drink in different countries. Margaret Thatcher approached the group and asked what they were talking about. 'Quick as a flash he said "architecture in Hyderabad" and proceeded to do so!'[75]

### New Labour, New Sobriety?

The New Labour decade coincided with a panic about how much alcohol Britain was consuming. Tales of binge drinking filled newspapers and television news bulletins. While teenagers were filmed staggering around town centres drunk on alcopops, middle-aged, middle-class boozers watched the reports from their sofas while unscrewing the evening's second bottle of pinot grigio. The government introduced longer licensing hours for pubs, and it seemed much of Britain was embracing the opportunities offered by 24-hour drinking. So it was fitting that the Prime Minister who oversaw this national inebriation was something of a lush himself.

When his autobiography was published, Tony Blair confessed to drinking a little more than his government recommended to deal with the pressures of running the country (and perhaps the pressures of living next door to Gordon Brown). 'If you took the thing everyone always lies about – units per week – I was definitely at the outer limit,' Blair wrote. 'Stiff whisky or G&T before dinner, couple of glasses of wine or even half a bottle with it. So not excessively excessive. I had a limit. But I was aware that it had become a prop.'[76] And his memoir included this self-help homily: 'You have to be honest: it's a drug, there's no getting away from it. So use it with care, maybe: but never misunderstand its nature and be honest about its relationship with your life.'[77] For Blair, and millions of others in Britain, breaking the government's drinking guidance every night had become an essential private pleasure, a tool to smooth away tension at the end of the day.

Blair's rumination on booze totalled only three small paragraphs in his 700-page doorstop, but it prompted much comment and some mockery. His six units a night boast did not impress his former Cabinet colleague Dr John Reid, a once heavy drinking Glaswegian who now does not touch a drop. Dr Reid told GMTV, 'Where I come from, a gin and tonic, two glasses of wine, you wouldn't give that to a budgie.' Alastair Campbell says he never saw Blair the worse for wear from drink: 'If you've gone from having two or three glasses of wine a week, which is what he was having at the start, to half a bottle of wine, you'll think it's a problem. He maybe was drinking more than we thought but I don't think he ever drank to excess.'[78] Campbell was at Blair's side from 1994 until 2003 and quit drinking after an alcoholic career working on Fleet Street. Blair drank most heavily towards the end of his premiership; perhaps he was missing Alastair Campbell.

In his book, Blair chats through his drinking dilemma. He says he could 'never work out' whether alcohol was good for him because it helped him relax, or bad because he could have been working instead. On balance he comes to the conclusion that the benefits of drink-assisted relaxation outweighed the cost to his work. 'I thought that escaping the pressure and relaxing was a vital part of keeping the job in proportion.'[79] If Robert Walpole had been in the market for confessional autobiography he might have said the same.

## Beyond Blair

Gordon Brown found it much more difficult to keep the job in proportion. He was a workaholic, phobic about holidays and prone to phoning his staff in the middle of the night to issue fresh orders. His Presbyterian conscience drove him to work and kept him away from a daily drink. But he was far from teetotal. As several people who worked closely with him told me, Brown's tipple was champagne. According to his long-time adviser Damian McBride, 'If Gordon could drink champagne he would drink champagne. It's always what he'd keep in the fridge in the Treasury and the flat in Downing Street. It was always his drink of choice. But he was always reluctant for other people to know that. So if he was at an event he would always say "give me a beer".'[80] McBride says that Brown was loyal to Moet & Chandon but never touched a drop until work was out of the way. And when he did drink it was not privately but convivially and in company. For instance, after a Downing Street drinks reception at which he would nurse an un-drunk glass of beer, he would invite close aides up to the flat and then the champagne would come out. But as McBride remembers, Brown was not inclined to savour the drink. 'He would knock it back. He would never consider two glasses of champagne as a big deal. He was like the cookie monster. Down in one, whoosh!'[81]

So was Gordon Brown ever drunk? 'I did undoubtedly see him tipsy. He would never have been laughing as hysterically as he used to at those Christmas parties if he hadn't been in drink. They were very entertaining affairs.'

McBride then proceeds to tell me an astonishing story about the drink-fuelled antics inside Downing Street while Brown was still Chancellor, but desperate for the occupant of Number 10 to clear off. 'There used to be some scandalous behaviour which did neighbourly relations no good. Downing Street shares a lot of staircases even though you've got independent flats. You cross a lot of walls that the Blairs would be on the other side of. And occasionally, in heavy drink after those Christmas parties, people walking down the stairs would hammer on the wall shouting "When are you going to fuck off! When are you going to fuck off!" You'd occasionally get the same thing back from Number 10 people saying, "Oh, have you been drinking again?" It was like a couple that had separated living in the same house occasionally coming together and shouting at each other for ten minutes and then going their separate ways. I never did that by the way ...'[82]

Echoing his political hero Margaret Thatcher, David Cameron was partial to a whisky, and his *Desert Island Discs* luxury item was a crate of Isle of Jura single malt. Like Gordon Brown, Cameron's consumption is modest and he does not drink every evening. But he does enjoy a Sunday afternoon pub lunch, as everyone discovered when he left behind his then eight-year-old daughter Nancy at the Plough Inn near

Chequers in 2012. A biography of Cameron published in 2012 described a Prime Minister who had mastered the art of 'chillaxing' – a man partial to a game of tennis, a TV box set and a couple of glasses of wine with his Sunday lunch. In fact, the same off-duty pursuits as the rest of us.

At a Downing Street Christmas drinks reception for journalists in 2013, Cameron sauntered around the room carrying a glass of water. When it was my turn for a two-minute chat, he told me that was all he drank at events like this or before a speech. 'But it's a different matter when they're done,' he chortled. I asked him whether he was drinking more the longer he was in the job, as many previous Prime Ministers did. Standing next to Cameron was his Director of Communications, who narrowed his eyes in a way that said 'watch it'. This was clearly a line of questioning that needed to be defused. 'No, I find sleep and exercise are by far the most important things,' Cameron replied, breezily tapping away the question.[83] He then claimed diplomatic meetings were rather dry these days, but revealed President Obama's fondness for Grey Goose vodka, the fashionable spirit favoured by Manhattan's cocktail sippers. In January 2016, pressed by Andrew Marr on the government's new drinking guidelines, Cameron said, 'I often have a drink in the evening after a long day.'[84]

The longest day of David Cameron's premiership came six months later, when he lost the referendum on Britain's EU membership, a vote he had called and expected to win. But as results started to come in on the night of 23 June 2016, the Prime Minister watched helplessly as Britain chose Brexit. At 1 a.m., David Cameron sent for a bottle of Scotch to help relieve the stress, according to one of the speechwriters in Number

10 that night.[85] At 3 a.m. the Prime Minister disappeared to get some sleep, his dreams of another five-year term in office crumbling along with the political legacy he hoped for.

The EU referendum terminated David Cameron's tenure in Number 10 and propelled Theresa May into office. The former Home Secretary had already paraded her serious-minded, alcohol-shunning credentials during the brief leadership race, so it was no surprise to see the new Prime Minister holding a glass of un-iced water at her first Christmas drinks reception for journalists. As we tucked into craft beers, wine and sausages on sticks, Theresa May was protectively guided around the room by an adviser. Guarded and enigmatic, the Prime Minister did not build her career schmoozing journalists over boozy lunches or drinks and is a mystery to most political correspondents. She has none of David Cameron's buoyant swagger, either. But she has a dry wit. When one journalist, fishing for some conversation, asked Mrs May if she ever popped round to Number 11 to borrow a cup of sugar from the Chancellor Phillip Hammond, she was overheard to say, 'I'm diabetic, why would I borrow sugar?' I talked to the Prime Minister briefly about this book and mentioned to her that almost all her predecessors drank more alcohol the longer they were in office. She gave her glass of water a wave in a manner that said, 'that won't be me'. When I asked what she did to relax, she said that she enjoyed hill walking, an activity that may not provide the nightly respite many of her predecessors found with the help of a drink. However, it seems unlikely that any future Prime Minister will match the drinking prowess of Walpole and Pitt, or of Asquith and Churchill, and even more unlikely that they would want to. Prime Ministers have sobered up too.

# CHAPTER 5

## Pubs, Clubs and Parties

Drink is the metronome of Westminster life. It paces the day like the chimes of Big Ben. 'A quick half?' is the question at lunchtime. 'A pint?' at the close of play. As the bell's six heavy tolls resound across Whitehall, the pubs begin to fill. The pavements outside will soon be packed with booze-guzzling smokers. Opening the doors, a visitor is greeted by a gust of beery hot air and cacophonous political chatter. All of Westminster life shoves its way towards the bar: civil servants, journalists, Members of Parliament, special advisers, press officers and political party staff.

The people change, but the fixtures don't. The Westminster pub, much like Parliament itself, is suspended in time. Dark mahogany bars, polished brass foot rails, etched mirror glass, beery carpets and real ale on tap. An American tourist's idea of what an English pub should be like? Perhaps, but no worse for that.

And it is in these Victorian drinking dens that political gossip is swapped, contacts are made and business is done. It's where the village meets. Listen in and you will hear civil servants complaining about a difficult minister or a policy they are trying to sign off. You might catch a couple of MPs conspiring over a pint. You will see political journalists truffling for stories and special advisers assisting their search. Politics is pollinated over amber nectar and ice buckets of wine. This chapter looks at political imbibing beyond the Houses of Parliament – in pubs, clubs, restaurants, receptions – and at the famously boozy antics of party conferences. It traces the influence of drink from the journey of a wannabe MP buying rounds in a pub to a Prime Minister sipping champagne on his plane.

Let's begin with a bar crawl around Westminster, where each pub has a distinctive but shifting political character. The Westminster Arms on Storey's Gate is crammed full of Conservative Party workers and special advisers. Close to the Treasury and the Tories' new HQ, it's a pub that has gone from red to blue. So too the Red Lion on Whitehall, perhaps the most famous Westminster boozer. Opposite Downing Street, the Red Lion is the domain of whichever party is in government. There has been an alcohol-selling watering hole on this site since 1435. Closest to Parliament is the touristy St Stephen's Tavern. It has its own division bell which rings when there is a vote, but there are few politicians to hear it.

Slightly further away are two more pubs, the Speaker and the Two Chairmen, useful meeting spots for a quieter pint. The Marquis of Granby on Romney Street was dominated by Tory drinkers when the party's headquarters was around the corner. For fifty years Conservative Central Office was at 32 Smith Square, where a victorious Margaret Thatcher waved from the windows. The building now houses the unlikely pairing of the European Commission and UKIP, which is why the Marquis of Granby is now the favourite drinking spot of Nigel Farage and the UKIP press team. It is also popular with civil servants, Labour drinkers and broadcast journalists from their offices on Millbank.

Pubs and pint-pulling for the cameras are important elements of the political scenery. Although drink is no longer used by candidates to bribe voters and elections have ceased to be carnivals of drunken excess, beer (never wine) drinking is a symbol. Want to prove you're a politician with a popular touch? Head to a pub and pull a pint. Few electioneering stunts are meant to say 'I'm a down to earth Brit who shares the hearty pleasures of my voters' more clearly than a posed photograph of the candidate drawing some ale from a barrel. The regular staff find themselves elbowed aside by people who have never stepped behind a bar before, grabbing the pump of a local brew and squirting the frothy beer into a glass. The usually unsellable pint is then triumphantly held aloft for the local press to take a snap. From prospective Prime Ministers to long-forgotten parliamentary candidates, the pub has always been commandeered by political wannabes eager to bridge the gulf between themselves and the electorate.

Yet this is very odd. No cameras follow our campaigning politician as they grab some dinner at Tesco on their way home from work. Or juggling the chaos of the morning breakfast melee or school run (though both Ed Miliband and David Cameron contrived kitchen scenes of dubious veracity). You can demonstrate your worth as a potential MP simply by showing how well you can fill a pint glass with beer. Even in an era of micro-targeted constituency propaganda, online adverts and ruthlessly focused attention on the small number of voters who swing an election, a photo opportunity in a pub is a constant of British election campaigning. The pub remains a political symbol of unpretentious good sense, particularly at a time when few words in the lexicon are as toxic as 'politician'.

And where did Jeremy Corbyn go first after trouncing his rivals? The Sanctuary pub in Westminster, where Labour's teetotal new leader roused his comrades and baffled visiting tourists by holding up a Tony Benn tea towel and joining in a rendition of 'The Red Flag'. Labour's first leader and most revered figure, Keir Hardie (like Corbyn a bearded non-drinker), may have approved, though not of the venue.

### Drinking for Britain

There is one politician who is seen in pubs more than any other. With his fag-rattle laugh and pinstriped suits, Nigel Farage is a throwback to a time when politicians didn't all look and sound the same. The ebullient former UKIP leader and MEP is rarely photographed without a pint of beer in his hand and he has never hidden his love of a drink, describing himself as 'a boozer not an alcoholic'. Farage is frequently to be found holding court in the Marquis of Granby in Westminster, around the corner from UKIP's headquarters.

Nigel Farage is one of the best political salesmen in the business, perhaps the only one who passes with ease that hoary old political question: which politician would you most like to have a pint with? He's the sort of 'hail fellow well met' raconteur who looks like he'd be entertaining down the pub. And he is. For Nigel Farage, a pint or five of frothy British ale is a pillar of his appeal, a sign that he doesn't take himself too seriously and that he shares the vices of voters. In recent years I have had the occasional pint with him in Westminster, Brussels and Strasbourg, the three places he habitually mocks and complains about. But when I talk to Farage about his drinking one morning in September 2015 it's outside a Westminster coffee shop, clouds of his cigarette smoke curling into the autumn air. The pubs aren't open yet, but he'll be in one again soon.

'I adore the pub,' he says. 'I think every pub's a parliament. We discuss the England football manager, the council, the left-wing local vicar. I've also been in pub conversations and through persuasion turned 180 degrees from the position I started an argument in. So I like that element of pubs. The other thing I love about the pub is the sheer classlessness of it. Every walk of life is there.'

While the main political parties spend vast sums of money on focus groups, Nigel Farage uses his local pubs in Kent as laboratories to test and shape his party's policies. There in Battle of Britain England, the party's brand of political nostalgia – for a Britain before the European Union, Polish immigrants and political correctness – is an easy sell. 'Have I sound-tested ideas in pubs? You bet your life I have! What makes me laugh is the cynical press corps think some brand image consultant behind me has decided that if I'm seen in the pub with a beer it's a man of the people image that fits in with UKIP and the demographic it's reaching, and this has all been carefully scripted. Cobblers! None of it's been carefully scripted. It's what I do!'

I ask him why the drinking seems to have become such an important plank of his appeal. 'The reason it works is because in a politically correct age where all this stuff is frowned upon I think people see it as two fingers up to the establishment and political correctness. And I think that's why it works and yet I'm not doing it for that reason. And it puts some people off. I might not be doing as well with the Methodist vote as we'd like. The upside is that wherever I go people are falling over themselves to buy me drinks,' he laughs.

When the latest official drinking guidelines were issued in early 2016, with reduced recommended limits, Farage was on hand to call for 'a mass protest against this form of nannying and we should all come out at lunch and have a glass of something'.

Nigel Farage's drinking is not a political affectation. He's been boozing heavily for years. 'On a personal level I've always drunk too much. There's no secret about that. I get up at five and work like stink, have a pint at lunchtime and generally have a drink with the team after work. Of the people I drank with in the City in the early days quite a few are dead; quite a lot drink mineral water now because they went over the edge – and I've seen that problem in my own family – but there are some of us who are lucky. And I'm one of the lucky ones. I can take it or I can leave it.'

You don't feel dependent on it?

'No. But it's like an incentive. It's like the reward. Is that dependency? Maybe psychologically it is.'

Do you drink more under pressure?

'No. I've never drunk a lot under pressure or when I've been down. I tend to be a celebratory drinker. My associations with it are positive – maybe that's why I've been spared.'

Farage firmly denies he's a functioning alcoholic. But I ask him, does he feel under pressure to keep up the consumption to maintain the image?

'No, I can do what I like can't I? There are certain pubs I have to avoid now because there's always a photographer around. I'm actually slightly cautious not to be seen to do it too much.'

Why?

'Because there's a slight reputational risk. I don't want to be thought of as a George Brown or a Charlie Kennedy. The public image as it is at the moment is fine. There's never been an implication in any cartoon that I'm a drunk – which I'm not. And that would be a disaster.'

Someone as ubiquitous on television as Nigel Farage might be wary of putting away pints all day, but he tells me he has firm rules about his drinking. First, he says, he never drinks in the office. Second, he will not do a broadcast interview if he's drunk more than five pints of beer. 'That's on the edge. That's the upper end. If I'm doing *Question Time* I'll have a couple of drinks before that. Enoch Powell told me he always had a glass of wine to loosen up before going on television,' he says, remembering a chat they had once at a public meeting, shortly before the controversial Conservative politician died. It was on an episode of *Question Time* in December 2014 that the comedian Russell Brand dismissed his fellow panellist as a 'pound shop Enoch Powell', but Farage's brand of politics won UKIP almost four million votes in the following year's general election and fuelled the vote for Brexit in 2016.

It's almost midday and Farage has a PFL in the diary. 'It's well known that I like a PFL – a proper fucking lunch!' he chortles. A Land Rover Discovery waits to whisk Farage off, two bodyguards by his side. 'I do think about my drinking sometimes,' he says. 'But this is the life I've got. It's fun, it's different.' And with that he stubs out his final fag and hops in the car.[1]

### Spinning with Bottles

Gordon Brown's former press chief, Damian McBride, described Westminster as the 'binge-drinking capital of Britain'. His memoir of life at the Treasury and then Number 10 is a queasy catalogue of lunchtime boozing, evenings in the pub and night-time karaoke: 'Lunch – booze; afternoon reception – booze; meeting a journalist – booze; 5 p.m. – traditional post-work booze even though it wasn't post-work; late night in the office or the House of Commons – booze; and always a nightcap or two at home.'[2] McBride said it took a huge toll on his health, but nobody ever took him aside and told him to stop. Building relationships with journalists, planting stories and sharing intelligence was his job. And like others before and since, McBride found that was easiest done with drink.

Journalists need politicians and their advisers to give them stories. The politicians want their latest policy wheeze or effort at self-promotion to be noticed and covered by the media. The two tribes are locked in a prickly, often hostile, but mutually dependent tryst. It's a symbiotic relationship that hinges on personal relationships and contacts, and one that is frequently oiled by alcohol.

It is important to separate the formal and informal channels of communication that generate much political news. For instance, twice-daily briefings are held for Westminster's lobby correspondents by the Prime Minister's official spokesperson. These on-the-record encounters are conducted by a politically neutral civil servant and are an opportunity for journalists to quiz Number 10 about the day's political stories. An MP or minister might say something in Parliament that generates a headline. Other political stories emerge from select committee or National Audit Office reports and a great deal of political news is churned out by the government and political parties themselves – everything from new policy initiatives to pre-briefed speeches, the creation of a task force to the appointment of a 'tsar'. There is a vast government communications machinery built to deliver all this, and legions of party press officers. Control and planning is at its heart. Downing Street directs what's called the 'grid', the master plan of what stories from which government departments will be released in the weeks and months ahead.

But running alongside this formal operation is a ceaseless churn of chatter, briefing and off-the-record gossip between politicians, their advisers and journalists. It's sifting this river every day that produces stories. Sometimes such conversations happen between an MP and journalist around the Members' Lobby at the entrance to the House of Commons chamber. This is where Westminster reporters have traditionally tapped the views of MPs and ministers, the journalist standing sheepishly in the shadows trying to catch the eye of a passing punter. The coffee bars and atrium of Portcullis House, MPs' modern office building, provide another popular place for politicians and journalists to talk. And of course a lot of business is now done by phone and text. But the pubs, bars and restaurants of Westminster are a crucial place for political trade.

I meet Damian McBride at the Mad Bishop & Bear pub in Paddington station. He has three hours to wait for his train, which gives us plenty of time to sample the beers and revisit his years as one of Gordon Brown's closest lieutenants, beginning as a Civil Service press officer before slipping the leash and becoming a political adviser. McBride's career imploded in 2009 after a leak of emails showing him prepared to smear leading Conservatives. Newspapers that had relied on his briefing and gossip for years formed a firing squad and he became a byword for everything squalid about politics.

Because I began my reporting career in Westminster just as the Labour government was beginning to crumble, I didn't really know him. But the McBride I meet doesn't bear much resemblance to the 'Mad Dog' of Westminster folklore. He is good company and it's clear why hacks enjoyed a drink with him.

And alcohol drove everything he did. 'I was a highly functioning alcoholic,' he tells me. 'It was the fuel that allowed me to do incredibly long hours.' Because he could do most business by phone (whether rewriting Civil Service submissions, writing articles for Gordon Brown or briefing journalists), he could also do it from the pub. 'It's not like I'm in a factory assembling Sky digiboxes. I was regarded as a top performer in my job while being pretty pissed ninety-nine per cent of the time.' McBride says he set out wanting to have the best press relations of anyone in Westminster and drink was the best lubricant for doing that. So where was business done?

'The Westminster Arms was where I went with civil servants, but it's a terrible place to drink with journalists. I found the best places to do proper trade were upstairs in the Two Chairmen, or other places you could be tucked away like the Sanctuary hotel bar. One journalist was so paranoid about being seen with me he insisted we would meet in Stringfellows. He didn't seem remotely interested in the girls, to the extent that we were asked to leave.' The drink greased the trade in information. Stories would be swapped for gossip about other government ministers or a degree of protection against reports that might harm Gordon Brown. 'Terms of trust were formed over drink,' McBride says.[3] And his predecessor did the same.

Charlie Whelan was Gordon Brown's ebullient spokesman until 1999, when he resigned after details of Peter Mandelson's mortgage arrangements were leaked. Whelan was notorious for conducting business in the pubs of Westminster. On a Friday evening in the autumn of 1997, he was overheard briefing journalists in the Red Lion that Britain would not be joining the European Single Currency in that parliament.

It was a defining moment of Tony Blair's first government. Gordon Brown, in an interview for the following day's *Times*, had hardened up the 'wait and see' approach on the euro. The bald headline said joining was off the agenda. Whelan, white wine spritzer in hand, guided hacks from other newspapers towards the true meaning of the Chancellor's words. In other words, the spin. Whelan's conversations were overheard by two Liberal Democrat press officers. They told the Press Association and the BBC about the briefing in the boozer and the fuse was lit.

But at the time one crucial detail was missing. Charlie Whelan was not just briefing the press that Britain wouldn't be joining the euro, he was informing the Prime Minister too. That evening Tony Blair was at Chequers, tipped off that his Chancellor had given an interview but clueless about what he'd said. Blair couldn't reach Gordon Brown or his own spokesman Alastair Campbell. Desperate to discover what was being briefed to the newspapers, Blair called Whelan, who answered his mobile phone in the Red Lion pub.

'I stepped outside,' says Whelan. 'And Blair said, "What's going on about not joining the euro?" He said we had to kill the story. I told him it's too late. It's already gone in.'[4]

This wasn't a minor policy. It was the single biggest political and economic decision the government would take. Tony Blair was much keener on joining the euro than his Chancellor, but this drink-assisted farce was an important moment in snuffing the idea out. It was a massive moment in history decided in a pub. It also symbolised the dysfunctional chaos that reigned between Tony Blair's Downing Street and Gordon Brown's Treasury for a decade.

'If I drank like that today I'd be dead,' Charlie Whelan told me. But he learned how to booze from years working for the Amalgamated Engineering and Electrical Union, the forerunner of Unite. The industrial correspondents were some of Fleet Street's hardest drinkers. Geoffrey Goodman, the most distinguished reporter of Britain's turbulent industrial relations in the decades after the war, said drink was used to fish for stories. 'You'd talk to your trade union leader and instinctively knew you weren't going to get the story until the guy had had enough to drink. That was regular practice. You'd lace them with drink. We had to school ourselves to withstand the physical damage it was doing us,' Goodman told me in his north London living room not long before he died at the age of ninety-one. The tribe of industry and labour correspondents has faded away, their beat dismantled along with government-owned industries and coal mines.

But Charlie Whelan carried on their tradition of industrial drinking. He had a habit of dreaming up policy ideas with journalists in the bars of Westminster. Shortly before the 1997 general election, Whelan briefed journalists over drinks that a Labour government would sell the Tote, the state-owned bookmaker. Robin Cook, later Foreign Secretary, racing fan and former tipster for the *Herald* newspaper, was furious and said the Tote would never be sold. But two years later the new Labour government announced that the Tote would be privatised after all. The sell-off didn't happen until 2011, fourteen years after Charlie Whelan set the hare running in a pub.

Another idea inspired by booze would reduce the Queen to tears. There's a special pressure on Sunday newspaper journalists to come up with a scoop. They have a week to traipse the corridors of Westminster and squeeze their contacts for a tale that will make waves and kick-start the week's news agenda. The royal yacht supposedly ruled the waves, but 1997 was a time of cool Britannia, not old *Britannia,* and the Treasury was keen to cut the £11 million a year cost of keeping the Queen's boat afloat. So when the Chancellor's spin doctor was drinking with a couple of Sunday newspaper journalists soon after the general election, they agreed to splash on *Britannia* being scrapped. 'We dreamed up the idea that doing in the royal yacht would be a good idea, a good story. That was dreamed up over a few drinks at the bar,' claims Whelan.[5] Like many Sunday newspaper stories it was a kite-flyer, a way of gauging reaction to a policy plan before formally announcing it. And within months the Queen was standing on the dock at Portsmouth naval base watching her beloved ship being decommissioned. She loved *Britannia* and was seen to weep during the ceremony. The Queen's yacht was sunk because of a story inspired by booze.

The pubs around Westminster are a particularly important source for the political reporters who work outside the closed world of the lobby system. It's here the new kids on the blogosphere quarry for trade. I meet Harry Cole for a pint at the Marquis of Granby. The sharp-witted, floppy-fringed young journalist is now the *Sun*'s Westminster correspondent but made his name as news editor at the Guido Fawkes website, the obsessively followed online bulletin board of Westminster gossip and rumours. It's contemptuous of politicians and Parliament, right-wing, acerbic, salacious and powerful. When Damian McBride was caught smearing Tory MPs, it was Guido Fawkes that obtained the incriminating emails.

The Guido bloggers have not been allowed passes to Parliament and are disdainful of the lobby. For that reason, much of the gossip that appears on Guido Fawkes is mopped up in Westminster's pubs. 'Most of my sources are behind-the-scenes people,' says Cole, who I talked to before he joined the *Sun*. 'They're the minister's bag carrier. They're the disgruntled staffer who's had a shit day and will slag off their boss. And that more often than not happens in pubs over pints.'

Thursday nights are usually best because MPs have gone home and the researchers, staffers and special advisers are out getting drunk. Cole would sometimes put his bank card behind the bar, an investment that was more than recouped in stories. 'After six pints someone's more likely to tell you something than after one pint or sober.' Drink, says Cole, helps build a bond that works both ways. It helps uncork the story, but the source receives some protection too.

'They'll slip us a few things, buy us a few drinks to remain on good terms. But obviously if a story's good enough a bottle of wine isn't going to save your neck,' he grins. Harry Cole has the same negotiation with his sources as any political journalist. It might be on the record, off the record or on background – the murkiest of the three. But if something's overheard in a pub he's not beholden by any rules and the blog is where it will end up. There have been Cabinet rows Guido Fawkes reported first that emerged only because people closely involved were drunk. 'The row happened and they were ranting about it. They've been drunk and given me the details or a quote. That wouldn't have happened if they weren't drunk. Everyone's a consummate professional until they can barely stand up.'

If he's meeting a researcher or special adviser with a document to leak, Cole reveals that the rendezvous is usually a quieter pub off the beaten track, like the Two Chairmen. 'Without booze my job would be joyless and a lot harder,' confirms Cole, who tells me the true mark of a Westminster drinker is a white wine spritzer. 'If you have to start putting soda water in you're probably drinking way too much.'[6]

Looking back on it all now, Damian McBride regrets the damage the drink did to his health and personal relations. 'I would never have been able to get my own drinking to some sort of sensible control if I'd stayed in Westminster. I'm a good drinker but it's a terrible thing to happen to anyone. Policemen in the 1970s and 1980s would probably say the same thing. If you're a lawyer doing your briefs or a teacher doing their marking you couldn't drink like this. The aggression, the arguments … alcohol is a lubricant in the wheel. It's not a million miles from the football terraces. It's a macho pissing contest.

'It's one of the reasons I never want to go back to politics,' he says, leaving to catch his train to Cardiff, where he's due to take part in a BBC Radio 4 discussion on when it's acceptable to lie.[7]

## The Political Lunch

It's one o'clock in a Westminster restaurant. A political correspondent and a government minister are examining their menus. The hack hopes his guest will pick the moderately priced two-course set special; the minister rather fancies the veal cutlet Milanese. A waiter asks if they've chosen some wine. After a bit of 'will we/won't we' they settle on two glasses of viognier. The bill will be picked up by the journalist, whose expenses are not what they were.

If the two haven't met for lunch before, the ritual resembles a bizarre blind date. They probe common ground, sketch out their families and share holiday plans. But at some point during the starter, conversation swerves sharply onto politics. Pop into any pukka Westminster restaurant between Monday and Thursday when Parliament's sitting and you'll see dozens of these assignations. Colleagues from the same newspaper and ministers from the same government will be having hushed conversations with each other at different tables in the same restaurant. They're trading gossip. Discussing the future. Sharing secrets and disparaging rivals. The politician may be suggesting a story. The journalist will certainly be fishing for one. But, like mating rabbits, these are quick encounters. And there's no fidelity here. A politician lunched a few months ago may be sitting at a neighbouring table with a journalist from a rival newspaper doing it all again. A polite nod of acknowledgment is enough.

The political lunch is a cherished feature of Westminster life. It is a chance to eat fine food with prominent politicians at the company's expense. Alan Watkins, the shrewd veteran of Fleet Street's El Vino wine bar, lunched politicians for more than fifty years. As a young reporter he learnt the principles of lunching from *Sunday Express* editor John Junor. 'One was always to order from the table d'hôte menu, because that would shame one's guest into doing likewise, so saving the company money. Another of Junor's principles of lunching was to have no truck with vintages or wine waiters but to order the house wine, red or white but on no account rose.'[8]

But politicians have always been eager to eat and drink at the expense of the Fourth Estate. The story is told of three journalists clubbing together to entertain Roy Jenkins in the early 1980s. 'When we got the bill it was £105, which in 1980 was impressive. Then a week or two later, we took Denis Healey out, and when we got the bill it was £115. One of us mentioned the comparison to him, which was terribly infra dig. But Denis didn't mind at all, and we heard later from one of the research assistants that he'd gone along the Shadow Cabinet corridor banging on doors and shouting, "I'm more expensive to lunch than Jenkins!"'[9]

Jenkins was a legend in his own lunchtime. Few politicians since have matched his reputation, although some continue the tradition. Political journalist Peter Oborne remembers taking the former Labour Paymaster General, Geoffrey Robinson, out for lunch at the Savoy Grill in 1998. 'We had several bottles of wine. I thought I could just about get it through on expenses. I went off to the loo, came back, and Geoffrey had bought a bottle of wine that cost about £350. I said "Geoffrey, I can't possibly pay for that!" It's obviously why he bought it. He said "You can't buy a bottle of decent red wine at a London restaurant these days for less than £400."[10]

The political lunch is not a discreet affair. In fact journalists enjoy the kudos of parading their date. As the *Mirror*'s Kevin Maguire puts it, 'never under-estimate the willingness of journalists to show off their contacts and be seen in public with a minister. It's appalling and it's showy but it goes on.'[11] This means it is fairly easy to guess the source of a story in the following day's paper or the identity of an unnamed Cabinet minister in a columnist's Sunday feature if you've seen the journalist in conspiratorial conversation at Indian restaurant the Cinnamon Club. And now everyone can play this game through social media, as *@eyespymp* logs the sightings of MPs – at lunch, buying coffee, chaining up their bicycles, enjoying free hospitality at the football, waiting for a train. Many contributors are the researchers and bag carriers who mill around Westminster and the tone is predictably mocking, a reflection of the disdain felt towards politicians by the public, rivalled only by their loathing of estate agents and bankers.

This is not a new phenomenon. A Gallup survey from 1944 found half of people thought politicians were in it for themselves or their party. Polls show that around 80 per cent of people do not trust politicians to tell the truth, a figure almost exactly the same as it was thirty years ago. But the elaborate fiddling of allowances exposed by the expenses scandal of 2009 unleashed a renewed rage against politicians. The receiptless claims seemed to symbolise what many voters view as the self-serving vacuity of modern politics, and condemnation was savage. The scandal's legacy continues to contaminate public life. But here in our Westminster restaurant politicians are still dined with respectful deference by journalists hungry for a story. And it's the journalist who pays, on expenses.

Journalists often lunch in pairs so they can compare notes, corroborate a story and split the cost. But what is the purpose of all this lunching? Peter Oborne is dismissive of the question. 'As Michael Oakeshott, the conservative political philosopher would have said, there is no purpose to a lunch. It is simply something you enjoy. If someone goes into a lunch with the purpose of extracting some piece of information from a politician it becomes a frightfully tedious and unpleasant business. The purpose of the lunch is the lunch itself,' he tells me emphatically.[12]

Oborne is someone who valiantly continues the lunching tradition of Alan Watkins and other Fleet Street ghosts. A lunch should be long, convivial, loosened with wine and formed on friendship. 'I find it very hard to meet a politician for lunch without having several drinks. Drink makes you feel more relaxed and at ease with the world. If you don't drink you feel ill at ease, particularly with someone you don't know.' Oborne laments the sobering up of lunch over the last twenty years. They've become, he believes, functional, transactional occasions at which younger journalists approach the politician in the same way a tearaway young bowler has a crack at the batsman's middle stump.

Many journalists do expect something in return for their hospitality. The *Guardian*'s Michael White says he's never believed in lunch as a means of story transmission, but there are tales of journalists throwing their knife down and crying, 'I've just bought you two bottles of wine and you haven't given me a thing!'[13] Politicians very rarely turn up to a lunch with a little gift-wrapped story. But in the meandering course of conversation something may be said about a colleague, a policy being cooked up, or a disagreement within the party, that makes the journalist's pulse jump. After scribbling some notes in the restaurant loo, 'Few pleasures on this little green planet are so glorious as tucking a real story into your breast pocket and returning for some cheese and a final glass of claret,' says Andrew Marr.[14]

Jon Sopel was a political correspondent for the BBC between 1989 and 1999, a decade that spanned the defenestration of Thatcher, the disintegration of Major and the early dominance of Blair. Lunch mirrored the drama of the time. Sopel remembers taking Alan Clark, then Minister for Defence Procurement, out to lunch in Belgravia. 'He turned up with this raven-haired beauty. Anything between nineteen and twenty-three years old. She didn't say a word during lunch, just sat there looking pouting and gorgeous. It was clear his lunch was preparation for afternoon activities that I suspect had nothing to do with the Ministry of Defence. I thought it was unbelievable. The brazenness!'[15] These were the days when broadcasters too would share a bottle of wine with their contact, maybe a couple of brandies, then trundle back to the office and go on air.

Gossip gleaned over lunch is easier to spin into a newspaper story than into a television or radio piece. A print journalist can construct a front page lead from an off-the-record lunchtime comment that shifts the political weather. 'Cabinet sources' make daily appearances in most newspapers, mischievously commenting on the Prime Minister's competence or another colleague's troubles. These

Plate 1  A three-bottle politician. Sir Francis Dashwood, Chancellor of the Exchequer.

Plate 2  "An Election Entertainment" by William Hogarth.

Plate 3  "Canvassing for Votes" by William Hogarth.

Plate 4  George Brown on the cover of *Private Eye*.

Plate 5  Draining the Valentia Vat c.1890.

Plate 6  Ted Heath meets Annie at the re-opening of Annie's Bar, House of Commons, 1968.

Plate 7  On the Palace of Westminster Terrace.

Plate 8  Charles Kennedy the day before he resigned as Liberal Democrat leader, January 6 2006.

Plate 9  "Sometimes I drink a prodigious amount". Boris Johnson at a London brewery in 2011.

Plate 10  Winston Churchill and General Eisenhower at Colonial Williamsburg in 1948.

Plate 11 Margaret Thatcher celebrates 25 years in Parliament with husband Dennis, 1984.

Plate 12 Pint-papped: Nigel Farage in a Westminster pub, May 2014.

Plate 13 Peter Mandelson at the Gay Hussar restaurant.

Plate 14  Tony Blair at Trimdon Labour Club, 2002.

Plate 15  US Congressmen celebrate the end of prohibition, 1933.

Plate 16  President Nixon and Soviet leader Leonid Brezhnev toast the Treaty of Moscow, 1972.

Plate 17 President Barack Obama at Hayes Bar in Moneygall, Ireland, May 2011.

Plate 18 Boris Yeltsin at a Kremlin ceremony for military graduates, 1999.

Plate 19  Roosevelt, Churchill and Stalin celebrating Churchill's birthday in Tehran, November 1943.

Plate 20  Poster criticising government plans to reduce the number of pubs, 1908.

stories are often plausible, but standing them up and putting a name to the quote is usually impossible. The deal is clear: off-the-record anonymity for a glimpse behind the curtain. But while these stories invaluably illuminate the rivalries, frictions, ambitions and tensions within the government or a political party, they are very rarely challenged for being wrong or misleading.

In contrast, it would be very unusual for a broadcast journalist to clatter onto the Ten O'clock News or the *Today* programme with a story sourced solely from an off-the-record lunchtime chat. The audiences are bigger, the stakes higher and the scrutiny by party and government press managers more intense. Off-the-record conversations are certainly used by political broadcasters, but usually to colour coverage of stories that are already up and running. For the broadcasters in particular, the political lunch is in part about building a relationship and establishing trust. Mobile phone numbers are usually swapped, and it's much easier to call an MP or minister with a question at 6.30 in the morning before appearing on the *Today* programme if you've previously met over lunch or a glass of wine. The politician may feel a vague sense of obligation to pick up your call.

If all this seems rather murky, that's because it is. There is no rigid set of rules underpinning these liaisons. What's the difference between an 'off-the-record chat' and a 'background briefing'? When can a reporter use 'senior Cabinet minister', 'friends of a senior Cabinet minister' or 'senior government source'? What does 'senior' even mean? Who decides? The political lunch often ends not only with coffee and tiramisu but an awkward haggle between politician and hack on the terms of the conversation that's just taken place. And that's no guarantee the delicate deal won't backfire. In the early 1990s Jon Sopel and his BBC colleague Mark Mardell took the Chancellor of the Exchequer, Kenneth Clarke, out to lunch at the now defunct Chez Nico at 90 Park Lane, then one of the best restaurants in London. At the time Clarke felt he was being undermined on Europe and economic policy by others in the Conservative Party. Over lunch he said: 'I'm going to tell the kids in Tory Central Office to get their scooters off my lawn!' It was characteristic Clarke, rumbustious and outspoken.

The next day Sopel reported these remarks on Radio 4's *World at One*, attributing them to a 'senior Tory' and saying they implied the source might resign. Pandemonium broke out at Prime Minister's Questions two hours later. The Opposition leadership gleefully leapt on the remarks, and then the Labour MP Frank Dobson revealed he'd seen Sopel and Mardell having lunch with Clarke at Chez Nico two days before. 'Ken's cover was totally blown and he had to make a statement saying he wasn't going to resign,' remembers a rather rueful Jon Sopel. He and Mark Mardell both wrote letters to the Chancellor apologising for the fact he'd been unmasked. But Sopel is certain they were right to report what Clarke had said. 'My job as a journalist is not to keep secrets, broadly speaking. You're not just going out to lunch. You want to get stuff on air.'[16]

It was this sort of napkin-dabbing indiscretion that the next government wanted to stamp out. Labour returned to power with the former political journalist (and former alcoholic) Alastair Campbell in charge of Downing Street communications. Iron message discipline was the party's mantra and Campbell knew how many unhelpful, embarrassing stories started life in Westminster's restaurants. So Number 10 insisted ministers should not fraternise with political journalists over lunch without telling the press office first. Campbell wanted to keep tabs on who was talking to whom. The most loyal ladder-climbers obeyed, while others found more discreet restaurants to subvert the edict.

But the political lunch was by now becoming a drearier date. It started to become routine for ministers to turn up with their special advisers, who would stiffen the atmosphere and make sure a pair of journalists didn't corroborate a story that wasn't entirely true. And today the political lunch can be as demoralising as a lifeless soufflé. In the view of Peter Oborne, 'There is no member of the current Cabinet or front bench who you could think of having a really agreeable lunch with. Not really, it's gone. Ken Clarke was the best. He didn't try and bore you with his latest policies.'[17]

What about the view from the other side of the table? Kenneth Clarke first became a Tory MP in 1970, and was a minister in every Conservative (or Conservative-led coalition) government from 1979 until he rejoined the backbenches in July 2014. The cigar-puffing jazz-lover has had a lot of lunches, but says today's are meaner and drier than the ones politicians used to enjoy. 'Politicians, journalists, lawyers all drank like fish thirty or forty years ago. They were much more proficient at their jobs than today's generation. But they had practice, they were able to do it. Today's generation are more earnest, more abstinent. Lunches are altogether cheaper, lighter things.'[18]

What are politicians thinking as they head off to meet a journalist for lunch? The former Liberal Democrat leader Sir Menzies Campbell says the successful lunch works if there's an exchange of information between the two sides of the Westminster village: 'I'm thinking how much I can tell him without causing trouble at party HQ. There's a clear understanding on these occasions that the journalist will give you some gossip you haven't heard but in return you're expected to provide some of the information that isn't publicly provided.'[19] Both the politician and the journalist are keen to enhance their standing in the eyes of the other, and swapping gossip proves they're in the know.

### Cherry Soup and Slivovitz

Several popular political lunch spots are a short walk from Parliament. Quirinale for delicate but pricey Italian; the Cinnamon Club for modern Indian set in a book-lined Victorian building that used to house Westminster Library. A more informal spot is St John's, in the crypt below Smith Square, whilst the fanciest restaurant close by is Roux at Parliament Square. Osteria Dell'Angol opposite the Home Office feeds a few politicians too.

To avoid being seen with their contact, journalists need to go further afield, and most have a preferred hideaway in Soho. For many years Shepherd's on Marsham Street has been a favourite destination for Tories who enjoy its posh pie and pudding. In 2013 Labour MPs feared the loss of their most treasured restaurant, but so far the Gay Hussar in Soho's Greek Street survives almost unchanged since it opened in 1953.

This Hungarian relic, sitting amid the frenetic churn of Soho's restaurant scene, has been defiantly cranking out food that has rarely been fashionable or refined. Typically, slabs of fish terrine, cherry soup or herring with sour cream to start, followed by goulash (beef, venison or veal), goose and crispy roast duck. There are schnitzels and fatty pink sausages as well as sides of cabbage and cucumber salad. Paprika makes an appearance in most of the dishes. This is belly-filling, snooze-inducing cuisine. As one enthusiast quipped, the Gay Hussar is a great restaurant so long as you don't eat the food or drink the wine.

But it's not the menu that has made this a dining shrine of the left (and some intrepid Conservatives) for decades. It's the experience of travelling back to a time of Bevanites and long political lunches. Political history is soaked into the wood-panelled dining room walls. It's easy to imagine Harold Wilson or Michael Foot having strolled out of the cramped, cosy restaurant just before you arrive. The faded club atmosphere echoes with past political gossip and plots. Every wall, nook and cranny is covered with political cartoons, photographs and books. Tony Blair's grin shines out over the restaurant, his autobiography squashed into a shelf. But this was never a New Labour sort of place. It's too louche, too old-fashioned, too eccentric. Now New Labour has closed its doors while the Gay Hussar stumbles on, just.

It was opened by Victor Sassie, its owner for thirty-four years. Victor (as regulars affectionately call the late proprietor) was actually not from Hungary but from Barrow-in-Furness. He launched the Gay Hussar after learning to cook in Budapest before the Second World War, and it soon became the Labour Party's salon.

Over several lunches, dinners and bottles of Hungarian wine with its most devoted patrons, I mop up its stories. Ian Aitken, the *Guardian*'s political editor from 1975 to

1990, recounts Victor asking regulars what they'd ordered. 'You can't have that,' he'd snap, 'that's rubbish. That's tourist rubbish.' He'd then march to the kitchen and change the order. Sometimes he'd snatch away the plates of food already delivered. The restaurant ran on political gossip and Victor would trundle between the tables spreading around the stories he'd just picked up.

It was the Bevanites (although not Nye Bevan himself) who first frequented the place in the late 1950s, and in the 1960s and 1970s it had a peerless reputation for political gossip and intrigue. The former Foreign Secretary George Brown was once thrown out for groping a woman on the next table. And in an upstairs room (still known today as the Tom Driberg Memorial Suite), the sexually voracious and eccentric Labour MP is said to have propositioned Mick Jagger while trying to entice the Rolling Stone into politics. Jagger fled.

'He may have been tempted to do things for the Labour Party but he didn't want to do things for Tom Driberg,' sighs the Gay Hussar's manager, John Wrobel, as he leads me around the creaky upper floors. He tells me the Gay Hussar has hosted Tory politicians as well as Labour. The 'wets' who were loathed by Margaret Thatcher sought refuge in the restaurant, as did the Eurosceptics famously branded 'bastards' by John Major. And after the 2010 election the whole Conservative Party whips' office had dinner in an upstairs room to put their stamp on the place and rub in their victory. They haven't been back since.

The Gay Hussar's glory years, the 1960s and 1970s, came to an end when journalists were relocated from Fleet Street to Canary Wharf and Wapping. The head count of hacks dropped, but it remained dear to Labour. In 1981 Tony Blair had several lunches at the Gay Hussar to discuss his search for a parliamentary seat with Tom Pendry, a Labour MP and drinking partner of Blair's Bennite father-in-law, Tony Booth. During the New Labour years the whips' office had its Christmas meals in a top-floor room, and a photograph on the stairs shows an angry-looking Gordon Brown leaving the restaurant with his spin chief Damian McBride at 1.30 in the morning, shortly before he became Prime Minister. It was the end of a long, tense dinner with newspaper editors upstairs. The late Northern Ireland secretary Mo Mowlam once surprised diners by swearing and crying after peeling a chilli and then rubbing her eyes. Regulars over the years have included Barbara Castle, Neil Kinnock, Roy Hattersley and Michael Foot, who celebrated his ninetieth birthday at the Gay Hussar in 2003.

Shirley Williams describes the establishment as a place for 'left-wing life-lovers'. But if you look around the restaurant you observe that it is – and always has been – predominantly full of men. The crimson wall of Martin Rowson caricatures is a political rogues' gallery of blokes. 'The clubbishness of England is a very deep feedstock for the way politics is run and lived and I think it's a shame. But that's how it is,' Williams says ruefully.[20]

But it is precisely the clubbishess of the Gay Hussar that its fans relish. The Labour MP Tom Watson – known in here as Tommy 'two dinners' Watson – says it's the nearest thing Labour has to the Conservative clubs of Pall Mall. 'The aspirational classes within the Labour Party need this place,' he laughs.[21] And with the food goes the booze. After a particularly liquid lunch, Watson once went upstairs for an afternoon nap. He was given a tablecloth as a pillow and revived with fresh mint and a glass of chilled wine. The *Mirror* journalist Kevin Maguire can often be found in the Gay Hussar too, and has seen many MPs stagger back to the Commons after a long lunch. He points out that there's been very little fighting in here over the years because diners have been so inebriated: 'They haven't had the power to throw a punch.'[22] There were wails of anguish when it seemed the Gay Hussar was poised to shut, but it's since had a new lease of life. Tom Watson is now Labour's Deputy Leader, and the left-wing nostalgia embodied by the restaurant is back on the party's menu for the first time in thirty years.

Yet the political lunch may be in permanent decline. Michael Frayn's 1967 novel *Towards the End of the Morning* captured the bibulous, nicotine-fingered, expenses-fiddling world of Fleet Street journalism:

> Various members of the staff emerged from Hand and Ball Passage during the last dark hour of the morning, walked with an air of sober responsibility towards the main entrance, greeted the commissionaire and vanished upstairs in the lift to telephone their friends and draw their expenses before going out again to have lunch.

Before newspapers went online a journalist could sink a bottle or two with a politician at lunchtime, but sober up enough to bash out their story in time for the presses. That world has vanished. Now lunch is snatched between tweets. The political hack's smartphone sits blinking on the table. There's no escape from the day's snowballing story. There's fresh copy to file and new lines to chase. News moves faster than Frayn could have imagined and the deadlines are continuous. So there's neither the time to booze at lunch nor the funds. The expenses racket that paid for the three-bottle lunch has been shut down. Most hacks and politicians have lost the habit of lunchtime drinking and sobered up. But so have pin-striped City boys and delivery van drivers. The boozy political lunch has gone the way of the footballer's half-time cigarette. Politics and journalism are now healthier trades, if rather less colourful ones. The lobby remains dominated by men, but there is less machismo and more professionalism. Before MPs' hours were changed by Robin Cook, they could saunter into Parliament after lunch to begin their day in the Commons at 2.30 p.m. Now their working day more closely mirrors the nation's, and this has squeezed out the time for lunchtime boozing.

Harriet Harman doesn't regret this one bit. 'When journalists took you out to lunch, if you didn't drink you were considered too guarded. For me, I'd been up four times a night with babies so going on the lash at lunchtime wasn't possible. I'd sip a quarter glass of wine to be polite but it was ridiculous,' she says, railing at the misty mateyness of it all.[23] It would now be unusual to drink anything with a Cabinet minister at lunchtime.

Some politicians and journalists are defiant. Like his anecdote-swapping colleagues in the Gay Hussar, Peter Oborne doesn't think drier politics is better politics. 'Political discourse in the last century was more humorous, kinder, more generous. Less earnestness, less dogmatism, more humanity at a personal level. I don't think it's entirely a gain that we've moved from a culture that was based on drinking alcohol together to a culture based on drinking coffee together.'[24]

## Members Only

Drink is still an important glue for binding the party faithful. Alcohol fosters political camaraderie, from the Pimm's poured at local Conservative Association summer BBQs to the pints pulled in working men's clubs. Today Tony Blair drinks champagne with plutocrats in Davos. But not so long ago he would sup pints in the bar of Trimdon Labour Club in his former County Durham constituency. It was where Blair announced he would stand for the Labour leadership in 1994, where he first celebrated victory in 1997 and where he announced he was bowing out as Prime Minister in 2007. There's a story – alas too good to be true – that, after answering the phone one evening, the barman shouted out, 'Where's Tony? Bloke called Clinton says he wants a word with you!' The club gave Blair a useful dusting of working-class cache and grassroots credibility at a time when New Labour was doing everything it could to distance itself from the party's past. The bar was formerly Trimdon Working Men's Club, one of the thousands that thrived throughout industrial Britain for a century.

Set up in 1862, the Working Men's Club and Institute Movement (CIU) was spearheaded by a temperance movement minister, the Reverend Henry Solly, and many clubs signed up to this national federation. Originally conceived as an alternative to the pub, they soon became social clubs renowned for heavy drinking, dominoes, concerts and comedy nights. They were the social centres of industrial communities and an antidote to the rigours of factory and pit life. In the early years particularly, the clubs had an educational role too; by 1903, of the 900 clubs almost half had lending libraries and many put on plays.[25] Seventy years later there were 4,000 CIU-associated clubs; smoke-filled, beer-sinking dens of camaraderie and pleasure. The working men's clubs hosted music acts and sports competitions. They were also home to sub-clubs of dog-racers, pigeon-flyers, card-players and leek-growers.

The Labour MP Ian Lavery is unlike most recent arrivals at Westminster. His accent is broad Geordie and his unshakable cough is a legacy of coal. Lavery took over the presidency of the National Union of Mineworkers from Arthur Scargill in 2002 and became MP for Wansbeck in 2010. We meet for a cup of tea in the Strangers' Bar of the Commons, a place once full of Labour MPs from trade union backgrounds and the country's vanished shipyards and pits.

Lavery tells me the bigger clubs used to have three or four thousand members and the drink and politics went together. 'There was a heavy drinking culture. There was a pecking order of drinkers. People had reputations as fast drinkers, good drinkers, big drinkers. You'd know who had fifteen pints yesterday morning, went home for his dinner and came back for another fifteen pints. People enjoyed the drink, they enjoyed the craic. Fantastic atmosphere. In these clubs you'd have people sitting together discussing trade unionism, politics, football. These people didn't have degrees and PhDs but they were bright and articulate.'[26]

The drinking was fierce. The Labour MP Kevan Jones used to be a trade union official on Tyneside, and he describes the clubs and drinking habits of the Newcastle shipyard workers. 'If you went to Swan Hunters in the early 1980s and visited the bars and clubs at lunchtime when the whistle went, they used to have all the pints on the bar ready for people to come in. These were people who'd go back to work in the afternoon to work with heavy machinery. It was simply part of the culture.'[27] Drink and shipbuilding go back a long way. A spectacular example comes from the Republic of Venice whose powerful fleet was built at the Arsenal, a massive shipyard that employed thousands of men. Wine was provided to workers for hydration and sustenance. It was stored in huge 2,000-litre casks and diluted to 4 or 5 per cent before being taken around the workers in buckets. By the late 1630s workers at the Venice Arsenal were drinking around five litres a day and a vast bronze wine fountain spewed out a continuous stream of wine.[28]

But the CIU clubs in 1980s Britain were not places for wine, or women. Wives and girlfriends might be taken along on a Saturday night, but these were clubs for blokes and beer. And to break the monopoly of the big brewers north-east clubs created their own beer, Federation, which was owned by the working men's clubs and provided beer and ales to the northern clubs as well as to the Strangers' Bar in the Commons. A CIU club membership card meant access to thousands of working men's clubs throughout the country. The beer was cheaper than in pubs but drunken misbehaviour could get a member barred.

The working men's clubs are threads in a once huge national tapestry of clubs and associations, most represented under the CIU umbrella. As well as the hundreds of Conservative and Labour associations, there are British Legion, RAF and naval social clubs. In 1977 the Queen popped into the Coventry

Working Men's Club, one of the oldest in the country. But this was their heyday and the visit was never repeated. The Coventry club was declared bankrupt in 2008 and closed its doors. Industrial decline, a dwindling membership and unaffordable debts finished it off. Sons no longer followed their fathers to these havens of cabaret, crooners and a cheap pint. When Kevan Jones first became an MP for the Durham coalfields in 2001, there were four or five working men's clubs in his constituency; they have since closed down. His Labour club shut its doors in 2002. There was also a CIU group of MPs that has disappeared too. As Jones says, the closure of thousands of working men's clubs over the last twenty years was inevitable. 'The decline of those industries broke the connection. If you worked at Saxon colliery you were also part of Saxon working men's club. When the pit went that link broke.'

There are now just 1,500 clubs in the Working Men's Club and Institute Movement and the number continues to shrink. The attractions of a night drinking pints of brown ale in front of a club circuit comic have faded too. People would rather watch Peter Kay affectionately parody the rusting northern clubs in *Phoenix Nights* on television than go to such a club themselves, while the smoking ban and even cheaper supermarket booze has accelerated the decline. When Trimdon Labour Club closed down in 2010, its last secretary, Paul Trippett, said their beer prices couldn't match the cost of drinking at home. 'In the club £10 will unfortunately only get you four pints of lager, but if you go to one of the big supermarkets, £10 will get you forty-eight cans. Really, you can't compete with that.'[29] The price of alcohol was once the big draw at these clubs. Now it is draining them of life.

But the jobs, traditions and habits of a working class that congregated in clubs are all vanishing. As the former Labour MP Roy Hattersley has said, the few remaining clubs are relics of another age: 'They are part of a lost civilisation in which working men never went out for the evening without being properly dressed in collar and tie, raised their cloth caps when coffin-bearing hearses passed them in the street, and knew nothing of "happy hours", giant television screens or karaoke machines.'[30]

So what has been the effect on politics of this decline? For a hundred years working men's clubs and trade unions were intertwined. Ian Lavery says the working men's clubs were where the ranks of trade unions and the Labour Party were replenished: 'Anybody who seemed fairly bright and articulate would be picked up by the local officials and given opportunities. Would you want to be a member of the Labour Party? A councillor? It was the political educational ladder that these clubs provided. It was a conveyor belt year after year. Nothing has replaced those structures.'[31] Lavery is adamant that the Labour Party is poorer for the disappearance of clubs that produced generations of councillors, canvassers and MPs who knew what it was like to work on the factory floor or hundreds of feet underground. But the unified political activism that he describes has faded away. Trade union membership has been falling for many years and the political allegiance of people in manual work has fractured. Even the term 'working class' is rarely used by political journalists now, nervously unsure what it means any more.

Ian Lavery is right to feel rather alone in Parliament. In his study of class voting between 1964 and 2010, the academic

Oliver Heath has found that the number of MPs with a background in manual work has fallen sharply. Although always smaller than the proportion of the working class in the population, in 1964 20 per cent of MPs had a working-class occupational background. By 2010, only 5 per cent had the same. The change is almost entirely due to the changing make-up of the Labour Party in Parliament. In 1964, 37 per cent of its MPs were from manual occupational backgrounds compared with just under 10 per cent in 2010.[32] Heath concludes that this shrinking working-class representation within the Labour Party is having a significant impact on how people vote, with working-class voters turning to the SNP and UKIP instead. The north of England and Scotland is still solid Labour territory, while the south of England is overwhelmingly Conservative. That geographical divide has hardened since Thatcher and Blair built huge majorities by winning non-traditional seats. But as Ian Lavery says, 'A good parliament should reflect the country a whole. And it doesn't.' To reverse this trend will take more than a few pint-drinking photo opportunities for politicians in the working men's clubs that soldier on.

## Clubland

The price of a pint is of no great concern to the denizens of Pall Mall drawing rooms. Inside the hushed temples of Georgian splendour that still dominate the streets around St James's, modern London stops at the door. While the brash, raucous, Tinder-browsing city rushes by outside, the clocks in the billiards room and library tick on with insouciant, timeless indifference. The quirks and rules of the gentlemen's clubs are a mystery to non-members and some of the most venerable institutions (White's and Brooks's for instance) still ban women from joining.

That discrimination is the main reason prominent politicians are no longer seen snoozing at their club following a lunch of cold meats, claret and custard. It's a toxic association for a modern politician. David Cameron's late father Ian was once a chairman of White's, the oldest and most aristocratic gentlemen's club in London. His son was a member until 2008, when the Conservative Party leader quietly handed in his resignation. The raffish, wealthy exclusivity of White's did not sit easily with the image of Cameron's rebranded party. The Carlton Club still lurks in the background of the Conservative Party's social life, but others have been drained of political importance.

It was very different in the nineteenth century, when the clubs of St James's and Pall Mall incubated the new era of party politics. The clubs where Charles James Fox and William Pitt met to gamble, gossip and drink in the previous century became overtly political. In the late 1700s White's cemented its status as the club for Tory gentlemen, while a few doors down Brooks's was the spiritual home of their political opponents. As Philip Ziegler writes, 'if the Church of England was later said to be the Tory party at prayer, Brooks's was the Whig party at dinner'.[33]

The arguments around parliamentary reform sharpened the party divide and spawned new clubs. A group of Tories including the Duke of Wellington formed the Carlton Club in 1832 after failing to halt the Reform Act of the same year. It effectively became the Tories' headquarters and a base for rebuilding their shattered party after electoral defeat. Four years later Whigs established the Reform Club to defend the wider franchise and counter the activities of the Carlton Club next door. This was when Pall Mall began to look as it does today. The Travellers' Club had been founded in 1819 and the Athenaeum in 1824. Not all clubs had a political stamp, but they did have characteristics in common, being exclusively male, elite, discreet retreats where men could network, gossip, dine and drink from the finest wine cellars in London. Then, as now, the profits of the clubs were in large part dependent on how much alcohol their members put away.

New political clubs followed, such as the Conservative-supporting St Stephen's (still used by the Tory Party today for press conferences and receptions) in 1870 and the National Liberal Club in 1882. Prospective members out of step with their party leaderships would find themselves blackballed and the clubs were vital to political advancement. As the historian Amy Milne-Smith writes, the clubs of Victorian London were far less raucous than the hard-drinking gambling dens of the Regency period but their political importance was clear: 'The conversations within club walls helped define politics not only in London, but also in Britain, the Empire, Europe and the world.'[34]

Nineteenth-century Liberal Prime Ministers continued to frequent Brooks's but the club was eclipsed in importance by the Reform, which first staged the long struggle between Whigs and Radicals and later the Liberal Party split over Irish Home Rule. This marked the beginning of the Reform Club's fade from formal Liberal politics. In the twentieth century it evolved into a purely social club with a liberal outlook, becoming the first traditional gentlemen's club to admit women members in 1981. But unlike their rivals in the

Conservative Party, Liberal politicians largely turned their backs on the rarefied world of London clubland. One significant exception was Roy Jenkins, who adored the silver-tray charms of Brooks's and noted with a touch of regret that the club had last produced a Prime Minister in the Edwardian era. That was Asquith, who used to slip out of Downing Street and stroll across St James's Park to the Athenaeum for a couple of hours to read the newspapers in the library.[35] In contrast, Tory politicians continued to tinkle the drinks bell at the Carlton despite the embarrassment its membership policy caused recent party leaders.

For over three decades Margaret Thatcher was the only woman signed up as a full member of the Carlton Club. When she became Tory Party leader in 1975, Thatcher was made an honorary member, getting around the awkward bar on women being able to join by right. The party's first female leader was unfazed by this eye-crossing hypocrisy and embraced the Carlton enthusiastically when Prime Minister. At the beginning of each parliamentary session she took most of the Cabinet to the club for a grand party, a tradition continued by her successor, John Major. It was a time that re-established the Carlton Club at the heart of the Tory Party's social life after years in the doldrums.

The Carlton Club had been the home of the party until Conservative Central Office was created in 1870. Benjamin Disraeli and Robert Peel built their careers in the club's Pall Mall home, which was destroyed in a 1940 air raid. The Carlton's most famous moment was a meeting held on Thursday 19 October 1922. The Tory Party was in coalition with the Liberals and the Conservative leader Austen Chamberlain shared Lloyd George's view that the coming election should be fought on a joint ticket. But many Tory MPs wanted their party to go it alone and a showdown meeting was held at the Carlton. At 11 a.m., large glasses of brandy and soda were passed around and the argument got under way.[36] Chamberlain failed to persuade the troops and when a vote was taken he lost by 187 to 87. This revolt by Tory MPs brought down the government, triggering a general election which the Conservatives won under the new leadership of Andrew Bonar Law, whose tenure as Prime Minister was the shortest of the twentieth century. Conservative MPs first elected in 1922 then established a new parliamentary committee the following year. The 1922 Committee – the '22, as it is familiarly known – was soon opened to all Tory MPs not serving in government and its weekly meetings are still the place for backbenchers to vent their views about policy, the state of the party and the leader. The committee's chairman and executive officers have significant clout in the party and the mood of the '22 cannot be ignored.

Despite this legacy, the Carlton Club's political importance then waned. Meetings of the 1922 Committee shifted to the House of Commons. After the war the Carlton was rehoused at 69 St James's Street and Tory MPs continued to drift in for dinner and drinks. A history of the club suggests it was far from a den of drunkenness and only one incident was brought to the organising committee's attention. On 11 January 1968 a complaint was received about a member who had left the club the previous evening 'so tight that he could not walk steadily through the hall. On getting to the doorway, he fell down the steps and groped around for all to see on his hands and knees. The hall porter's comment was: "He is always like that".'[37]

Harold Macmillan would not have approved of such uncouth behaviour, but his fondness for club life did revive the Carlton. As Prime Minister he enjoyed lunching there with colleagues and there is a delicious story told by John Boyd-Carpenter, the government's Paymaster General, of Macmillan's decision to skip Prime Minister's Questions one day for another glass of port:

Macmillan used to lunch at what was the Parliamentary Table at the far end of the dining room about twice a week. A number of other senior Ministers took the cue from him and did the same. He would talk amusingly and sometimes very indiscreetly on the basis that the Parliamentary Table was occupied by discreet Parliamentarians. Sometimes he would drink port after lunch. On one occasion, after I had given the Prime Minister a glass of port, he gave me one and we were approaching a third glass when his Parliamentary Private Secretary, Sir Knox Cunningham MP, came bustling in clutching a folder containing the Prime Minister's answers to Prime Minister's questions. He drew the Prime Minister's attention to the fact that he should go quickly to the House to answer them. Mr Macmillan was undeterred. Pausing for a moment in the course of an anecdote of a somewhat scandalous character which he was telling, he said 'Please ask Mr Butler to answer for me.' He then resumed his story.[38]

In 1977 Macmillan became chairman of the Carlton, a club he had joined in 1929. He was now eighty-three years old but had lost none of his twinkly élan. At the club in

1979 he unveiled a sculpture of Margaret Thatcher by the Croatian artist, Oscar Nemon. Thatcher was in the audience when Macmillan murmured in an elegant stage whisper, so everyone could hear, 'Now I must remember that I am unveiling a bust of Margaret Thatcher, not Margaret Thatcher's bust.'[39]

Macmillan helped revive the Carlton's financial and social fortunes, staunching the falling membership and restoring some political glitz. But with the club still stopping women from gaining full membership, it was becoming the party's embarrassing, sexist uncle. In 1963 women were allowed to visit the first-floor library but only if they used the lift or a small back staircase. The portrait-lined grand staircase was strictly off limits to heels. This was, apparently, to stop Tory gentlemen sitting in the corner of the hall from seeing too much of a lady's leg, and that part of the lobby became known as Cads' Corner.[40] In the 1970s women were allowed to become associate members, which meant they could only use certain rooms and were prohibited from taking part in club elections.

There followed three decades of often anguished debate. A number of MPs resigned from the club and votes held in 1998, 2000 and 2007 failed to get the two-thirds majority needed to change the rules. Conservative Party leaders Iain Duncan Smith and David Cameron both shunned the club and turned down membership because of its antiquated entrance policy.

Duncan Smith did, however, retain his membership of the men-only Beefsteak Club, an institution where all the waiters are addressed as 'Charles' so as to spare members the bother of learning their names. Faced with a choice between political extinction and tradition, the Carlton Club eventually did vote to accept female members in May 2008, Ann Widdecombe becoming the club's first full woman member.

Today the Carlton seems to be the sort of place that non-toff Tories are keen to join. The former Defence Secretary Liam Fox holds an annual New Year's party there and MPs such as Brian Binley (secondary modern school followed by a career in business) are proud members. Support of the Conservative Party remains a qualification for membership, and a proposer and seconder are needed to get hopefuls through the door. Its current chairman, the effortlessly aristocratic Lord Strathclyde, tells me the club today is vibrant, having put the 'terrible blight' of its gender agonies behind it. The executive of the 1922 Committee no longer holds its meetings there and its political function is faint. But it does provide a place for like-minded Conservatives from all over the country to meet. 'It serves good food, good drink and excellent wine at reasonable prices. That is part of the conviviality of politics which is very necessary,' Strathclyde tells me. And he insists the leadership's allergy to the Carlton has been cured. 'I assure you Cameron does go to the Carlton. And not just for big events. He occasionally slips in.'[41]

But the Pall Mall clubs serving claret and custard, while doing far better than the working men's clubs, are not where top politicians congregate now. Instead you'll find them jockeying to get into the new breed of private members' clubs that are thriving across London. Soho House, Shoreditch House, Home House and Mark's Club (which includes David Cameron among its members): these are the clubs that are booming and today it's where the media aristocracy, actors, celebrities and politicians fraternise in privacy.

## Party Time

It's 6.30 in the morning at the Midland Hotel in central Manchester. The Conservative Party conference is trudging into its third day. The lobby smells of baked beans, bacon and booze, the morning after slowly eclipsing the night before. While keener party members begin to appear for their breakfast, the huge lounge bar is still scattered with politicos looking glassy-eyed at their dregs. There are about thirty people still drinking and the bar is ready to serve more. The shutters will only come down once the last customers have staggered off to bed. A trio of tight-suited delegates from Conservative Future (the party's youth wing and successor to the Young Conservatives) are slumped on sofas, their feet planted on a table covered with half-empty wine glasses and shrivelled lemons in puddles of gin.

I'm on my way to the conference hall to do an interview for BBC Breakfast on David Cameron's speech to conference later that day. Key lines and themes were briefed to journalists the night before, so there's something for the newspapers and people like me to say before a word of the speech is uttered. With a few minutes to spare I go and sample the mood in the bar. 'We're Liberal Democrats,' one of the occupants slurs. He's probably about twenty years old and he and his friends have been drinking since late afternoon yesterday. They may be hammered but this group is still savvy, flipping over their passes to hide their names from the nosey hack. Not that there is anything outlandish in having a skinful at conference. Indeed, it is why many people want to come. It's a chance to drink colossal quantities of alcohol with fellow believers. Party conferences are, wrote Jeremy

Paxman, 'part revivalist gospel meeting, part boozy party, part ineffably tedious evening class'.[42] Evening classes with free drink thrown in. Because almost every fringe event, from a think tank's worthy panel discussion on the future of social housing or the third sector to a newspaper-sponsored public conversation with a Cabinet minister, will lay on a long table of free food and drink to entice an audience. With conference hotel bar prices high, it's a very useful place for the politicos to pre-load on white wine before the evening's serious drinking.

Party conferences have shrunk in size, importance and character over the last three decades. They've moved from the huge Victorian ballrooms of English seaside towns to city centre conference venues, where the dwindling number of delegates can be disguised by rearranging the chairs into ever smaller auditoriums. The public are kept away by Green Zone levels of security. The politicos and press appreciate the superior hotel rooms and the quality of the cappuccino. And it's for them that party conferences still exist. Deterred by the cost, the security and the stale theatre of the conference schedule, fewer ordinary party members turn up each year. Instead it's a gathering for professional party workers, lobbyists, journalists and charities who pay the parties much-needed cash to exhibit their stands on the conference fringe. If there was a time when party conferences really mattered, few can now remember it. The Tory Prime Minister Arthur Balfour said he would sooner take advice from his valet than the Conservative Party conference; and its role has always been to rally the faithful rather than set party policy. Votes are still taken at Labour's annual gathering, but for years politically awkward results were simply ignored by the leadership. However, Jeremy Corbyn has promised to breathe new life into Labour conferences and revive the policy-making power of party members, freeing them from the grip of spin doctors terrified by any squeak of dissent. In that respect they could become more like Liberal Democrat conferences where debate is held and policy set. But at all three it's the leader's speech – and its reception on the teatime TV news – that matters most.

Writing about party conferences in the early 1980s, the Conservative MP Julian Critchley observed the various tribes:

> The Social Democrats seem to attract the examination-taking classes, *Guardian* readers with yellow Volvos and two children, one of whom suffers from dyslexia; the Liberals are a blend of the old middle classes and the bearded practitioners of 'community politics', whereby broken paving stones acquire a curious doctrinal significance; the Labour Party is not a band of brothers; and the Conservative Party has, under Margaret Thatcher's populist leadership, become, to all intents and purposes, a working class festival.[43]

The differences haven't completely vanished; you'll find more hemp bags sported at the Liberal Democrat conference and more Guards ties at the Tories. Labour still rounds off its conference with a time-warp rendition of 'The Red Flag'. But the distinctions are fading. As are the parties themselves, which have been losing members since the 1950s. Then the Conservative Party had almost three million members; today it has fewer than 200,000. Just one per cent of the population is a member of a political party, compared with nearly four per cent a generation ago. More people pay money to belong to the Caravan Club or the Royal Society for the Protection of Birds than all of Britain's political parties put together.[44] Political activism is now very much a minority pursuit, although Jeremy Corbyn's success at rallying disillusioned older Labour members and young activists in 2015 may yet harbinger a new era of political participation that other parties will try and copy.

For the diminished number of party members who still attend the annual get-together, along with the legions of political journalists who dutifully cover it and the scores of advisers, bag carriers, press officers, lobbyists and policy wonks who also pack their suitcases for conference, the promise of bacchanalia and drink remains a draw. Television cameras never choose to capture and broadcast the sweaty, boozy, fetid scrum to be found at the bar of the main party conference hotels each year. The political parties hire the hotel and try to control what's filmed. The hacks are usually in the thick of it too. And it's been like this for as long as anyone can remember. Bernard Donoughue shudders at the memory of Labour Party conferences of the 1960s and 1970s: 'They were Romanesque grotesque occasions with people often drinking all day, people going from party to party. For a number of people it was clearly the most exciting occasion of the year. For me it was an appalling experience and I hated every minute of it.'[45]

Party conferences are boozy school trips for the politics industry and the bars always do business until dawn. Fabulous snapshots of status anxiety can be glimpsed outside the main bashes. MPs can be found trying to charm their way into the

*Spectator* magazine's party, horrified they've been left off the list. Inside, Cabinet ministers, journalists, lobbyists and party bosses mingle and schmooze their way through crates of Pol Roger champagne.

Conference drinking is a useful measure of political hypocrisy too. In September 2009 the Labour Party assembled in Brighton for its final pre-election conference – tired, deflated, depressed. In his leader's speech, Prime Minister Gordon Brown took a populist swipe at 'binge drinkers' – the scourge of Britain's town centres, whose antics were fodder for the tabloids at the time. Labour had introduced 24-hour licensing but Brown said local authorities should now have the right to scrap it. And he promised new rights for people to make clubs and pubs pay for cleaning up the broken glass and vomit in areas where there was persistent trouble from young drinkers.

It was all enthusiastically applauded. But hours later the *Sun* newspaper ditched its support for Labour and the binge drinking began in earnest in Brighton. 'Labour's Lost It' would be the next day's front page, ending Rupert Murdoch's decade-long love affair with New Labour.

Party bosses showed their fury and disgust by boycotting the free drinks being laid on at the News International party in one of the Grand Hotel's conference rooms. Instead Labour members, politicians and staff crammed into the Grand's main bar to drink, some in defiance, others despair. As the night went on the sweaty, beery crush spilled onto the terrace. Inside, the then Culture Secretary, Ben Bradshaw, led his comrades in a hearty singalong of 'Hey Jude' around the bar's grand piano.

Labour's conference the year before in Manchester had witnessed another night of drink-fuelled confusion around

Ruth Kelly's resignation from the Cabinet. At a chaotic press briefing in the bar of the Midland Hotel at 3.15 in the morning Damian McBride, beer in hand, confirmed rumours the Transport Secretary wanted to go. According to McBride, a party conference resembles a stag do. There's the odd speech or fringe event a delegate might want to attend, but the rest is about boozing. In the Blair/Brown years their respective warring teams of advisers would race to colonise a hotel bar for themselves in the style of an Italian gangster film. 'At the 2008 conference there was a vitriolic atmosphere,' McBride tells me: 'All these plots and coups going on. The atmosphere in the bars was absolutely poison and that was fuelled by drink.' When Gordon Brown was still Chancellor, McBride was woken up one morning by his ringing mobile phone. It was Sue Nye, Brown's gatekeeper, reminding him that the editor of the *Sunday Times* was due to meet the Chancellor in five minutes' time. 'I said I'd be up in a minute. But I looked at the lift and realised it wasn't my hotel. I went outside and saw I was at a Travelodge on the motorway twenty miles outside Manchester. No idea how I'd got there. No idea what I was doing there or who I'd come with. They were the kind of things that happened at party conference.'[46]

One of the most surreal scenes to be found at a party conference is the final night at the Liberal Democrat conference. In a packed hotel suite, familiar faces can be seen belting out songs with chorus lines like 'Tony Blair can fuck off and die' to the tune of 'American Pie'. This is the Glee Club, the bizarrely savage side of the hemp-and-beards brigade. This singalong has been a conference highlight longer than the Lib Dems have existed and is organised by the grassroots group known as The Liberator. Satirical lyrics are paired to well-known tunes ranging from old hymns to Amy Winehouse.

The 2015 Glee Club was held in the Dorchester Suite of Bournemouth's Marriott Hotel and the song sheet was dedicated to their late leader Charles Kennedy, whose name cropped up in a number of ditties including one about the drinking habits of politicians. There was a song about Trident sung to the tune of the Beatles' 'Yellow Submarine', an old favourite called 'Iraqi Cokey' and another number, 'Coalition', matched to the melody of 'Twelve Days of Christmas'. Here's a flavour:

On the first day of coalition
The Tories gave to me,
A referendum on A.V.

On the second day of coalition
The Tories gave to me,
Absolutely zilch,
And a referendum on A.V.
(which we lost!)

And so on for ten more increasingly irate verses. Other songs skewer past and present Liberal Democrat figures with varying degrees of affection, and the whole raucous cabaret manages to be self-mocking, pugnacious and despairing all at the same time. It's a bizarre window into what the party really thinks about itself. And of course most of those singing along have had a few sherbets beforehand. At least you hope they have.

It always seems there are more gin and tonics and wine bottles being drained at Conservative Party conferences than at Labour's, which remain a brotherhood of beer-drinkers. And it was the Tories who felt the need to have a 'champagne ban' at its conferences in 2009 and 2010. Party workers and MPs were told not to be snapped holding anything that looked like a glass of bubbly, for fear the press would condemn such indulgence in a time of austerity. While working-class Nye Bevan could get away with being a 'Bollinger Bolshevik', the wealthy duo of David Cameron and George Osborne were determined to try and stop their party looking posh, and that meant no champagne. Even Lord Strathclyde, the Conservative Leader in the House of Lords, cancelled his lavish annual drinks party, held in his suite at the conference hotel.

'I stopped doing them in around 2006,' he tells me in the House of Lords tea room. 'There had been a rich tradition in the 1980s, Alistair McAlpine and Jeffrey Archer threw shepherd's pie and Krug parties. Being in opposition was very miserable. It was appalling for us and conferences became rather miserable places. And one or two of us decided to hold a party. The magic was not to invite anybody apart from the Shadow Cabinet but to let people know there might be a party somewhere on the eighth floor of the Blackpool hotel. All of these things used to be at the seaside. Following on from the example set by Lord Hesketh we produced a plate of oysters, a plate of smoked salmon sandwiches and champagne that we kept in bottles in the bath. I once met a Labour peer who asked if I poured it all in! It was bottles on ice in the bath.

'It all sounds so incredibly dated now. Anyone with any nous like lobby correspondents would find their way and it was great fun. A great mixture of senior journalists, Shadow Cabinet ministers, and one or two very junior people who found their way there and it was fun. It was good for party morale and people wrote about it. There was no dress code. No guest list. To begin with the only invites under doors were to Shadow Cabinet ministers, although it gradually became more sophisticated and we eventually succumbed to printed invitations.'

Lord Strathclyde takes a sheepish pride in his party-throwing past. Everyone wanted to join the convivial crush in his Blackpool hotel room at two in the morning and drink from the champagne-filled bathtub. But then party conferences and the Tory Party began to change. 'As part of the modernisation we moved to modern hotels in nice city centres which started to exclude normal members. The rooms became boring. More importantly there was a feeling that conferences should be more than about whether or not someone threw a good party. So the fun party died. It was a good decision to sober up, look more professional,' he says rather unconvincingly.

I ask Lord Strathclyde if politics and the public are better served by this new seriousness. 'That is something for historians to decide. Certainly politics has a little less colour, less character.'[47]

Away from the public bars, discreet and exclusive soirees, hosted by party donors, newspaper publishers and lobbyists, are still held at all party conferences. And despite the champagne ban, top Tories still found a way to drink the best. During the 2010 conference the outgoing party treasurer Michael Spencer held a party at Simpsons, a swish Birmingham restaurant. Honouring a promise he had made to the leadership if the Tories won the election, the billionaire Mr Spencer dipped into his cellar and pulled out crates of 2001 Petrus. At around £1,000 a bottle, there was plenty of the magnificent Bordeaux red for guests to quaff. Next time there's talk of a party conference champagne ban, my advice would be not to believe a word of it.

## Supping with the Leader

Apart from the well-courted political editors of newspapers and broadcast media, most political journalists are not on first name terms with the Prime Minister and their most senior Cabinet colleagues. Of course there are friendships, usually formed when the politician was on their way up the ladder and looking for flattering press coverage. But once they make it to the top, the gap grows. Old mobile numbers are used very sparingly. Conversation and questioning is mostly conducted through special advisers, the young political spinners and loyal lieutenants who work for Cabinet ministers. Many of these, as we have seen, can be found doing business in the back of Whitehall pubs.

It is sad to report that run-of-the-mill political correspondents do not spend their evenings sipping brandy and swapping gossip behind the doors of Numbers 10 and 11 Downing Street. So it is a rare treat when this happens. Twice a year, in summer and winter, the hacks are let in, after a stiff envelope has arrived in the post containing an invitation for drinks with the Prime Minister.

Even the most jaded journalists run their hands up the polished wooden banister of Number 10 and wonder what it must be like to live there, up past the portraits of Pitt,

Disraeli, Attlee and Thatcher. Mobile phones have to be handed in at the front door, where they're held in a mahogany sideboard. Political journalists are a self-important tribe but this surrender reminds them where power really lies. If it's winter, it is up to one of the large reception rooms where a large table is laid out with drink. In summer, trays of glasses and nibbles are passed around in the garden. Everybody already knows everybody else. Except the person hosting the party.

We know them, of course, or think we do. And they know most of our names and who we work for from press conferences and encounters on foreign trips. But it's an odd situation. Someone whom the journalists spend so long talking and writing about with casual familiarity doesn't really know them at all. And they have the same frisson when the Prime Minister comes into the room as any other visitor to Downing Street would. It must be peculiar for the Prime Minister too, hosting a jolly reception for a Westminster press corps composed of people who inevitably spend much of their time making life difficult for them and their government.

For Gordon Brown the whole thing seemed to be agony. He would try and make conversation with the hacks which invariably began with 'Did you see the game?' followed by an update on the fortunes of his own football team, Raith Rovers. For most of his time in Number 10 Brown was torn to pieces in the papers. But his torturers still showed up for the free drinks twice a year and the chance to share stilted observations about football. These occasions are not the moment to ask about his mutinous Cabinet, the date of the general election or rumours about his phone-throwing. To do so would jeopardise the return of your own phone.

David Cameron was far more insouciant at these receptions. The drink's improved too. At a recent Christmas do there was red and white wine from Berry Bros. & Rudd in St James's, as well as bottles of craft beer, served below the chandeliers and portraits. The format's the same though. Journalists go straight to the drinks table to get a glass and then mill around talking to each other while keeping an eye out for the Prime Minister, who is being steered around the room by their official spokesman. Not everyone gets a word, so you need to catch their minder's eye. Small groups of journalists then stand in a doughnut around the PM and try to think of something to say while the spokesman discreetly reminds their boss who they are.

For the journalists, the alcohol is a useful lubricant at this point, while Prime Ministers have mastered the art of polite but perfunctory conversation and the quick getaway. Once the circuit of the room is done, they're out of there, leaving the journalists to carry on consuming as much free drink as they can before being gently shown the door by Downing Street staff. And whether it's winter or summer the jaded, seen-it-all-before cynics of the Westminster press corps will then snap selfies and pose for photographs on the steps of Number 10 before trundling down the street for further drinks at the Red Lion on Whitehall.

And the point of all this? It's a chance for the journalists to glean a bit of gossip from the Prime Minister, of course. But this biannual brush with the PM over drinks at their place flatters the lobby correspondents too. It's a perk of belonging to Westminster's small club of political hacks and makes them feel important. Prime Ministers are not naïve enough to believe some free drink and a chat will change what's written or said about them. But it's a bridge between the two trenches and a reminder that both the press and politicians are in the same game.

Downing Street isn't the only corner of political London handing out alcohol to grateful journalists. Before the Christmas and summer recesses thirsty hacks can fill their diaries with evening drinks at Number 11 and the Leader of the Opposition's knees-up in his parliamentary office. Lobbyists and think tanks also lay on seasonal parties where journalists and politicians can be found swigging the free booze. Invitations pour in from all sides, from Welsh Labour to the Institute of Economic Affairs. The Mayor of London hosts a bash at City Hall. The venues are different but the crowd and conversation are the same. In the throng will be some teetotallers and others having a night off from the grog. But these gatherings float along on a sea of warm wine. They pull in the politicos and grease the gossip. Who's up, who's down, who's going to win, who's doomed?

## A Height for Drinks

The most memorable political drinks – from a journalist's perspective – are usually those served at 36,000 feet during a long flight back from a Prime Minister's foreign trip. The last report has been filed, mobile phones won't work for hours and the aircraft's galley is groaning with free booze. Often these trips are on scheduled flights, but the best are those on specially chartered planes, where the Prime Minster and their Number 10 team, a contingent of political journalists and a few rows of business leaders mingle, drink and gossip. The news organisations and the business people pay to be on these trips. Thus it was that I covered David Cameron's four-day dash around South-East Asia in 2015, spending almost as much time in the air as we did on the ground. Every take-off was further lifted with a glass of champagne and the atmosphere soon resembled a bizarre political package tour. The Prime Minister would occasionally amble down to the back of the plane for a chat with the hacks, for whom these trips can be a valuable source of stories. It's also a rare chance to hobnob up close, dressed down, with the person we spend a great deal of time talking and writing about but rarely meet outside a press conference or drinks reception. As the trip wears on, the jet lag kicks in, the drinks keep coming, and the formality on board dissolves. By the time we begin our final leg from Kuala Lumpur to London the plane is up for a party.

The alcohol is provided by the airline – not the taxpayer – and everyone tucks in with gusto. It's champagne to start and David Cameron comes to chat holding a plastic cup of fizz. The forbearing cabin crew then attempt to steer a drinks trolley up the aisle through the crush of politicians, advisers, CEOs and journalists, all stretching out for a top-up. The flow of booze is ceaseless and the trolley barely makes it to the wing before it is wheeled back for a refill. This is hardly Led Zeppelin on tour, but it's the closest we will ever get.

Previous trips have seen quizzes, charades and karaoke without machines. On this one, speakers were wired up to an iPad and somewhere over the Arabian Sea a disco kicked off at the back of the plane. The Prime Minister had long since retreated to his seclusion at the front and several hours later Number 10 told us to pull the plug because he was trying to sleep. We woke up on the descent to Heathrow, empty miniature wine bottles wedged into seats and cracked plastic cups at our feet. Drink had briefly brought the two halves of the aeroplane together.

But on the ground, David Cameron was straight down the steps and into a convoy of cars waiting to take him to a meeting of the government's emergency committee, a reminder of just how gruellingly relentless modern prime ministerial life can be. There is a world of difference between journalistic access to political power and the exercise of it. For us, the bubble had burst. We just had a slow trudge home with our hangovers.

# CHAPTER 6

## Cocktails and Congress: Political Drinking in the United States

This story of political drinking now takes a detour, to the United States, to fill out the picture from over there. Like its Cold War rival Russia, the land of Alcoholics Anonymous and Betty Ford Centers is one of the very few countries to have experimented with banning alcohol altogether. Prohibition was a policy debacle that few politicians bothered obeying. Yet its legacy lasts in a nation where a third of people don't drink at all and per capita consumption is far less than in other comparably prosperous countries. But America wasn't always so temperate.

The colonists were champion drinkers, firm believers that alcohol could cure the sick, improve digestion and prolong life, making it more enjoyable along the way. Their various distilled liquors – gin, brandy, whisky and rum – were also safer to drink than the water. Before and after the Revolution, America was one of the hardest-drinking countries in the world. The annual amount consumed by each colonist is believed to be in the range of five to six gallons of pure alcohol. By 1830 Americans were knocking back a colossal seven gallons a year. In comparison, per capita consumption in the

United States in 2007 was 2.3 gallons.[1] As the historian W.J. Rorabaugh says, in the early nineteenth century, 'Americans drank from the crack of dawn to the crack of dawn.'[2] They drank at breakfast, before meals, with meals and after meals, bingeing their way through the first decades of the new Republic.

So it's no surprise that alcohol sloshed through the politics of the era too. As in Britain, taverns were places for political argument and organisation. They were rallying points for the militia and recruiting stations for the Continental Army.

John Adams, a Founding Father and the United States' second President, described public houses as the 'nurseries of our legislators', places where British rule was condemned and independence plotted.[3] Drink oiled elections in colonial America too, with voters demanding and receiving spirits in return for their ballots. Candidates needed to be generous with their liquor. Electoral success, said one Kentucky politico, hinged on understanding that 'the way to men's hearts is down their throats'.[4] When the young George Washington failed to win a seat in the Virginia House of Burgesses at the age of twenty-four, he blamed the defeat on the failure to lavish alcohol on voters. Two years later he made sure they were plied with 144 gallons of rum, punch and cider.[5]

It was important for a politician to imbibe with his voters too, proof that he was like them. As Rorabaugh writes, 'a candidate's good nature and congeniality in his cups demonstrated his respect for his peers, the voters, and thereby confirmed his egalitarianism'.[6] Many a politician in colonial America became inebriated to prove he was independent, an equal and a true republican.

The Founding Fathers knocked it back with gusto. John Adams drank a tankard of strong cider every morning while wondering whether it was 'not mortifying ... that we, Americans, should succeed all other people in the world in this degrading, beastly vice of intemperance?'[7]

No such angst afflicted Thomas Jefferson, who as well as writing the Declaration of Independence, became sommelier to the other Founding Fathers. In his early life Jefferson carried on the colonial tradition of drinking fortified wines like madeira and port, but he became passionate about wine while in Paris as Minister to France from 1784 to 1789. His travels through the vineyards of Burgundy and Bordeaux in 1787 prompted an interest in lighter red and white wines which he later had shipped across the Atlantic to fill his Monticello cellar. At Jefferson's Virginian villa, wine was winched up to the dinner table by a dumb waiter, and guests would receive tutorials on Old World wines from the New World's most knowledgeable connoisseur. Not all diners were dazzled. 'There was, as usual, a dissertation upon wines,' John Quincy Adams noted in his diary after dining with Jefferson in November 1807; 'Not very edifying.'[8]

So Jefferson may also have been America's first wine bore. The household at Monticello emptied 400 bottles a year and fresh supplies were ordered annually from Europe. He ordered around 600 bottles a year when he lived at the President's House. An oenophile but not a drunk, Jefferson savoured the pleasure of three or four glasses at dinner and didn't imbibe at any other time of day. But for the same reason that he soaked his feet in a bowl of cold water every morning, Jefferson believed wine drinking improved his constitution. 'Wine from long habit has become indispensable for my health,' he wrote to the wine merchant John F. Oliveira Fernandes in December 1815.[9]

America's third President was also one of its wine-growing pioneers. Or at least he wanted to be. Jefferson tried many times to make a Monticello-grown wine, but none of his attempts to cultivate imported vines worked. He persevered into his retirement, by which time he was importing less expensive wines from southern Italy and France instead of the earlier bottles of Chateau Margaux and Chateau Latour. And during these years, wine made from the scuppernong grape of north California began to appear on the shelves of Monticello's cellar. Jefferson couldn't grow his own grapes; but the author of the Declaration of Independence, third US President, multilingual polymath, philosopher, founder of the University of Virginia, amateur architect and inventor makes contemporary politicians look as nugatory as a nickel, on which his head is now stamped.

Two centuries later, rich men would squabble over the provenance of wine believed to have belonged to Jefferson when he lived in France. In 1985 the publisher Christopher Forbes paid $156,450 for a bottle of 1787 Chateau Lafite – a record auction sum for a single bottle of wine. Etched into the dark green glass were the initials 'Th.J'. Four other bottles from the cache reputedly found behind a bricked-up wall in Paris were bought by the US billionaire Edward Koch in 1987 and 1988. When he wanted to display them at the Boston Museum of Fine Arts in 2005, Koch had to prove their authenticity. But the Thomas Jefferson Foundation at Monticello, on being asked to give the bottles their stamp of approval, found no evidence of the Paris haul in Jefferson's own records.

As it began to look like the bottles were fake, Koch launched a succession of legal actions in the US for alleged fraud against both the German wine dealer who put the bottles on the market and Christie's auction house. But in October 2012 a New York judge ruled that Koch had waited too long to file the suit against Christie's. Already, in 2009, the former director of Christie's wine department, Michael Broadbent, had won an apology and damages from Random House after it published a book on the saga called *The Billionaire's Vinegar*.

Thomas Jefferson could not have imagined any of this as he sat on the edge of his bed, refreshing his feet, watching the sun rise over Monticello's plantation. Would he have been amused or appalled by the antics of America's wealthiest wine collectors and the prices they are prepared to pay? After all, it was Jefferson who had begun weaning America's political aristocracy off madeira and onto the pleasures of wine two hundred years earlier. The Jefferson wine frenzy reached its ludicrous climax at New York's Four Seasons hotel in April 1989. One of Manhattan's most publicity-hungry wine merchants, William Sokolin, possessed a 1787 Margaux, believed to be one of Jefferson's lost bottles. He had been trying to sell it for $519,750 but nobody had bitten. So Sokolin took it along to a banquet for New York's wine buffs, held to greet the arrival of the latest Bordeaux vintage. But as he twirled his treasure around the room he collided with a metal-topped tray table and punctured the back of the bottle. Guests watched aghast as red wine, possibly 202 years old, possibly once belonging to Thomas Jefferson, soaked into the Four Seasons carpet.

Back to America's founders. Evidence offered to prove they heartily filled their cups is a session that supposedly took place in a Philadelphia tavern in 1797, two days before the delegates to the Constitutional Convention signed off the Constitution. The bill from the evening is said to detail what must be one of the biggest political drinking binges in history. The fifty-five delegates drained fifty-four bottles of madeira, sixty bottles of claret, eight of whisky, twenty-two of port, eight of hard cider, twelve of beer and seven bowls of alcoholic punch. Clearly an impossible amount to drink. And not all of them were heavy boozers.

Benjamin Franklin – another extraordinary polymath and leader of the American Enlightenment – thought drunks tiresome and urged people to drink moderately. But he enjoyed the conviviality of taverns and it was there he mopped up more than 200 synonyms for 'drunk', publishing them in a piece for the *Pennsylvania Gazette* in January 1737. The alphabetical list includes the following, many of which time has rendered nonsensical:

A – addled, afflicted, in his airs
B – biggy, boozy, buskey, buzzey, been at Baradoes, drunk as a wheel-barrow, he's kissed black Betty
C – cherubimical, cracked, juicy, halfway to Concord. He's been too free with the creature. Sir Richard has taken off his considering cap
E – he's eat a toad and a half for breakfast, cock ey'd
F – fishey, fox'd, fuddled, sore footed, been to France
G – groatable, gold-headed, as dizzy as a goose, been with Sir John Goa, got the glanders
J – jagg'd, jambled, going to Jerusalem, been to Jericho, juicy
R – rocky, raddled, rich, lost his rudder, ragged

S – steady, stiff, stew'd, stubb'd, soak'd, soft
V – he makes Virginia fence, got the Indian vapours[10]

In the US, a million college T-shirts carry a quote attributed to Benjamin Franklin about beer. In fact Franklin chose wine, not beer, as 'a constant proof that God loves us, and loves to see us happy'.[11] The quote is from a letter Franklin wrote to his friend Andre Morellet in 1779. It's a hymn to the pleasures of wine and an argument that God wanted us to drink because he gave us elbows:

> You see in animals, who are intended to drink the waters that flow upon the earth, that if they have long legs, they also have a long neck, so that they can get at their drink without kneeling down. But man, who was destined to drink wine, must be able to raise the glass to his mouth. If the elbow had been placed nearer the hand, the part in advance would have been too short to bring the glass up to the mouth; and if it had been placed nearer the shoulder, that part would have been so long that it would have carried the wine far beyond the mouth. But by the actual situation, we are enabled to drink at our ease, the glass going exactly to the mouth. Let us, then, with glass in hand, adore this benevolent wisdom – let us adore and drink![12]

Benjamin Franklin appreciated and celebrated the pleasures of drink. Not so his fellow Founding Father Benjamin Rush, a physician and pioneering advocate of temperate behaviour. He was one of the first Americans to question whether booze was in fact good health in a glass. From his experience treating patients and a stint as the Continental Army's surgeon general, Rush came to the view that drink, specifically distilled spirits, had several downsides. These included vomiting, liver disease, hand tremors, stomach sickness, dropsy, madness, palsy, apoplexy and epilepsy.[13] He published his findings in a pamphlet, 'An Inquiry into the Effects of Spirituous Liquors', which in 1784 came as quite a shock to binge-drinking Americans. Deploying medical evidence, Rush began to cut through where the preachers and puritans had failed. Americans would continue to drink heavily into the nineteenth century, with whisky replacing rum as the popular tipple of choice, but the work of Benjamin Rush would be a weapon for the temperance movement more than a century later.

By the mid-nineteenth century societies such as the Sons of Temperance had sprung up to help Americans dry out. In 1851, while posted to Sackets Harbor on Lake Ontario, a young army lieutenant called Ulysses S. Grant turned to the group for support. Grant the President is barely remembered. Grant the soldier and Union Army commander is revered. But it's his drinking that has gripped and split historians of the Civil War for decades. In his biography of Grant, William McFeely writes: 'The idea that he drank prodigiously is as fixed in American history as the idea that the Pilgrims ate turkey on Thanksgiving, but the evidence for it is far more elusive.'[14] That hasn't stopped Grant becoming one of the most famous drunks in American political history. Throughout his military career, even while leading the fight against the Confederate forces, Grant was dogged by rumours of excessive drinking and intemperance.

The West Point graduate and Mexican war veteran started to drink heavily when he was dispatched to California and the Pacific Northwest in the early 1850s. Desperately missing his family, Grant turned to alcohol to relieve the loneliness. Most biographers agree that Grant preferred occasional binges to everyday drinking. He could go for weeks without touching a drop. And nor was Grant unusual in America's hard-drinking army. But in 1854 Captain Grant was discovered to be drunk on parade and resigned his commission.

Grant's thirties were spent failing at various jobs and when war broke out he was working as a clerk in his father's store in Illinois. He decided to re-enlist, and his meteoric rise up the ranks over the next four years was even more remarkable considering the sniping he battled from rivals about his drinking. After he led the Union Army to a brutal, blood-soaked victory at Shiloh in 1862, the press devoured planted stories about Grant's supposed intoxication. When he fell from his horse near New Orleans in September 1863, drunkenness was blamed. One of the most notorious examples of Grant's inebriation occurred during a trip up the Yazoo River on the steamer *Diligent* in June 1863 to flush out Confederate forces. A *Chicago Times* reporter on board, Sylvanus Cadwallader, witnessed Grant indulge in a two-day bender. But instead of filing a sensational story that could have terminated Grant's command, Cadwallader buried it. The manuscript of his account was finally published in 1955, triggering decades of argument between historians about its veracity.

Throughout the war, Grant's chief of staff John A. Rawlins had the job of steering the general away from the bottle. Grant's rivals tried to undermine his standing in Washington by focusing on his drinking. But the star of the Union Army was defended at the top. In part that was because he seems to have drunk only during quiet periods of the campaign. In the view of the historian Geoffrey Perret, '[Grant's] drinking was not allowed to jeopardise operations. It was a release, but a controlled one, like the ignition of a gas flare about a high-pressure oil well.'[15]

And, most importantly, President Lincoln believed Ulysses S. Grant was the only man in America who had the guts, talent and drive to deliver victory and repair the Union. There is a quote attributed to Lincoln in response to complaints by Congressmen about Grant's drinking habits: 'I then began to ask them if they knew what brand of whisky he used,' confided the president to John Eaton. 'They conferred with each other and concluded they could not tell … I urged them to ascertain and let me know, for if it made fighting generals like Grant, I should like to get some of it for distribution.'[16] In other words, drench the troops in whatever Ulysses S. Grant was drinking.

The misery of war strained the nerves of those fighting it. When the Civil War general William Sherman suffered a nervous breakdown, he and Grant became brothers in battle. 'Grant stood by me when I was crazy, and I stood by him when he was drunk; and now we stand by each other always.'[17]

## Prohibition

With typical brio, Churchill described America's thirteen-year booze ban as an 'affront to the whole history of mankind'. The culmination of decades of pressure from temperance societies, dry religious denominations and anti-saloon activists, prohibition was meant to cut crime and corruption while improving America's moral and physical health. The movement had particular momentum in southern and western rural states, where it had clearly become a vote-winning cause.

By the First World War many states were partially or completely dry and the pressure to act was building in Washington. Despite President Wilson's attempt to veto the prohibitionist Volstead Act, Congress passed it into law. It then needed to be ratified by thirty-six states, and in January 1919 Nebraska became the last to do so. The Eighteenth Amendment was grafted onto the Constitution and precisely a year later America's liquor stores were closed, its saloons padlocked, wine cellars sealed off and distilleries mothballed. The manufacture, sale, advertising, transport and import of alcohol was banned. Existing private stocks of liquor could be drunk at home, but otherwise the shutters were pulled down.

But what was meant to herald a new era of American sobriety instead spawned a decade of bootleggers, rum-runners, speakeasies, smugglers and gangsters. The story of prohibition's spectacular failure has been told many times before. But it's the two-faced behaviour of the politicians who banned the booze that is the focus here.

The beginning of prohibition coincided with the start of Warren Harding's presidency, by most measures reckoned to be one of the worst in American history. Corrupt and incompetent, Harding did like a drink and had no intention of obeying the spirit of prohibition. In the words of one contemporary, the President had a sociable nature, one 'not at all averse to putting a foot on the brass rail'. But since the public bars had been shut, Harding was forced to drink at home. He arranged to have $1,800 worth of liquor transferred from his private home to the White House, which became a salon for members of his administration. A friend of Harding's wife, Alice Longworth, recalled the White House air, 'heavy with tobacco smoke, trays with bottles containing every imaginable brand of whisky … cards and poker chips ready at hand – a general atmosphere of the waistcoat unbuttoned, feet on the desk, and the spittoon alongside'.[18] According to Daniel Okrent, Harding's Washington was 'awash in alcohol from the moment of his inauguration'.[19]

The Attorney General, Harry Daugherty, arranged for Justice Department employees to deliver stocks of seized liquor to his private drinking den. Up on Capitol Hill, many Congressmen and Senators who trumpeted the benefits of prohibition in public were determined to get their hands on a drink, a habit known as a drinking wet but voting dry. H.L. Mencken called the prohibition era the 'Thirteen Awful Years' and lampooned the deceptive hypocrisy of politicians: 'Today the voter chooses his rulers as he buys bootleg whisky, never knowing precisely what he is getting, only certain that it is not what it pretends to be. The Scotch may turn out to be wood alcohol or may turn out to be gasoline; in either case it is not Scotch'.[20]

Herbert Hoover, Warren Harding's successor in the White House, did try to beef up the enforcement of prohibition, but throughout the 1920s Washington was so wet it squelched. A pervasive liquor trade had become essential to the lives of politicians and the press revelled in exposing the deceit. In 1929 there was a deluge of stories. On 19 November, police raided a speakeasy across the road from the White House and found an admittance list that included members of the Cabinet and a Congressman.

Some politicians tried to source their own supplies, rarely with success. There was Congressman William M. Morgan of Ohio, who represented a bone-dry district. He was caught by customs officers returning into the port of New York with two bottles of whisky and two bottles of champagne in his bags. Representative Edward E. Denison from Illinois, a supporter of the tough new prohibition penalties introduced by the Jones Law, was caught smuggling eighteen bottles of Scotch and six of gin from Panama into his office in the Capitol building. Others were caught with leaking luggage at ports and railway stations.

More sensible members of Congress relied on the services of Capitol Hill's own bootlegger. In October 1930, the *Washington Post* ran a series of front-page articles written by George Cassiday, who smuggled drink into Congress for a decade. Cassiday began the series with a confession: 'For nearly ten years I have been supplying liquor at the order of United States senators and representatives at their offices at Washington. On Capitol Hill I am known as "The Man in the Green Hat."'[21] Cassiday was given a key and a storeroom in the House Office Building which served as his off-licence and he claimed that four out of five Congressmen guzzled alcohol at their homes or in their offices during prohibition. After he smuggled the goods in at night, Congressmen carried the bottles out during the day, exempt from the security bag check at the door. In 1925 Cassiday was arrested carrying a briefcase of booze into the House Office Building. After lying low for a while, he transferred his business to the Senate side of the Hill.

In November 1928 the *Washington Post* ran another exposé of D.C.'s political drinking. The article began: 'Here is the nation's capital – where they made the law. Here in little back rooms, men gather and violate the law.'[22] But politicians weren't the only Washingtonians ignoring prohibition. Drinking thrived in the jazz clubs of U Street and in the speakeasies of Dupont Circle, while hundreds of bootleggers made discreet home deliveries.

It was the same in cities across America. People who had never drunk before embraced the thrill of beating the ban. Criminality and corruption flourished. Because the home-made hooch being illegally brewed often tasted awful, fruit-flavoured cocktails became popular. It was therefore fitting that the policy debacle of prohibition was finally repealed by the martini-sipping Franklin Roosevelt. Writing shortly before the capital's bars were reopened and glasses could again be clinked without the threat of a raid and arrest, the *Washington Post* columnist George Rothwell Brown mourned the culture that had gone. Without drink, he wrote, politics was poorer:

> Something has gone out of life with the passing of famous old Washington institutions as Mullany's, the historic bar of the original Willard's, Shoomaker's, Hancock's and the old Whitney House, of an earlier day. Here were absolutely open forums for the discussion of the principal problems of the day by men who spoke freely under the inspiration of more or less strong drink; which had a tendency to promote eloquence and bust asunder the shackles of convention, conservatism and caution. The poet has said truth lies at the bottom

of a well, but in reality it lies at the bottom of a wine bottle.[23]

## The Presidents

When Donald Trump was inaugurated US President in January 2017, many people across the world anxiously reached for a drink. With no previous political or military experience, the billionaire businessman was unlike any incoming President in US history; a tangerine-hued Twitter obsessive who was widely seen as impetuous, sexist and thuggish by people who did not vote for him, and heroically anti-establishment by those who did. Something else set Trump apart from his predecessors: he has eschewed alcohol his whole life. 'I've never had a drink', he told Fox News in an interview broadcast shortly after his election victory, a statement that might have surprised people who follow Trump's nocturnal rants on social media.

The reason for his sobriety is that his adored older brother Freddie died of an illness stemming from alcoholism at the age of 42. 'It was a very tough period of time', Trump said, that convinced him never to drink. 'If you don't start you're never going to have a problem. If you do start you might have a problem. And it's a tough problem to stop', he told Fox. What is fascinating is Trump's view that one drink could spiral into addiction. He discussed his fear that he might have a gene that would make moderate drinking impossible. His approach to alcohol is also a window into a personality that appears to crave control over others. Trump ordered his children to follow his example. Every day he would drum the message into them: no drugs, no alcohol, no cigarettes. 'I've been very tough on my children with respect to drink,' Trump said.[24] While many politicians seek to persuade voters that they are like them by posing with a drink, Trump tore up the campaign rulebook when it came to alcohol, too.

His predecessor Barack Obama was happy to be snapped with a beer in his hand on the campaign trail or at home. In July 2009, he hosted what was imaginatively dubbed a 'beer summit' on the Rose Garden patio. The arrest of a black Harvard professor by a Massachusetts police sergeant had triggered a huge row about racial profiling in the United States, and in an effort to calm down the furore, Obama got the two men together for a drink in front of the cameras. The President supped a glass mug of Bud Light while the US press went into a frenzy over the pictures. This was beer to symbolise – and perhaps facilitiate – bridge-building and reconciliation. A signal to Americans that the President deliberated over a drink, too.

Obama told reporters: 'This is three folks having a drink at the end of the day, and hopefully giving people an opportunity to listen to each other. And that's really all it is.' It was in fact a carefully contrived photo opportunity that probably did little to harmonise race relations, but did send a signal to Americans that he was still a bit like them. And as US voters weighed up Donald Trump, some may have remembered the gloomily sober administrations of two previous non-drinking Presidents.

Jimmy Carter and George W. Bush had little in common apart from unpopularity, evangelicalism and teetotalism. In 1976 Carter successfully campaigned against the tax deductibility of the three-martini lunch, a move that helped kill off the boozy lunch in corporate America. After the election a defeated Gerald Ford said the three-martini lunch was the epitome of American efficiency: 'Where else can you get an earful, a bellyful and a snootful at the same time?'

Life in the Carter White House was drearily dry and a chore for its more sociable visitors. Senator Ted Kennedy remembered arid evenings of earnest discussion: 'You'd arrive about 6:00 or 6:30 p.m., and the first thing you would be reminded of, in case you needed reminding, was that he and Rosalynn had removed all the liquor in the White House. No liquor was ever served during Jimmy Carter's term. He wanted no luxuries nor any sign of worldly living.'[25]

George W. Bush went dry after discovering God at the bottom of a glass. His years of partying, heavy drinking and frat house frolics ended abruptly on 28 July 1986, when he woke up with a hangover and decided it would be his last. The previous night had been spent at the Broadmoor Hotel in Colorado Springs, where he and a group of Texas friends celebrated their collective fortieth birthdays. Bush had long liked to drink what he called the four Bs: beer, bourbon and B&B (brandy and Benedictine). He claimed never to have been an alcoholic but he did drink heavily, getting arrested for drink driving in 1976 near the Bush retreat at Kennebunkport, Maine. Another session ended with Bush drunkenly smashing his car into some neighbours' bins and then challenging his father to go *mano a mano* outside the family's home in Washington. The senior Bush – patrician, serious, successful – was not amused.

Was the drinking an escape from the pressure of having to live up to his name? Certainly by the age of forty Bush junior had failed at business and made no impact in politics. It seems a conversation with the Reverend Billy Graham in Kennebunkport the year before his birthday persuaded him it might be time to swap grog for God and get his life in shape. In 1986 George W. went cold turkey and hasn't touched alcohol since. Instead, he swapped a compulsion to drink for an obsession with fitness and propelled himself into politics.

So does a tippling President make for a better commander in chief? US historians and political scientists love ranking their political leaders and Franklin D. Roosevelt is always placed near the top of the table. The four-time President first defeated the Great Depression and then led America through the Second World War. And throughout these tumultuous years the cheerfully patrician FDR kept a martini close at hand. Roosevelt prized his pre-dinner cocktail hour, when friends and colleagues would meet at the White House to unwind over a drink. Samuel I. Rosenman was one of Roosevelt's speech writers and later described the ritual:

The President made quite a ceremony out of this daily cocktail hour, mixing the drinks himself from various ingredients brought to his desk on a large tray. People who were more accustomed to drinking than I, and who knew more about the mixing of drinks, were a little nonplussed at the nonchalance with which the President, without bothering to measure, would add one ingredient after another to his cocktails. To my unpracticed eye he seemed to experiment on each occasion with a different percentage of vermouth, gin and fruit juice. At times he varied it with rum – especially rum from the Virgin Islands. The President liked to press a second, and at times a third, cocktail upon any guest who was at all willing. His usual expression, on noticing an empty glass, was: 'How about another little sippy?'[26]

It was sometimes too much for Rosenman, who used to pour second servings into a plant pot. Other witnesses to this presidential bartending say Roosevelt used to add drops of absinthe to his martini concoctions for extra flavour.

Cocktail hour took place in the President's second-floor study, his favourite room in the White House. Among the leather sofas and piles of books, the pressures of politics and war were swapped for drinks, storytelling and gossip. The former Attorney General and Supreme Court Justice, Robert H. Jackson, said Roosevelt took huge pleasure in the conviviality of cocktail hour but rarely had more than a couple of drinks: 'Any impression that the President was given to any considerable amount of drinking ... is a mistake. I never knew him to take more than a couple of cocktails, nor did he want anyone about him who drank to excess.'[27]

Jackson was trying to correct the impression left by Roosevelt's son Elliott that drinking formed a large part of the President's wartime diplomacy. His 1946 memoir frequently finds the younger Roosevelt fixing his dad an Old Fashioned, or buzzing around the margins of meetings filling up glasses for his father and Churchill while they argued about the future of the British Empire and post-war Europe.[28] When Churchill first visited President Roosevelt at the White House in December 1941, the two leaders cemented their fraternity over drink, despite Eleanor Roosevelt's disapproval. Decades later Elliott Roosevelt wrote: 'Winston liked to down a few brandies as the night wore on, so Father would have himself an extra cocktail or two to keep him company, which was another reason for Mother's objections.'[29]

The Cold War Franklin Roosevelt had striven to avoid was well under way by the time two of America's heaviest-drinking Presidents occupied the White House. The daiquiri-sipping John F. Kennedy was not a big drinker (like Clinton, Kennedy preferred women to wine) and kept a clear head through the Cuban Missile Crisis. It might have been different if two of his successors had been in the Oval Office in 1962.

On his political ascent through the Senate in the 1950s, Lyndon Johnson made a show of being a clubbable heavy drinker, one of the boys. But in the early years it was something of a charade, according to Robert A. Caro, Johnson's magisterial biographer. The Senator used to say, 'drinking makes you let your guard down,' and he was careful not to lose control. Staff in his Senate office were instructed to make drinks for visitors stronger than his own glass of Cutty Sark Scotch and soda.[30] But after becoming the Democrat majority leader in 1955, Johnson began to drink more. Returning to his office after the Senate had recessed for the day, he would be given a drink and sink into a big leather chair. There, writes Caro, Johnson 'would throw back his head, empty the glass in a single gulp, immediately hold it out and rattle the ice cubes for another Cutty Sark and soda, and another and another. More and more, the man who never wanted to be "out of control" because of drinking was out of control.'[31]

Reports of Johnson drinking and chain-smoking like someone facing the electric chair began to circulate around Washington dinner parties. But he saved the serious drinking binges for the privacy of his Texas ranch. Once, while recovering from a heart attack there, Johnson's doctors told him to relax and do more of the things he enjoyed. He told them he enjoyed nothing but 'whisky, sunshine and sex'.[32] Johnson craved sensation and escape, whether with women or a whisky bottle. It didn't stop him getting to the White House though; and one of the most vivid snapshots of presidential drinking was captured by Joseph A. Califano Jr, Johnson's special assistant for domestic affairs. Califano had been summoned to the ranch in July 1965, shortly after being offered the job. Here he recalls a ride with President Johnson:

> In the early afternoon, the President, with me next to him in the front seat, took his white Lincoln convertible, top down, for a drive around the ranch. It was incredibly hot; the dust clouds made it hard to breathe. But there was relief. As we drove around we were followed by a car and a station wagon with Secret Service agents. The President drank Cutty Sark scotch and soda out of a large white plastic foam cup. Periodically, Johnson would slow down and hold his left arm outside the car, shaking the cup and ice. A Secret Service agent would run up to the car, take the cup and go back to the station wagon. There another agent would refill it with ice, scotch, and soda as the first agent trotted behind the wagon. Then the first agent would run the refilled cup up to LBJ's outstretched and waiting hand, as the President's car moved slowly along.[33]

Donald Trump's first months in office revealed a man quick to anger and take offence at any perceived slight. He intends to be a political iconoclast who tears up the rulebook, and to push the US constitution to its limits. Perhaps we should be grateful that drink is not in the mix, too. Or maybe the perspective and balance many previous presidents found through alcohol is exactly what Trump needs.

## Nixon's Nemesis

Perhaps only Franklin Pierce was as dependent on and damaged by alcohol as Richard Nixon when President; and both careers ended in humiliation. Often ranked among the worst US Presidents, the amiable but frequently drunk Pierce managed to split his own Democratic Party and accelerate the United States' slide towards civil war. In 1974 Richard Nixon became the only President to resign the office after facing certain impeachment following the Watergate cover-up. As Air Force One flew him back to California for the final time, Nixon nursed a martini, the drink he had consoled himself with during the long nights of his presidency.

When asked by the press about the President's drinking, the White House would claim Nixon only sipped the occasional glass of white wine. But it was a lie, as several biographies have since revealed. By 1972, both Henry Kissinger, Nixon's Secretary of State, and his Chief of Staff, Alexander Haig, were referring to the President behind his back as 'our drunk'.[34] But his propensity to hit the bottle when under strain had been evident twenty years earlier. After losing the governorship of California in 1962, Nixon went on a 'roaring bender', according to the Washington journalist Don Fulsom and corroborated by others.[35] The following morning, hungover, red-eyed and trembling, Nixon appeared in front of the cameras and famously declared he was quitting politics. 'Just think what you'll be missing,' he said. 'You won't have Nixon to kick around anymore, gentlemen, because this is my last press conference.' A propensity for embittered self-pity was already evident, but the press did not comment on Nixon's haggard state, even though it must have been obvious to reporters. For much of Nixon's life, the American people were completely unaware of his drinking.

Richard Nixon didn't bow out of politics in 1962. Instead he won the presidency six years later. John Ehrlichman served as domestic affairs adviser in the Nixon White House, but only agreed to work on the 1968 campaign if the candidate laid off the booze. He believed Nixon's drinking was serious enough to cost him any chance of a return to public life.[36] And to begin with, Nixon hoped to keep his alcohol intake under control, telling the journalist Theodore White in 1969 that now he was President he wouldn't drink in the way he had done: 'You can't drink and think clearly ... two drinks and your mind isn't quite as sharp and you may not be able to think clearly when that phone rings at night ... no more drinking ... no more late hours.'[37]

It was a pledge he failed to keep. Slurred and rambling late-night telephone calls to aides were a fixture of the Nixon presidency until it collapsed in 1974. White House Chief of Staff Bob Haldeman put them down to a mixture of fatigue and drink. 'One beer would transform his speech into the rambling elocution of a Bowery wino,' he wrote.[38]

Most witnesses agree it didn't take much alcohol to release a snarling, unpleasant and paranoid drunk. Nixon's character was one of the most complicated of any President and not that of a typical politician. He was socially awkward,

introverted, insecure and self-pitying. He loathed small talk
and had no time for flattery or charm. In Henry Kissinger's
view, Nixon drank in part to compensate for the political
skills he lacked. According to Kissinger, 'alcohol had a way
of destroying the defences he had so carefully constructed to
enable him to succeed in a profession based on a conviviality
unnatural to him'.[39] But Kissinger dismisses as 'absurd' the
suggestion that Nixon staggered through his presidency with
a bottle by his side and claims the President only drank at
night, never in the Oval Office and never in the context of
major decisions. 'The trouble was that Nixon could not hold
even a small quantity of alcohol. Two glasses of wine were
quite enough to make him boisterous, just one more to grow
bellicose or sentimental with slurred speech … The few of us
who actually witnessed such conduct never acted on what he
might have said.'[40]

Since Nixon could have ordered a nuclear attack with the
power to obliterate the planet, we should all be grateful that
Henry Kissinger at least was sober. According to Kissinger's
biographer, Walter Isaacson, the Secretary of State used
to tell aides he was the one man who kept that 'drunken
lunatic' from doing things that would 'blow up the world'.[41]
And late-night threats of military action were actually
made. When North Korea shot down a US spy plane in
April 1969, an enraged Nixon ordered a tactical nuclear
strike and told the Joint Chiefs to recommend targets.
According to the historian Anthony Summers, citing the
CIA's top Vietnam specialist at the time, George Carver,
Kissinger spoke to military commanders on the phone
and agreed not to do anything until Nixon sobered up in
the morning.[42] A memo from June 1969 obtained by the

National Security Archive in Washington in 2010 showed the Pentagon had drawn up plans for a tactical nuclear strike against North Korea, codenamed Freedom Drop. A former US bomber pilot, Bruce Charles, told National Public Radio in 2010 that he was put on alert to attack North Korea with a nuclear bomb hours after the US plane was shot down. After several hours of waiting an order to stand down came through.

Whether President Nixon did actually order an immediate drink-fuelled nuclear strike on North Korea isn't clear. But a nuclear response was considered. As it was in October 1973, when it seemed the Soviet Union was poised to send forces into the Middle East and Brezhnev issued a letter to Nixon warning that the Soviet Union was prepared to act unilaterally. But on the night of 24 October, the President had crashed out early and gone to sleep. Some believed he was drunk, others that he was merely tired.

Alexander Haig decided Nixon should not be involved, so the President was left to sleep upstairs while defence chiefs gathered in the White House situation room. The world was closer to nuclear war than it had been since the Cuban Missile Crisis and US forces were notched up to DEFCON III alert, two away from war. At US bases, B-52s loaded with nuclear bombs lined up on runways and nuclear-armed submarines waited for orders close to the Soviet coast.

The next morning another letter from Brezhnev arrived as if none of the previous threats had been made and the crisis petered out. But at this critical moment the US President had been out of action. Later, in 1997, the chief of naval operations, Admiral Elmo Zumwalt, remembered the night: 'We had to go on nuclear alert without his permission. The reason we had to do that was because he could not be awakened. Nixon obviously had too much to drink … I was told at the time that they were not able to waken him.'[43]

By now, Watergate was beginning to choke Nixon's presidency and he was relying ever more on drink and sleeping pills to cope with the pressure. On the evening of 11 October 1973 he was incapable of speaking to the British Prime Minister, Edward Heath, on the phone. Heath was keen to discuss the latest developments in the Arab-Israeli War, but a transcript of the conversation between Henry Kissinger and his assistant Brent Scowcroft revealed that the President was too drunk to talk to the Prime Minister. 'Can we tell them no?' Kissinger asks his assistant. 'When I talked to the President, he was loaded.' Scowcroft replies: 'Right. OK. I will say the President will not be available until first thing in the morning but you will be this evening.'

By 1974 the pressure on Nixon was immense. He was drinking excessively and unable to sleep, prone to wandering the halls of the White House at night talking to the portraits of former Presidents on the walls.[44] Nixon's aides were afraid Watergate might end with a presidential suicide. But in the end he capitulated to the inevitability of resignation, spending one of his final nights in the White House drinking uncontrollably, weeping and praying with Henry Kissinger in the Lincoln Sitting Room. Kissinger tried to convince the broken President that historians would treat him more kindly than his contemporaries, while knowing that Watergate would be Nixon's epitaph. He is a warning to future Presidents on the danger of mixing hubris with drink.

## D.C. Drinking

Kyle sat stiffly on a bar stool sipping a mint julep. His $200 suit and schoolboy side-parting jarred with the clubby red leather, brass fittings and marble-covered counter of the Round Robin Bar. He had heard the Willard Hotel was the place in town to mint new political contacts.

An ice cube's throw from the White House, the Willard is said to be where the term 'lobbyist' was first coined, after Ulysses S. Grant was collared by people wanting favours every time he arrived at the hotel hoping to have a quiet brandy and cigar at the bar. However, the *Oxford English Dictionary* records that in America the verb 'lobbying' first appeared in an Ohio newspaper in 1837, thirty years before Grant went to Washington. And in Britain, 'lobby' was the name given to the place where people met Members of Parliament as early as the 1640s.

But none of this mattered to Kyle. He was a young man in his early twenties who had migrated from Alabama to Washington in the hunt for politics, power and a like-minded tribe. A few weeks into his adventure, Kyle had done some unpaid photocopying at a conservative think tank and was now bombarding Congressional offices with his resume. But getting a foothold in Washington, he told me, was about who you know. And he didn't seem to know anyone. So he spent his evenings hunting out drinks parties and receptions where he hoped to meet the contact who would unlock a political career. And when the drinks were over he slept on the couches of people he hardly knew. Tonight Kyle had taken himself off to the Willard alone. More drinks, more awkward introductions, more hopes.

Unluckily for him, it was only me who was perched on the neighbouring bar stool, able to offer nothing more than sympathy and encouragement. Elsewhere in Washington that evening, an army of Capitol Hill staffers were fanning out into Happy Hour. At the renovated Hawk 'n' Dove, a once legendarily political dive bar on Pennsylvania Avenue, the cream chino-clad bag carriers of Congress were eating 'Filibuster Flatbreads' and 'Opening Statement' appetisers with their beers. It was the same crowd at Tune Inn a few doors down, where towers of cheese-covered nachos were washed down with pints of Fat Tire. In bars like these, thousands of press secretaries, diary schedulers, errand-runners and letter-openers drink and dream of something better. Most, like Kyle, are fresh out of college and will soon quit Capitol Hill for something better paid and less precarious. But others will stick at it, looking for the key that will open a world of Georgetown cocktail parties, lobbying lucre and political clout.

'Suck-up City' is what one Obama adviser called Washington during the 2008 campaign and sucking up is essential to getting on. 'Sucking up is as basic to Washington as humidity,' wrote Mark Leibovich in an excoriating dissection of the city.[45] Others have compared D.C. to a school, full of bullies, over-achievers, nerds and life's natural milk monitors. Kyle, I feared (or hoped), wasn't cut out for it. I left him to his mint julep and his yearning for a serendipitous encounter with a Congressman.

At the other end of Washington's social ladder are the ones who have clambered to the top: the Congressmen, Senators, White House advisers and lobbyists. Governor

Haley Barbour glows with his own good fortune. Rotund and ebullient with a helmet of silver hair, Barbour has been at the heart of Republican politics for decades. He was political director in the Reagan White House, chaired the Republican National Committee in the 1990s and served two terms as Governor of Mississippi. Barbour founded the lobbying firm BRG and thought about a run for President in 2012. He's also a throwback to a time when US politicians did business over bourbon and cross-party friendships were sealed with a drink. I meet him at his wood-panelled Washington office. Bottles of Maker's Mark bourbon stamped with Barbour's face line the top shelf of a bookcase, presents from the Kentucky distillery to one of its favourite Washington friends. In his Mississippi drawl, Haley Barbour describes how Capitol Hill drinking has changed over five decades.

'When I was a college boy I came up to Washington to see Senator Eastland from Mississippi. He was having a drink. Teddy Kennedy was there having a drink. Two or three conservative Republicans having a drink together. Couple of other Southern Democrats. Seven or eight Senators. Liberal Democrats, conservative Democrats, conservative Republicans. And they did that all the time. They were friends, and they were very social. It was very bipartisan. Lots of stuff they disagreed on but they spent time in each other's offices. You don't see that any more. There is not as much social bipartisanship.'

In contrast to the bar crawl possibilities of the Houses of Parliament, the US Congress is as dry as a box of cigars. Its House and Senate restaurants do not serve alcohol and there are no taverns tucked away offering refreshment to thirsty Congressmen. For much of its history, drinking was instead done in secret cubbyholes and members' rooms. Tip O'Neill, a Democrat Congressman and Speaker of the House of Representatives for a decade, describes a drinking den known for years as the 'Board of Education', a place where senior Democrats would ply junior members with drink to discover what they knew and what they could do.[46] It was established in the 1940s by Speaker Nicholas Longworth and continued by his successors. Hidden on the first floor of the Capitol behind the members' restaurant (Room H-128), its door was unmarked and a guard stood outside. On the table would be a bottle of Virginia Gentleman bourbon, water and a bucket of ice. It was a place where the Democrat leadership, committee chairmen and the occasional Republican would meet to drink, puff cigars, chew over politics, gossip, plot, play poker and discuss ways to push legislation along.

The longest-serving Speaker, Sam Rayburn, loved his politics spiced with a slug of bourbon. It was while kicking back at one of Rayburn's Board of Education gatherings that Vice-President Harry Truman received a phone call from the White House telling him FDR had died. Truman turned pale, hung up, told the room he had to go and was then heard running down the marble corridor towards the presidency.

Sinking deeper into his sofa, Haley Barbour warily reveals the names of convivial Congressional drinkers he has known over the years such as Tip O'Neill, Senators Ted Kennedy and Chris Dodd. He mentions Wilbur Mills, the Democrat Chairman of the House Ways and Means Committee who was caught by police, drunk and in the company of a stripper, while driving past the Tidal Basin in the early hours of 9 October 1974. After a second scandal involving drink, Mills left politics and set up the Wilbur D. Mills Treatment Center for alcoholism in Arkansas. But the days when members of Congress room-hopped with bottles of whisky as the sun set over the Mall have largely gone. There are still nightly receptions, fundraisers and cocktail parties where politicos mingle over a drink, but the sort of clubby, cross-aisle glass clinking of Tip O'Neill's day is no more. There are still certainly politicians on Capitol Hill who like a drink (the merlot-drinking former Republican Speaker of the House of Representatives John Boehner is one), but the fraternity has faded, along with the bipartisanship. 'People aren't around like they used to be,' says Donald Ritchie, the Senate's historian. 'The arrival of the jet plane changed everything. And then in 1994 the Speaker encouraged members to spend time in their states and keep their families there so it concentrated the political week from Tuesday morning to Thursday evening. And when they do have an evening free they're busy fundraising.'[47]

It's worse in the House, where politics has become a permanent election campaign. As district boundaries are gerrymandered to make them less competitive, for most members of Congress, particularly Republicans, the electoral threat is from their own party in primaries. There is neither the time nor the motivation to forge friendships over a drink with colleagues or political opponents. 'Forty years ago they didn't raise money all the time like they do now,' Haley Barbour tells me. 'There weren't lots of special interest functions and fundraisers. They had more time to spend on the Hill, to talk, drink, get to know one another.'

In October 2013 the first government shutdown for seventeen years took the US to the brink of a default. The stand-off between House Republicans and the Obama

White House known as 'the sequester' was the latest flare-up of systemic political dysfunction and polarisation in Washington. Compromise is now a toxic concept in US politics. Haley Barbour contrasts this era with the 1980s, when Reagan got a conservative agenda passed although Democrats controlled the House. 'When I was in the White House Tip O'Neill would come over and have a drink with Reagan. They both got it done because they figured out how to work with their opponents.'

I wonder if a decline of bipartisan drinking is a small contributor to this polarisation or merely a symptom. Barbour reels off a long list of reasons for the current atmosphere, from electoral gerrymandering to the shrill, obnoxious commentary of rolling news, and says this can't be blamed on a lack of booze. 'But I regret that camaraderie is so diminished now,' he muses. 'If people drank more would it make them better members of Congress? No. But maybe having a drink together would help. We'd all be better off if they had that sort of relationship.'

As a southern Governor, Barbour remembers hammering out the annual budget with members of the Mississippi legislature, Democrat and Republican, a bottle of Maker's Mark on the table. 'The drink was good lubrication. And sometimes lubrication is needed to get the process over the finishing line.'[48] Of course it has been lucrative for Barbour to have friends throughout Washington's web of politicians, wonks, lobbyists and hacks. But he's a rare bon viveur in an increasingly sour and strait-laced town. The tweeters and bloggers who feed on the city's gossip are poised to pounce on anything that smacks of indulgence or good living, demanding a puritanism they do not practise themselves.

Governor Barbour leaves me with a copy of the 'whisky speech', delivered on the floor of the Mississippi state legislature in 1952 by Noah S. 'Soggy' Sweat. At the time, alcohol was still prohibited in Mississippi and remained so until 1966. The speech was a rousing argument both for and against the ban on booze. The young politician toiled over his argument for two months before delivering this passionate masterpiece of political equivocation:

My friends,
I had not intended to discuss this controversial subject at this particular time. However, I want you to know that I do not shun controversy. On the contrary, I will take a stand on any issue at any time, regardless of how fraught with controversy it might be. You have asked me how I feel about whisky. All right, here is how I feel about whisky.

If when you say whisky you mean the devil's brew, the poison scourge, the bloody monster, that defiles innocence, dethrones reason, destroys the home, creates misery and poverty, yea, literally takes the bread from the mouths of little children; if you mean the evil drink that topples the Christian man and woman from the pinnacle of righteous, gracious living into the bottomless pit of degradation, and despair, and shame and helplessness, and hopelessness, then certainly I am against it.

But;

If when you say whisky you mean the oil of conversation, the philosophic wine, the ale that is consumed when good fellows get together, that puts a song in their hearts and laughter on their lips, and the warm glow of contentment in their eyes; if you mean Christmas cheer; if you mean the stimulating drink that puts the spring in the old gentleman's step on a frosty, crispy morning; if you mean the drink which enables a man to magnify his joy, and his happiness, and to forget, if only for a little while, life's great tragedies, and heartaches, and sorrows; if you mean that drink, the sale of which pours into our treasuries untold millions of dollars, which are used to provide tender care for our little crippled children, our blind, our deaf, our dumb, our pitiful aged and infirm; to build highways and hospitals and schools, then certainly I am for it.

This is my stand. I will not retreat from it. I will not compromise.[49]

# CHAPTER 7

## From Canberra to the Kremlin

A 2009 meeting of finance ministers from the G7 group of wealthy nations would not have merited a footnote in summit history if Shoichi Nakagawa had stuck to mineral water. But Japan's then Finance Minister appeared to be drunk at a press conference in Rome and resigned days later, accused of embarrassing one of the world's major economics. Mr Nakagawa claimed he had only had a sip of water during lunch and attributed his comatose appearance in front of the television cameras to cold medicine and jet lag. Japanese journalists knew about his fondness for alcohol and during that summer's general election Mr Nakagawa said he had given up drinking for the 'sake of Japan'. But the charismatic politician, tipped as a future Prime Minister, died in October 2009 at the age of just fifty-six, a month after losing his seat in parliament.[1]

This doleful story is a recent window into the drinking habits of politicians beyond the UK and the United States. Some, like Mr Nakagawa, were casualties. Others thrived with a drink in their hand. Which in the ritualistic world of diplomacy is a central part of the theatre, from toasts of sake to champagne. Alcohol runs through the chronicles of presidents, prime ministers and parliaments around the world.

The frequent inebriation of Australia's first Prime Minister, Edmund Toby Barton, earned him the nickname 'Tosspot Toby' and provoked one politician, John Norton, to publish an open letter to the PM in 1902 concerning his 'disgusting drinking habits'. But ask an Australian, Britain's closest drinking cousin, for an example of political imbibing and they'll probably mention Bob Hawke, one of the country's longest serving and most liked leaders. His drinking was epic enough to win him an entry in the *Guinness Book of Records*. As a Rhodes scholar at Oxford in 1955, the young Hawke drained two and a half pints of beer (a yard of ale) in eleven seconds, a world speed drinking record at the time. The legions of beer drinking voters in Australia were appreciative of the accolade. As Hawke wrote in his memoir, 'this feat was to endear me to some of my fellow Australians more than anything else I ever achieved', even though he renounced drink for the duration of his time in office.[2]

Another future Australian Prime Minister also gained a poll bounce from booze. In 2003, when he was the Opposition's foreign affairs spokesman, a drunk Kevin Rudd visited a New York strip club. He said he was too inebriated to remember what happened inside the club, called Storms, but the revelation helped rather than harmed him during the general election campaign. One newspaper poll found 85 per cent of people thought the evening's escapade showed the strait-laced Rudd to be a 'normal bloke' after all and he was voted into office.[3]

The drinking binges of John Gorton, Prime Minister from 1968 to 1971, made him equally popular with the Australian public. Once, after a long drinking session in Melbourne, he was driven to the airport to fly back to Canberra. Soon after settling into his seat, Gorton felt queasy, leant over the side of the chair and threw up onto the floor. The stewardess appeared to mop up the mess and the twinkly, womanising old charmer said, 'Well, my dear, I suppose you find it a bit strange that an old RAAF man like me can still get air sick.' According to the journalist Mungo McCallum, the stewardess looked at him and said, 'Yes, Prime Minister, I do actually because the plane hasn't taken off yet.'[4]

Occasionally, when Gorton was the worse for wear, his press secretary would announce the Prime Minister's absence from Parliament by saying he was a feeling a 'bit fluey'. 'Gorton flu' soon became a Canberra euphemism for a hangover. Eventually, his Liberal Party colleagues tired of his larking around and Gorton became the first and only Australian Prime Minister to vote himself out of office.

In neighbouring New Zealand in 1984, Prime Minister Robert Muldoon called what's still known as the Schnapps election, a reminder to political leaders everywhere not to roll the electoral dice when drunk. Muldoon had been the country's belligerent, outspoken and polarising Prime Minister since 1975. But by 1984 his National Party was limping along with a majority of one in parliament and rebelliousness had erupted in its ranks. One member of his party, Marilyn Waring, had threatened to cross the floor and vote with the opposition Labour Party on nuclear policy. On the evening of 14 June, there was a fractious, drunken and abusive meeting between Muldoon, Waring and other leading members of the party. When Waring arrived, Muldoon barked, 'You perverted little liar. What the fuck do you think you're up to now?'[5] At this stage in the evening the Prime Minister was draining tumblers of brandy and ginger ale. Through the fug of shouting, tears, drink and cigarette smoke, Muldoon was suddenly seized with clarity: a snap general election would catch the opposition unprepared and a win would crush his party rebels.

The Prime Minister then headed off to Government House to tell the Governor General, Sir David Beattie, about his plan to go to the country. This was followed by an extraordinary appearance on New Zealand television which is preserved for posterity on YouTube. At 11.15 p.m. a glazed-looking Muldoon made a slurred, intoxicated statement to the TV cameras. After announcing the election date, the Prime Minister then went back to his office, said, 'I'm not going to drink coffee at this time of night,' poured another glass of Scotch and started to plan the election campaign. That night several National MPs worried that their leader had made an irrational decision while drunk. Which he had. 'In addition to the half-dozen whiskies and brandies he had consumed earlier in the evening he had consumed several more at Government House,' recounted Muldoon's biographer.[6]

Muldoon was also exhausted, frustrated and taking tablets for diabetes. Had he not been plastered, he may have thought of another way to prolong the life of his government. But the sight of a clammy, drunk Prime Minister announcing the general election was not the smartest way for Robert Muldoon to convince New Zealanders he should be given another term. A month later Labour won the election and Muldoon's political career was over.

It's not known what North Koreans made of their revered late leader's drinking habits. As well as a penchant for shark's fin soup and James Bond movies, Kim Jong-Il had a taste for the finest alcohol. He reportedly kept a cellar of over 10,000 bottles and spent $720,000 a year on Hennessy cognac. In the 1990s he was one of the company's biggest single customers. Dictatorship underpinned by a fiercely enforced cult of personality, a state-run press and complete isolation from the outside world meant North Koreans would have had no idea about Kim's drinking indulgences. In a country of relentless poverty and food shortages, where the average annual wage is $900, alcohol of any kind is an unimaginable luxury for nearly all North Koreans. Their despotic ruler's spending on the world's priciest alcohol is probably the most grotesque example of political drinking, a perfect symbol of Kim Jong-Il's contempt for his millions of deluded disciples.

### Comrade Vodka

In the Soviet Union at least, people could endure the miseries of totalitarian dictatorship with the help of a drink. According to legend, vodka was invented in 1503 by Kremlin monks, who used it first as an antiseptic. Then they started to swig it for pleasure. Some historians believe vodka production was under way in Moscow as early as the 1440s.[7] In the words of the writer Victor Erofeyev, 'more than by any political system, we are all held hostage by vodka. It menaces and it chastises; it demands sacrifices. It is both a catalyst of procreation and its scourge. It dictates who is born and who dies. In short, vodka is the Russian god.'[8] Tasteless, colourless and flavourless, vodka has inspired, consoled, warmed and ruined Russians for centuries. And its presence in politics stretches back to the drunkenness of Ivan the Terrible and

Peter the Great. The latter was a prodigious drinker and insisted members of his court and visiting foreign dignitaries join him in guzzling vast amounts of alcohol at festive events.[9] Tsar Nicholas II was a moderate supper of fine wines and realised that by the early twentieth century imperial Russia was in the grip of rampant alcoholism. With war approaching, it needed to sober up. As Russia mobilised in August 1914, Nicholas introduced prohibition, banning the sale of vodka anywhere except in first-class restaurants and clubs.

After the Bolshevik Revolution three years later, Lenin, himself quite indifferent to alcohol, kept the prohibition of vodka in place until the mid-1920s. He said that 'to permit the sale of vodka would mean one step back to capitalism', and he might have hoped to keep the proletariat clear-headed for longer than he managed. But with the ban unpopular and tax revenues needing a lift, Lenin legalised vodka and established a new state monopoly which was in place by 1925, the year after his death. In the decades that followed, Russians clutched their vodka bottles even more tightly than they had before the Revolution. Throughout the twentieth century, the Soviet Union's political elite wrestled with the country's vodka addiction as well as their own. The production of spirits trebled between 1940 and 1980, an acceleration driven by Joseph Stalin.

A megalomaniacal tyrant who ruled the Soviet Union for a quarter of a century, Stalin enforced the collectivisation of agriculture, industrialised the economy and terrorised and killed millions during the Great Terror of the 1930s. He led the Soviet Union through the Second World War, first in a pact with Germany and then in a brutal battle against

Hitler's armies on the Eastern Front. The savage four-year fight was unprecedented in its destruction and human cost. At least twenty-five million Soviet citizens died. In part, Russia's post-war problem with alcohol germinated during that grinding military campaign. After the Russian victory at Stalingrad in 1943, a ration of 100 grams of vodka per day was given to Red Army soldiers. And since by 1945 nearly the whole active male population of the Soviet Union was in the army, by the end of the war they were all drinking vodka too.

Throughout this period Stalin drank like a Russian and revelled in the toasting rituals of his native Georgia. His Kremlin was saturated in vodka. Memoirs catalogue stories of leading Communists being carried out legless, after which they were administered caviar, chopped onions and raw eggs in a traditional attempt to absorb the alcohol. The Kremlin was where leading officials indulged in loud parties, heavy eating and riotous drinking. And at the centre of the excess was Stalin himself. The Yugoslav Communist Milovan Djilas, at first a fan of Stalinism and then one of its most prominent dissenters, remembered dinners in Moscow with the Soviet leader. On cold winter nights, instead of discussing socialist theory, Stalin insisted his guests play a game. They each had to guess the temperature outside and, for every degree they were wrong, they had to drink a glass of vodka.[10] An amusement for Stalin; and a threatening ordeal for his guests, all of whom lived with the threat of arbitrary imprisonment, torture and execution.

Stalin's appetite for food and drink was immense. According to his third wife, Rosa, breakfast was a massive affair that began with drinking a quarter pint of vodka.

After some salt herrings and raw onion he would have another quarter pint of vodka as a chaser. Then he'd have lamb chops, steak and potatoes. For lunch Stalin would start with a quarter pint of vodka, followed by a salt herring, lots of chopped raw onions, rounding this all off with another quarter pint of vodka. For dinner he'd start with Borscht rather than vodka, followed by smoked salmon, fried eggs, roast chicken, pork or venison. During the meal he usually drank a bottle of light Caucasian wine.[11]

This description of gastronomic gorging is probably exaggerated, so too its drinks tally. Stalin drank for effect, but the performance was illusory. As the Soviet Union and Germany cooked up the Nazi-Soviet pact in 1939, Hitler sent his Foreign Minister, Ribbentrop, to Moscow. Stalin and his visitor flattered each other with endless toasts of vodka and champagne. But an SS officer noticed that Stalin was filling his glass from a special flask and the German managed to do the same. It was water, not vodka. Stalin smiled weakly at the discovery of his secret.[12] It was the smallest deception of the trip; the Germans had no intention of honouring their new alliance with the USSR and within two years Germany and the Soviet Union were at war.

Stalin was not in fact much of a drinker, according to the historian Simon Sebag Montefiore, and he expected others to be sober. But the grind of war seems to have made him drink more. As the Germans were closing in on Moscow in October 1941, he hosted a lavish banquet at the Kremlin for a hundred guests, including the newspaper tycoon Lord Beaverbrook. Champagne, vodka, wine and Armenian brandy clouded the reality of the catastrophe confronting the Soviet Union and there were thirty-two toasts to victory before the night was out, with Stalin drinking continuously from a small glass. And as the threat of defeat turned into the euphoria of inevitable victory, Stalin drank still more. When Charles de Gaulle visited Moscow in 1944, Stalin was a swaggering, bullying drunk. The Frenchman was there to negotiate a treaty of mutual assistance. Stalin threatened and humiliated the French and his own entourage to the accompaniment of endlessly clinking vodka glasses, at one point saying: 'Bring out the machine guns. Let's liquidate the diplomats.' Stalin was, noted future President Nikita Khrushchev, 'completely drunk'.[13]

After the war, Stalin hosted drink-sodden bacchanals at his home in the Moscow suburbs. For the Soviet apparatchiks compelled to attend, these were death-dicing ordeals. Simon Sebag Montefiore writes, 'as the evening went on, the toasts of vodka, pepper vodka and brandy became more insistent until even these iron-bellied drinkers were blind drunk'.[14] The leaders of the vast Soviet empire staggered around, legless and vomiting. Forcing his party comrades to lose control with drink was a way for Stalin to tyrannise and humiliate them. Failure to drink, or saying a wrong word when drunk, could be met with a bullet to the head.

As dawn approached, cars were summoned to carry the comatose comrades away. Once, on the drive home, Khrushchev and Nikolai Bulganin (a Soviet Defence Minister) slumped into their seats, relieved to have survived another ordeal: 'One never knows', whispered Bulganin, 'if one's going home or to prison.'[15] As sadistic political drinking goes, Stalin has no rival.

Today, annual consumption of alcohol in Russia is higher than anywhere else in the world. More than thirty thousand Russians die of alcohol poisoning every year. It was a problem allowed to grow in the Soviet Union left by Stalin. The state budget relied on the tax revenue from vodka to fill its coffers and successive Soviet leaders were wary of restricting its availability. But during the seventy years of Soviet rule, the country lost four times as much wealth in working hours lost to alcohol as it raised in revenue.[16] An epidemic of alcoholism began to rot the country's foundations and Russian life expectancy started to decline in the 1960s. The last Soviet leader, Mikhail Gorbachev, recognised this and was the only one to try and eradicate vodka.

Gorbachev had been horrified by the drinking he witnessed on his way up the Communist Party ladder. 'In the course of my career I saw massive drunkenness in the Party. Brezhnev drank, especially at the beginning. Yeltsin even used the fact that he drank to attract women – "He's just the same as we are!" Women couldn't keep their hands out of his pants. But in the West they were afraid. He had his finger on the nuclear button.'[17] Gorbachev's efforts to curb Russian drinking were unpopular but effective. When he came to power in 1985 he closed 90 per cent of Moscow's alcohol shops and shut down distilleries. The following year saw the highest number of births since 1962 and life expectancy rocketed. But by 1991 both the policy and the Soviet Union were gone. Russia's first democratically elected leader, Boris Yeltsin, was a drinker who paraded his dependency on the world stage, to the amusement and horror of the watching press.

Boris Yeltsin drank big. But until the late 1980s, he had not been known as an excessive imbiber. He enjoyed convivial, comradely libations rather than solitary glasses of vodka. But when he got the keys to the Kremlin, his intake increased. The presidential limousine carried a satchel containing drinks, shot glasses and appetisers that were replenished daily. By now his preference was for grass-flavoured Tarkhum vodka and cocktails of champagne mixed with cognac. Foreign leaders soon learnt to live with Yeltsin's inebriation. During Bill Clinton's first phone call to the Russian leader after becoming President, Yeltsin's speech was slurred and he failed to follow what Clinton had to say. Over the next seven years, the White House was careful to put calls through to the Kremlin before the dinner hour in Moscow.[18]

In the edgy, uncertain years after the collapse of the Soviet Union, the two superpowers continued to point ten thousand nuclear warheads at each other's cities, ready to launch within minutes. While the US President relieved the pressures of the job with the assistance of a White House intern, his Russian counterpart relied on alcohol to cope with his awesome responsibilities. Clinton and Yeltsin had a natural rapport, but the US President was well aware of his counterpart's drinking.

Interviews with Clinton published in 2009 revealed a drunken visit to Washington by Yeltsin in 1995. The Russian President was staying at Blair House, across the road from the White House. According to Clinton, Secret Service agents found Yeltsin late one night standing alone in Pennsylvania Avenue, dressed only in his underwear, trying to hail a cab. In slurring Russian he told them he wanted a pizza. The next night Yeltsin evaded security and made it down to the Blair House basement, where a guard mistook him for a drunken intruder.[19] According to Taylor Branch, 'President Clinton said [Yeltsin's] escapes into alcohol were far more serious than the cultivated pose of a jolly Russia.' But, unsure of his place or of the consequences, Clinton never counselled Yeltsin about the drinking. Instead, the US and the rest of the world had to hope that the Russian President's alcoholism did not distort his decision making and tip the world into nuclear war.

In fact, it once triggered a dramatic pledge of détente, when in 1997 Yeltsin said during a visit to Sweden that Russia would unilaterally cut its nuclear arsenal by a third. There was consternation at the Kremlin, and Yeltsin's long-suffering press secretary had to explain that the President actually meant Russia was not cutting back its nuclear weapons at all. Two years later Yeltsin's boozing was blamed when he blurted out a threat to 'send a missile' if the United States overstepped the mark during the Kosovo conflict. Again, his press spokesman had to mop up the confusion and extinguish the threat of his master's statement.

Boris Yeltsin's drunkenness was visible at home and abroad. On 22 April 1993 he appeared at a rally in Moscow far from sober and an aide wisely removed the microphone from his hand before he could say anything dangerous or damaging. But one of the most memorable images of Yeltsin's time in office dates from 31 August 1994. The Russian President was in Berlin to mark the departure of Russian forces from the former East Germany. He had been drinking enthusiastically since the morning and by the time he arrived at the square in front of Berlin's town hall he was banjaxed. A brass band from the local police was entertaining the crowds. Spotting a chance to have some fun, the Russian President commandeered the baton from the conductor.

He flailed his arms around in an inebriated imitation of a band leader, leaning towards the musicians and jabbing his stick at various sections of the band. He later grabbed the microphone, leading a short rendition of a Russian folk song before giving a thumbs up to the crowd, blowing some kisses and staggering off the stage. Several of Yeltsin's aides were tempted to resign immediately. Instead, they wrote him a letter telling him that his dependency on the 'well-known Russian vice' was damaging him and had to stop.

During a trip to Britain in September of the same year, Prime Minister John Major took Yeltsin to a pub close to Chequers in the village of Great Kimble. When they knocked on the door asking the owner to open up, Yeltsin said he was the President of Russia. If that was true, said the landlord from behind the door, then he was the Kaiser of Germany. At dinner that evening Yeltsin arrived drunk and decided he didn't want to sit where he'd been placed. The journalist Max Hastings described the scene: 'He picked up his own table card, next door to that of Princess Alexandria, and deposited both the card and himself next to John Major, with whom he chatted amiably, if incoherently, all evening.'[20]

The nadir came during a stopover visit in Ireland a month later. The presidential plane had circled inexplicably over Dublin for an hour before eventually landing at Shannon airport. There, on the tarmac, a delegation of dignitaries accompanied by a military band waited for the Russian President to appear. The door opened but nobody came out. Yeltsin was due to attend a lunch with the Irish Prime Minister, Albert Reynolds, and eventually his deputy emerged to report that the Russian President was too tired and ill to leave the plane. A magnanimous Reynolds said he completely understood that Yeltsin was only acting on doctor's orders, and later in Moscow the Russian leader blamed his security team for not waking him up. But it was obvious to everyone else that Yeltsin had hit the hospitality hard on the flight over from Washington and was too drunk to leave the plane.

In his memoir, *Presidential Marathon*, Yeltsin tried to explain the allure of drink to an under-pressure politician. 'At a certain time, I sensed that alcohol is a means that rapidly relieves stress.' But as his biographer Timothy J. Colton has written, 'drinking immoderately and on the government's time was a self-inflicted wound that brought no good to anyone'.[21] Yeltsin's drinking was embarrassing, certainly, and detrimental to his health. But Colton doesn't believe it interfered with Yeltsin's performance at foreign summits or influenced domestic policy decisions taken during his first term as President. It did, though, become a political liability. As Yeltsin's health worsened, he finally forswore daily heavy drinking in 1996 after a quintuple heart bypass. But by then his boisterous drunken shenanigans had defined his image.

There was of course more to Yeltsin than drink. Mounting a Moscow tank in 1991 to protect the reforms of Mikhail Gorbachev made him a hero to many; and he defended the fledgling Russian democracy in 1993 when he ordered tanks to fire on the Russian parliament after it was occupied by hardline political opponents. But he also began a bloody, disastrous military campaign in Chechnya and oversaw a decade of economic chaos. Nor did he show any inclination to stem Russia's alcohol dependency. Yeltsin abolished the state monopoly on vodka production and opened up the country to cheap imports. Perhaps his own drinking made him blind to the damage it was doing to everyone else. But his teetotal successor Vladimir Putin doesn't have that excuse. By 2050, it is estimated, Russia's population will be thirty million people fewer than it was in 2000 and life expectancy is falling again. The country's vodka habit is crippling its future, but Russia's political leadership is too timid to take away the bottle.

## Protocol and Alcohol

Lord Lyons was a canny chap. 'If you are given champagne at lunch there's a catch somewhere,' he observed.[22] His job was to discern what that catch was. Britain's ambassador to Paris from 1867 to 1887 knew that drink and diplomacy make a ready but risky mix. According to America's urbane and intellectual ambassador to the United Nations during the Cuban Missile Crisis, Adlai Stevenson, a diplomat's life comprises three ingredients: 'Protocol, Geritol and alcohol'.

In 2013 the Deputy US Ambassador to the United Nations for Management and Reform declared it was time the era of alcohol-driven diplomacy came to an end. It was, he said, difficult enough corralling representatives from 193 countries into agreeing the United Nations' budget. But what made it even tougher was that many of the members turned up to meetings completely drunk. Joseph Torsella's bold suggestion was that UN diplomats should desist from drinking before the deal was done. 'We make the modest proposal that the negotiating rooms should in future be an inebriation-free zone,' Mr Torsella told the General Assembly's Budget Committee.[23]

Alcohol has long been present at the set-piece summits and embassy drinks parties that form the cornerstones of diplomacy. Perhaps the most important summits of the twentieth century took place towards the end of the Second World War – and at these tripartite meetings at Tehran, Yalta and Potsdam the quantities of drink consumed were staggering.

Elliott Roosevelt witnessed the first banquet of the Tehran conference in late 1943, at which Stalin, Churchill and Roosevelt coordinated the next stage of the war in Europe and Asia, including the planned invasion of France. As they hammered out a strategy, and tried to decipher each other's motives, they ate and drank. Roosevelt later recalled one evening's beverage list:

> Of course, vodka; and fortunately also a still light wine, light and dry, and a Russian champagne, to my taste very good. I say 'fortunately,' for there was no conversation without a drink; it would have been a contradiction in terms. The only way we talked was through the medium of proposing a toast. It may sound cumbersome, but if your staying power is good you find that it develops into quite a lot of fun.[24]

The bacchanalia was repeated the next night on Churchill's birthday at the British Embassy, an evening of countless toasts at which most of the conversation was done standing up on increasingly unsteady feet.

It was the same in February 1945 at Yalta, the summit intended to shape the post-war world. The US Secretary of State, Edward R. Stettinius, remembered how the ailing FDR had to endure a merry-go-round of toast-making on the first day of the summit. "There were dozens of toasts. I was highly amused to notice that Stalin would drink half of his glass of vodka and, when he thought no one was watching, surreptitiously pour water into the glass', Stettinius wrote four years later.[25] It was at this first American-hosted dinner of southern fried chicken washed down with Russian champagne that Franklin Roosevelt revealed that he and Churchill called Stalin 'Uncle Joe'. The Soviet leader was indignant and the mood was only lightened with more champagne.

At a Russian-hosted dinner on 7 February, there was more relentless toasting, each leader taking it in turns to make ever more ludicrously gushing tributes to their allies. Raising his glass to Stalin, Churchill praised the 'mighty leader of a mighty country, which took the full shock of the German war machine, broke its back, and drove the tyrants from her soil'.[26] With dinner guests discreetly pouring vodka into plant pots and diluting their champagne with water, most successfully stopped the slide towards intoxication.

That was the fear of Alexander Haig, Henry Kissinger's right-hand man, as he rolled the pitch for Nixon's trip to China in 1972. It would be the first visit of any American President to the country and the rapprochement would be marked by a banquet at the Great Hall of the People. Americans would be watching every chopstick pinch and liquid toast up close on live television and the White House was worried about the drink. Specifically, mao-tai, China's explosively strong rice wine. When he visited China a few months before the summit, Alexander Haig sampled the brew and fretted about its effect on Nixon. 'Under no, repeat no, circumstances should the President actually drink from his glass in response to banquet toasts,' he cabled.[27] Whether Nixon swallowed or not isn't known, but he kept his eye on the prize and toasted in a new era of US–China relations without trouble, the high point of his presidency.

Foreign policy during Bill Clinton's presidency was dominated by war in the Balkans, brutal conflicts punctuated by all-night brandy-fuelled talks. Following Slovenia and Croatia, Bosnia-Herzegovina declared its independence from Yugoslavia in 1992 but this country of Serbs, Catholic Croats and Muslim Slavs became a battleground of competing nationalisms and religions. For three years the Bosnian Serbs waged a genocidal war on the country's Muslims and Croats, armed and supported by Serbia's strongman President Slobodan Milosevic. NATO finally began bombing Bosnian Serb forces in the summer of 1995 following the massacre at Srebrenica and into this chaos barrelled the US diplomat Richard Holbrooke. Nicknamed 'the Bulldozer', Holbrooke combined table-thumping fury with charm and intellect, becoming one of the United States' most famous post-war diplomats. In the autumn of 1995 his mission was to get the warring sides to the negotiating table and construct a peace in Bosnia. That involved many trips to Belgrade, where Slobodan Milosevic enjoyed subjecting foreign dignitaries and journalists to late-night drinking sessions. Milosevic was a whisky and cigars man and the talks were awash with alcohol.

Richard Holbrooke wrote about his experience of Balkan diplomacy in his book *To End a War*, in which he recounts deal-making by drinks. The day is Friday 1 September 1995, the location a hunting lodge at Dobanovci, near Belgrade. An American delegation is meeting with Milosevic and his cronies for talks about ending the war in Bosnia:

The meeting at the hunting lodge rambled on for twelve hours, with a break during which we returned to our hotel for a press conference. Milosevic had changed the venue in order to create a more relaxed atmosphere. There was heavy drinking for much of the day, which clearly affected Koljevic, but I saw no evidence – then or later – that the alcohol affected Milosevic's judgements. The Americans drank little, and I began a policy of accepting Milosevic's frequent offers of drinks only when we reached agreements.[28]

Another US diplomat, James Pardew, called it the day of 'bonding with the godfather', and the plum brandy and whisky played its part in coaxing Milosevic towards the peace talks at Dayton, Ohio, later that year.

The agreement that followed stopped the fighting in Bosnia, but alcohol-assisted negotiation failed to prevent the West's next confrontation with Milosevic in 1999 after his crackdown on Kosovo's Albanians. At their last meeting, on the eve of the NATO bombing campaign that would lead to Milosevic's fall and trial in The Hague for war crimes, he pleaded with the US diplomat he had shared many drinks with: 'Don't you have anything more to say to me?' Holbrooke's deadpan reply to the Serbian leader: 'Hasta la vista, baby.'[29]

For the more lowly diplomat in a distant posting, the remorseless hospitality is an important part of the day job too, as the leaked US cables published by WikiLeaks confirmed. An August 2006 dispatch described how a three-hour 'alcohol-sodden lunch' between the United States Ambassador to Tajikistan, Richard E. Hoagland, and Tajikistan's Minister of Defence, Sherali Khairulloyev, had 'helped place another brick in the wall of U.S.-Tajikistan military relations'. The US ambassador lost count of the toasts after the tenth and later provided this summary to the State Department: 'Although this drunk-fest is how many old-guard former Soviets do mutual business, it was most unusual for an American guest. It was, to a degree, a mark of respect.' The cable finishes with this proud boast: 'We were pleased to have drunk Khairulloyev well under the table.'[30]

The former British Foreign Secretary, Jack Straw, thought better of a head-to-head drinking bout with the Russians, even as he tried to soften their hostility to war against Iraq in 2003. Alcohol still oils Russian diplomacy, as Straw discovered on his visits to Moscow. 'I had some convivial evenings with Sergey Lavrov and Igor Ivanov, his predecessor,' he told me over coffee in the Houses of Parliament.[31] 'In Moscow it was vodka shots and you have to be very, very careful. It can be a lubricant but it can leave you very exposed. Drinking is useful if you're trying to develop a relationship *à deux*. I had meals with Sergey Lavrov and I certainly found drink helpful with the Russians and some of the Eastern Europeans.' Relationships, rapport, chemistry and empathy: such words as these are frequently used in discussions of diplomatic drinking. Politics and diplomacy are powered by the personal; and alcohol certainly helps bridge the divide when politicians from different cultures meet.

But this sort of drinking can be dangerous. In September 2014 the Labour MP for Heywood and Middleton, Jim Dobbin, drank a fatal quantity of spirits during an official visit to Poland organised by the Council of Europe. After drinking a shot with each course during a dinner in the city of Slupsk, the 73-year-old went to bed feeling unwell. He died hours later and a post-mortem examination revealed he was nearly five times over the drink-drive limit in England. The Coroner's Court heard how Mr Dobbin never drank at home and only did so socially. The trip, which was also attended by several other MPs, was to honour the award to Slupsk of the Council's 2014 prize for 'promoting the European ideal'.

The foreign visits made by groups of MPs often consist at least as much of drink-consuming as fact-finding. On one such trip to Australia, the liberally lubricated chair of a select committee regaled his colleagues at dinner with scathing anecdotes about his constituents, one of whom happened to be sitting at the next table and duly passed the story to the newspapers.

When Paul Flynn MP joined the British parliamentary group on the Council of Europe, he 'heard legendary tales of wild living and drunken fights among past delegations'. Although today's MPs are more serious and sober, he is nevertheless able to recount an unforgettable story involving two MPs who had a competition one evening to see who could drink the most champagne. It ended with one of them projectile vomiting at a dinner attended by delegations from many countries, with the consequence that 'the reputation of the British is still damaged by this incident'.[32] It seems that it is not just at Europe's tourist resorts that the British are observed to have a problem with drink.

Drop into almost any embassy on any evening in any country and you will find a drinks reception under way. The British Embassy in Washington might be seducing US businesses and lobbyists with wine, fishing for foreign trade. The Swedish Embassy may be exhibiting photography from Norrland accompanied by Scandinavian nibbles and aquavit. And Irish embassies around the world are cherished by foreign journalists for their willingness to give away free pints of Guinness several times a year.

Then there is the familiar image of diplomatic field work being conducted on the warm veranda of a bustling hotel bar. Think Saigon's Continental Shelf in Graham Greene's *The Quiet American*, where diplomats and journalists swapped tips in wicker chairs over chilled martinis. In 1961 the British diplomat and politician Harold Nicolson wrote about the importance of saloon intelligence-sharing in an article for *Foreign Affairs*:

> My own advice to the junior diplomat is not to confine himself lazily to the easy circle of his own embassy but to cultivate the society of journalists, both foreign and native. It is from them that he will derive useful advice and commentary. When I look back on the years before Hitler that I spent in the British Embassy in Berlin, I am grateful for the hours I devoted talking to journalists in the Adlon Bar. I learned more from them than I did from any other form of social relations … It was the journalists of the Adlon Bar who first warned me of the coming of the Nazi movement.[33]

Not that this drink-inspired glimpse of the future managed to stop it.

Alcohol can be meal-breaking too. Drink clearly plays no part in the politics of Muslim countries such as Pakistan, Saudi Arabia or Afghanistan. Foreign diplomats posted there have no chance to build bonhomie and cross-cultural understanding with government ministers over an icy G&T.

This dry policy can also make for brittle overseas visits. A particular flare-up has been between France and Iran over the presence of wine at French state banquets. In 1999, Iran postponed a visit to Paris by its then President, Mohammed Khatami, because the French insisted wine should be served to those who wanted it at official receptions. The spat over protocol went on for weeks, with Iranian officials saying Islamic codes were normally respected when the President travelled overseas. But France refused to jettison its secular, republican tradition of serving wine at state meals.

The same disagreement soured a visit by President Rouhani to Paris in November 2015, the first trip to Europe by an Iranian President for a decade. Again, Iran asked for bottles of the finest Bordeaux and champagne to be banished from the table at a planned lunch at the Elysée Palace hosted by President François Hollande. The Iranian request for a drink-free, halal menu was met with a firm refusal by Paris and the two presidents settled for a less convivial face-to-face meeting instead. Months before, France and Iran had managed to compromise enough to agree a deal between the Islamic Republic and the West that lifted sanctions on Iran in return for curbs on its nuclear programme. It marked a huge rapprochement after years of negotiation but, for Iran and France, a bottle of wine was a diplomatic hurdle too high.

In the European Union today alcohol remains an essential political oil. On a Thursday evening in Brussels, the picturesque Place Luxembourg becomes a 28-nation drinking binge as MEPs, their staff, lobbyists, journalists and diplomats from across the EU swarm into the square to gossip, network and flirt over gallons of Belgian beer. 'It's like a rave, it's totally astonishing!' bellows Nigel Farage, a big drinker in a town where alcohol is still wired into the political culture.

It's the same in Strasbourg, where the European Parliament decamps once a month. 'It's like being on holiday,' Farage says. 'Five thousand people go to a city they don't live in and go berserk. Les Aviateurs bar is still heaving with political assistants and a few MEPS at 4 a.m. every morning. And the lunch culture in Strasbourg and Brussels is like it used to be in the UK thirty years ago.' Farage can usually be found in the Old Hack bar in Brussels with other members of UKIP, raising their glasses in raspberry-blowing defiance at the European Commission opposite. 'All the Commission drink in there,' he laughs. 'They all know I want them fired.'[34]

There are a number of characterless open-plan bars dotted around the European Parliament that do steady trade through the day. And the scene at Place Luxembourg on a Thursday does resemble an Oktoberfest for politicians. Farage nevertheless exaggerates. The Commission used to have a bar in its briefing room, run by a Belgian lady named Annie, where the daily briefings for journalists were made more bearable with glasses of wine. Summits of EU leaders used to rotate around Europe, depending on who held the presidency, and the food and booze was free. That has all stopped. When he was President of the Commission in the late 1970s, Roy Jenkins adored his ride on the Brussels gravy train, eating in the city's best restaurants, which he thought rivalled the best in Paris, and seeking out the finest wines, which he meticulously described in his diary.[35] But as Geoff Meade, a legendary figure of Brussels journalism, told me, 'you try to get someone out for lunch now and it's quite difficult. If you do it's on a tight rein.'[36] Brussels has also sobered up, as a political industry of think tanks and lobbyists has grown up alongside the expanding EU membership. It's not the small club it once was and much Brussels business is now done at breakfast meetings and briefings over coffee and croissants.

At summits of EU leaders and ministers, however, wine and brandy still fortify the formal evening dinners, where late-night negotiations often stretch into the early hours. And as European heads of government wrestle with EU budgets over bottles of Chateau Angelus Premier Grand Cru, bleary journalists pass the time in the press bar at the Justus Lipsius building, the headquarters of the European Council. It's a very convivial place to meet journalists from other EU countries and compare how a story looks from a different perspective. And then it's into the press briefing rooms, where you notice how flushed this or that leader is looking at two in the morning.

The President of the European Commission, Jean-Claude Juncker, is the ultimate Brussels insider and a veteran of backroom deal making. Juncker was Prime Minister of Luxembourg before taking charge of Europe's executive branch, and during the European Parliament elections in 2014 that led to his Commission presidency, there was plenty of press speculation, mainly in Britain, about his appetite for drink; meanwhile a handful of anonymous EU officials were briefing that he might not be suitable for the job. He wouldn't have been the first Commission President to allegedly enjoy a drink. Another former Luxembourg Prime Minister who ran the Berlaymont, Jacques Santer, the man who oversaw the introduction of the euro, acquired the soubriquet 'Jacques Sancerre' among some Brussels journalists.

There has never been any proof that Jean-Claude Juncker drinks excessively, and Juncker's team were furious at what they saw as an effort to smear him when he was running for the presidency. But he and his friends have had to respond to the persistent rumours. The German Finance Minister, Wolfgang Schäuble, talking to the Foreign Correspondents Association in Berlin in June 2014 after many years sitting in meetings with Mr Juncker, was able to attest to his sobriety: 'I never said Jean-Claude Juncker was abstinent. I also drink sometimes, including in Eurogroup meetings, where it can happen that I have a glass of wine with dinner. Then he drinks beer. But I've never experienced him drunk.'[37] Juncker himself hit back at an article in *Der Spiegel* titled 'Achtung Alkoholkontrolle' (Attention, Breath Test), snapping, 'I have no problems with drink, that's enough now! Leave me alone with these accusations that are not true.'[38]

But why should there be this kind of sanctimonious interrogation in the first place? Nobody has ever suggested Jean-Claude Juncker's judgment has been impaired by alcohol. And after the issues he has had to deal with, from the near collapse of the euro to the continent's refugee crisis in 2015, it might seem reasonable to allow the poor man a drink. But the experience of politicians and alcohol has always been clouded in contradiction. We expect them to drink as a mark of ordinariness, but condemn them if their consumption is judged excessive. Even then, some heavy political drinkers are celebrated while others are mocked and ridiculed. It's been the same for hundreds of years and is, perhaps, a mirror of alcohol's own conflicting charms. Some politicians have discovered booze makes life better. It rewards success, disperses boredom and unpicks the locks of conversation and relationships. At the same time drink can bite back, imprisoning some in dependency and despair. Winston Churchill believed that, on balance, he had got more out of drink that it had taken out of him. This has clearly not been true of others. As long as there are politicians, and drinks to be had, the story of their relationship is destined to continue.

# CHAPTER 8

## Time, Gentlemen!

Not only have politicians through the ages, from Alexander the Great to Boris Johnson, experienced the exhilarating balm of drinking alcohol themselves, but for as long as politicians have been consuming drink they have also been trying to control and regulate it. It has been a policy preoccupation across time and place. A nineteenth-century sake-drinking Japanese emperor, a bourbon-sipping US President, a wine-drinking English Whig and a present-day Swedish Prime Minister have all tried to police the alcohol habits of their people. The result is a global patchwork of different drinking rules that have evolved over centuries, their unifying aim being to limit the damage alcohol can do. This chapter looks at the politics of alcohol control.

According to the World Health Organisation in 2015, 3.3 million deaths every year result from the harmful use of alcohol. That's 5.9 per cent of all deaths. But laws relating to alcohol use vary widely. In France, for instance, alcohol sponsorship of sport has been banned since 1991. You won't see advertisements for spirits on Austrian television. A sixteen-year-old can buy a beer in an Italian bar, but a teenager in the US has to wait until they're twenty-one.

Scotland has a minimum unit price for alcohol, while in Sweden booze for drinking at home can only be bought from a state-owned monopoly called the Systembolaget. Burkina Faso and the Democratic Republic of Congo are among the handful of countries to have no drink driving limits at all.

Britain has always had a reputation for boozing. From the jolly ale drinkers described by Charles Dickens to the rampaging stag tribes that descend on Prague, the world knows we like to drink (and that we have trouble behaving when we do). Even Debrett's, the snooty guide to British titles and manners, lists drunkenness as one of the nation's notable characteristics:

> Despite their reputation for reticence and reserve, British people love to drink. Alcohol oils the wheels of British social life – from the rarefied glamour of Royal Ascot and the traditional British wedding to the conviviality of a night out at the local pub or socialising after a day at work. For many people, alcohol is an effective de-inhibitor, a failsafe way of breaking down social barriers and bringing people closer together. But the emollient effects of alcohol can easily tip into drunkenness, as the rowdy Saturday-night streets of many British towns will testify.

For centuries, politicians have been the nation's landlords, deciding when the rest of us can drink and how much. Current arguments around the price, control and availability of alcohol reprise age-old debates about the rights of people to drink freely and the duty of the state to protect its citizens from harm.

Until the Licensing Act of 1552, there were very few rules governing the sale and purchase of beer. In 1266 the price of ale was pegged to the price of bread and from 1393 alehouses had to identify themselves by displaying a stake in the ground by the door – a medieval pub signboard. The cultivation of hops in the early 1400s turned beer production into an industry for the first time and introduced many more people to the pleasures of booze. But as drinking became more popular, so did the fear of social chaos. The 1552 Act was passed to counter what it described as the 'intolerable hurts and troubles to the commonwealth of this realm' which 'daily grow and increase through such abuses and disorders as are had and used in common alehouses'.[1] This was the earliest attempt at licensing, and anyone wanting to keep an alehouse had to obtain a certificate from two local magistrates and prove their good character. Drunkenness was first made an offence in 1606; twelve years later James I brought in charges for licences, beginning the state's practice of pocketing money from the sale of drink.

But it was the 'Gin Craze' of the early 1700s that first ignited mass panic about the dangers of drink. Invented in Holland, gin was imported to Britain around the same time as William of Orange, who became monarch along with his wife Mary in 1689. To begin with, gin distilling was encouraged because it was patriotically free of any French connection – unlike brandy, imports of which had been banned by Parliament. Gin was cheap, easy to produce at home, safer to drink than water and could be made with what was grown in British fields. Landowners were delighted to make money from the surplus grain produced thanks to more advanced farming methods and Parliament was happy to scoop up the duties.

Crucially, there was at first no licensing, while government stimulated production by breaking up the London Guild of Distillers monopoly in 1690. It was the biggest drinking free-for-all in British history, with anyone able to distil and sell gin. And for the next fifty years gin fuelled an unprecedented epidemic of drunkenness that governments initially encouraged and then consistently failed to curb.

Gin anaesthetised the urban poor with devastating effect, especially in London. For a city of 700,000 people, there were 9,000 gin shops by the 1730s. In addition, 15,000 of the city's 96,000 homes had a room set aside for people to buy and drink gin.[2] Wheelbarrows sloshing with the drink were carted around for people too drunk or desperate to walk to a shop. In 1700 consumption of gin was less than half a gallon per person a year.[3] But by 1729, a colossal five million gallons of gin were being drunk every year, enough for every man, woman and child in London to drain a pint of gin a week. The drunkenness, despair and social rot that had begun to calcify in London's poorer streets was soon the focus of heated debate.

In 1726 Daniel Defoe wrote that self-destructive gin drinking was the responsibility of the drinker, not the fault of the market: 'The people will destroy themselves by their own excess ... 'tis the magistrates' business to help that, not the distillers.' To Defoe, the distilleries were merely providing a drink that people bored with beer wanted to buy.[4] He didn't think it was the job of the distillers or the state to meddle. But other voices, in the Church and in Parliament, began to argue that direct intervention was needed to prevent people drinking themselves to death. Throughout the following two centuries the same arguments have flared up at regular intervals. And they frame today's debate about the government's role in policing alcohol consumption.

Defoe soon changed his mind about the virtues of an unregulated gin market. Eventually so did Parliament, which in 1729 passed the first of many Acts it hoped would calm the gin drinking mania. A licence was introduced for the first time and a new duty was placed on every gallon of compound spirits. Unsurprisingly, distillers produced a raw spirit instead, popularly known as 'Parliamentary Brandy', which got round the law.

The Act did nothing to dent the epidemic of drunkenness. Gin drinking continued to rise and in 1733 the measure was repealed.[5] Three years later, however, against a backdrop of vigorous public argument about drink, Parliament had another go. The 1736 Gin Act placed very high duties on the sale and production of the spirit and new £50 licences were slapped on sellers in what effectively amounted to prohibition. The Act stated that gin drinking had become 'very common especially amongst the people of lower and inferior rank … rendering them unfit for useful labour and business, debauching their morals, and inciting them to all manner of vices'.

It was the raucous gin-dependent proletariat that frightened the frequently sozzled upper classes of Georgian England. They saw the foundations of London rotting from the bottom up, corrupting women and their unborn children in particular. Those fears are most famously captured in William Hogarth's 1751 engraving 'Gin Lane'.

Hogarth sets his portrait of desperation and death within the parish of St Giles in Holborn. Beggars share a bone with a dog; people crowd around the pawnbrokers with their kettles and tools, selling the means of earning their livelihoods so they can buy another drink. One corpse is placed in a coffin while her child cries on the ground; another hangs in the window of a crumbling house. A drunken mob fights outside the distillery while a mother pours gin into the mouth of her baby. And at the centre of the scene, a ragged, drink-broken woman sits slumped on the steps as her baby falls to her death. It's a hellish depiction of Madame Gin's dangers and a dramatic contrast to Hogarth's companion engraving 'Beer Street', full of hearty, jolly chaps enjoying foaming pints of beer while women make a living from their abundant baskets of fish.

Who does Hogarth hold responsible for the misery in Gin Lane? Is it the distillers who make the addictive drink? Is it the weak-willed poor of London who've capitulated to the booze? Or is it the country's failure to care about the inhabitants of Gin Lane that has driven them to suicidal drinking? Hogarth doesn't provide an answer, but he does reflect the anxieties of the age. And similar questions were asked 250 years later as Britain staggered through another era of binge drinking. Photographs of inebriated late-night revellers regularly filled the tabloid newspapers in the early 2000s, particularly pictures of young women in mini-skirts, legs buckled, sprawling on the street. There was a Hogarthian reflection in the images and a Georgian echo in the commentary. Newspapers wrung their hands about young women drinking, the anti-social behaviour of the mob and the evidence that public morals were on the slide.

'Gin Lane' was published in 1751, fifteen years after the drink was meant to have been prohibited. That's because the 1736 Gin Act had been another epic failure. The huge unlicensed gin trade was run by backroom hawkers, grocers and from street stalls and consumption continued to increase. As Jenny Uglow has written, gin made the miserable lives of London's poor feel a little better: 'To the desperate and destitute gin was cheap and warming … It tasted vile, more like rubbing alcohol than subtle juniper berries, and it was horribly potent, leaving drinking dens and gutters littered with collapsed bodies.'[6]

A further Gin Act in 1743 repriced annual licences at a much cheaper twenty shillings and restricted them to existing tavern and alehouse keepers. Levels of gin drinking fell but the arguments in the press, among politicians and from the pulpit still raged, leading to the final Gin Act of the era, in 1751, shortly after Hogarth's engravings were printed. Licensing restrictions were tightened further, taxes on spirits were increased and a minimum rent had to be paid by sellers. At the same time the cost of grain began to rise and gin production fell, hastening the end of a fifty-year drinking frenzy. However in 1835, Charles Dickens was still shocked by what he found on a walk through the squalid streets of St Giles:

> Gin-drinking is a great vice in England, but wretchedness and dirt are a greater; and until you improve the homes of the poor, or persuade a half-famished wretch not to seek relief in the temporary oblivion of his own misery, with the pittance which, divided among his family, would furnish a morsel of bread for each, gin-shops will increase in number and splendour.[7]

The Gin Craze showed the difficulty of finding an effective political response to the social problems thrown up by drink.

The competing arguments between state restriction of the alcohol trade and a belief in liberalisation went back and forth through the nineteenth century. For instance, the 1830 Beer Act tore up the system of magistrate-approved licensing in an attempt to bring more competition to the beer trade and break the stranglehold of big breweries with their tied alehouses and pubs. Under the Act, anyone could sell beer so long as they paid a small tax and within a year of it being passed 24,000 beer shops had opened.[8]

There were two main consequences. People got plastered on the widely available beer and the British temperance movement began to mobilise. In 1834 a House of Commons select committee held an inquiry into drunkenness, concluding that the 1830 Act had been a mistake. Among the committee's witnesses was Joseph Livesey, a cheese-maker from Preston who had set up the first temperance society in the town years earlier. Livesey was convinced that much of the misery endured by the poor stemmed from alcohol abuse and only teetotalism could break the dependency. Many thought the zealous, evangelical advocates of temperance dotty and ignored their warnings about the dangers of even moderate drinking.

But by the late 1840s every large town in England had a local temperance society and the drink question sparked into life again.[9] In 1853 the societies organised themselves into a powerful political pressure group, the UK Alliance, and found fertile ground in many working-class communities. Magistrates' control over licensing was revived in 1849, but the argument over drink remained polarised between liberal free-trade disciples and those who believed the government's duty was to dragoon the public into sobriety. Belief in individual liberty clashed with demands for moral progress. As James Nicholls writes, for John Stuart Mill and like-minded liberals,

> the job of the State was to allow individuals to make their own choices and their own mistakes so long as those choices and mistakes did not actively restrict the opportunity of others to do the same. For prohibitionists, the role of the State was actively to create the conditions in which individuals would be able to apprehend moral truths – and since that required sobriety, the State had a responsibility to outlaw the drinks trade.[10]

The Victorian struggle with alcohol culminated in the 1872 Licensing Act, which reduced the number of licences and restricted pub opening hours, forcing pubs in London to close by midnight and by 11 p.m. everywhere else and not to reopen until six in the morning. The Act also introduced the offence of being drunk and disorderly in the street, which still exists today, and it remains illegal to be drunk in charge of a carriage, horse, cow or steam engine, or whilst carrying a loaded firearm.[11] The brewers and publicans were furious at the Gladstone government's original 1871 Bill, while temperance campaigners thought it was a wishy-washy fudge. A compromise Act was eventually pushed through Parliament the following year with sizeable Tory support. Despite that, and both parties' wariness about getting too close either to the brewers or the temperance zealots, the Conservative leader Benjamin Disraeli successfully painted the Liberals as a party that planned to snatch voters' beer away. After losing the general election in 1874 Gladstone wrote to his brother Robert, rather melodramatically, 'we have been borne down in a torrent of gin and beer.'

The Act failed to slow Britain's headlong march towards intoxication, the second great industrial epidemic of alcohol consumption. In the 1870s, an average of 40.5 gallons of beer was being drunk per capita per year, a colossal amount.[12] Urban drinking was on the rise in the factory towns and cities of the Midlands and northern England and there was a boom in brewer-backed pub building to assuage the thirst of working-class drinkers. At this time taxes on booze brought in a quarter of the state's revenue, which meant that governments were wary of staunching such a valuable income stream even if the social effects of mass drunkenness were clear.

This kept the temperance movement at the centre of the debate about drink. It was just as busy lobbying as the brewers, another echo of today's struggle between groups such as Alcohol Concern and the drinks industry. At the close of the century a Royal Commission was set up to examine the drink question, but it was not until 1908 that the new Liberal government resolved to rein in the pubs. The plan was to restrict the number of licences to one per 1,000 people in cities and to compensate pubs that lost their licences using money raised from a levy on all public houses. The plan envisaged that a third of the pubs in England and Wales would eventually close. In an attempt to end the Monday morning hangover, the Bill also squeezed Sunday opening hours and proposed a ban on women working in pubs. The aim of the latter measure was twofold: both to protect female bar staff from the unwanted attentions of drunken men and to make pubs less inviting by prohibiting women servers. 'The nation ought not to allow the natural attractions of a young girl to be used for trading purposes,' mused a supportive Bishop of Southwark.[13]

But the Bill managed to unite suffragettes, brewers and the nation's drinkers in opposition to it. At its Second Reading in the House of Commons, Prime Minister Herbert Asquith spelt out the government's ambition to break the brewers' control over 90 per cent of licences through tied pubs: 'The second great and governing purpose ... is the recovery for the State of complete and unfettered control of this monopoly.' Many saw the proposal as an attack on property.

The drinks trade, more closely aligned to the Conservative Party since it had helped scupper the 1872 Licensing Act, mobilised against the plans with unprecedented force. A national campaign reached its zenith in September 1908 when a quarter of a million people poured into London to demonstrate against the Bill in Hyde Park, many ferried to the capital on charter trains laid on by Midland and northern breweries. Protesters pinned sprigs of hops to their buttonholes and wore badges that proclaimed 'Honesty and Liberty'. Publicans and their customers, bar staff and brewers wanted to defend a working man's freedom to drink – and the brewers' freedom to profit handsomely from it. The dynamic Irish suffragette, social activist and poet Eva Gore-Booth led the fight against the proposed ban on barmaids. With her lover and fellow suffragette, Esther Roper, she launched the Barmaids Political Defence League to champion the rights of women to work, in and beyond the nation's pubs. In April 1908 the two women contributed to an extraordinary by-election upset when they helped unseat Winston Churchill as Liberal MP in Manchester North-West. Asquith had just promoted young Churchill to the post of President of the Board of Trade. But at that time newly appointed Cabinet ministers were obliged to stand for re-election in their constituencies first. It was a convention for such by-elections to go unopposed but, in backing the barmaid ban, Churchill became the target of suffragette campaigners. Eva Gore-Booth, together with her sister Countess Markievicz, whipped up support for the Conservative candidate by denouncing Churchill and the government's pub plans at packed public rallies. The women did not yet have the right to vote but their enthusiastic campaign scuppered Churchill's re-election hopes. Following defeat, the future Prime Minister had to scout for another seat and re-entered the Commons as MP for Dundee at a by-election later in the year. While Churchill went on to be Number 10's heavyweight drinker, his belief that the removal of women from behind the bar in pubs would make booze less tempting to susceptible working men derailed his career, if only briefly.

After scraping through the Commons, the Licensing Bill was vetoed by the Tory-dominated House of Lords in November 1908. To the ears of peers, the angry complaints of drinkers and brewers made a more powerful appeal than the pious temperance campaigners. Many Conservatives shared the concerns of the Liberal Party (and businesses) about the country's drunken intemperance, but they flinched at the radicalism of the Licensing Bill. But in killing off the Bill the House of Lords quickened its own demise. A year later peers blocked Lloyd George's 'People's Budget' and by 1911 the Asquith government's exasperation with the Lords tipped into constitutional crisis. The Parliament Act was passed, ensuring that the Lords could never again veto the will of the Commons.

It was not decades of debate, temperance pressure for prohibition, parliamentary battles or a decisive shift in public opinion that finally shunted Edwardian Britain into sobriety. It was war. The government called time on intemperance with several sweeping interventions to sober Britain up for the fight. The 1914 Defence of the Realm Act brought the axe down on day-long drinking and the following year direct state control over the supply and sale of alcohol in some areas was established through the Central Control Board. In towns where drunken munitions workers would have damaged the war effort, pubs were effectively nationalised and in 1916 the government took over the management of the entire drinks industry in the Carlisle area, an experiment that would continue until 1974. Taxes on alcohol were increased, while beer and spirits were diluted in strength. This unprecedented move to limit the country's drinking had a dramatic effect on alcohol consumption and on levels of recorded drunkenness. By 1918 beer intake per head was half what it had been before the war and it was only in the late 1970s that alcohol consumption in Britain returned to levels last seen at the start of the twentieth century. Since then it has been a boom in the drinking of wine and spirits that has continued the rise.[14]

In comparison, France pursued a quite different approach to alcohol after the First World War. The state embarked on an extraordinary campaign of encouraging its citizens to drink as much wine as possible. Sales were hit by the disappearance of many wine-buying aristocratic families. Prohibition in the United States depressed demand further and good wine harvests were producing gallons of surplus wine. In 1931 the government launched a campaign urging patriotic Frenchmen to knock back more of the national drink. Advertisements stressed the health benefits of wine; billboards were placed at railway stations and neon signs around Paris. It was suggested that wine should be given to children during their lunch breaks, while a series tracing the country's history through drink, run on French state radio, posited the view that Louis XIV's pre-Revolution reign was so abysmal partly because he diluted his wine with water, which stopped him thinking deeply enough.[15]

In Britain, though, the government gradually began to grapple with the problem of drink again. Victorian questions about the morality of excessive drinking and the nature of liberty were eclipsed by more practical concerns. How should drivers be deterred and punished if they were drunk behind the wheel of a car? The first drink driving limits and breathalyser tests were introduced in 1967. How should responsible drinking be encouraged? By setting safe drinking limits. The idea of units was first proposed in the Royal College of Psychiatrists' report, 'Alcohol and Alcoholism', published in 1979. It suggested that safe drinking limits should be set at what now seems an extraordinary four pints of beer, four doubles of spirits or one bottle of wine a day.[16] The report argued for government intervention to stop Britain's alcohol consumption rising any further and concluded bluntly: 'When price goes up, consumption falls. When prices go down, consumption rises.' Thirty-five years later, that assertion still prompts fierce disagreement between politicians, the alcohol industry and public health campaigners.

## Barcelona Comes to Britain

On the eve of the 2001 general election, the Labour Party sent out a text message to young voters which read, 'cdnt give a xxxx 4 lst orders? Thn vte Lbr on Thursday 4 extra time.' The technology had evolved but William Hogarth would have recognised the tactic of seducing the electorate with drink. Labour was not talking about an extra hour in the Royal Oak to finish a pint of bitter. Instead, it was promising to tear up licensing rules and free Britain to enjoy a continental culture of round-the-clock drinking.

The boulevards of Reading would be lined with café tables in the early hours of a balmy morning, humming with convivial wine-sipping conversation. Freed from the pressure to binge drink until 11 p.m., the salons of Newcastle would see a gentle ebb and flow of custom through the evening and into the night. Of course, some people might still have a little too much to drink, but the end of last orders would put an end to the closing time punch-up.

The backdrop to this vision was an urban drinking environment that had changed considerably in the preceding decade. After the 'Beer Orders' were introduced in 1989, brewers had to sell off thousands of their pubs, which were then bought up by new pub companies that sold but didn't produce alcohol. And as local authorities tried to breathe new life into run-down town centres, these cash-rich 'pubcos' planted large new chain bars along the country's high streets. Alcohol became an important motor of regional economies and late-night drinking licences for music and entertainment venues were handed out much more liberally by local planning authorities. As James Nicholls has written, 'faced with the prospect of watching their cities go the way of Flint, Michigan or the way of Barcelona, it is hardly surprising that most planning authorities opted for the latter, especially when the architectural models never depicted the scene at a taxi-rank at 2 a.m.'[17] With drink now considered a leisure activity to promote rather than a problem to control, an overhaul of the opening hours was a logical next step.

In 2000 a Home Office White Paper called 'Time for Reform' concluded that the existing licensing laws were a tangled mess and recommended the abandonment of fixed closing times. After Labour was re-elected in 2001, it introduced a Licensing Bill the following year which proposed an end to fixed licensing hours. In the end, only a tiny minority of licensed premises chose to take out 24-hour licences, but the effects of the 2003 Act were fodder for the tabloids and 'binge-drinking Britain' became a national obsession. The vomit-splattered pandemonium of towns after dark was proof, many said, that the Act had been a disaster. In fact, a government-commissioned report in 2008 concluded that the Act had had a negligible impact on levels of drink-related anti-social behaviour and alcohol consumption. Its effect had been neutral. But by the time Labour left office, Britain's drinking culture was no more Spanish than the Last Night of the Proms.

At the same time, though, the Act had not unleashed a new epidemic of drunkenness. Overall alcohol consumption in the UK had dropped a little in the preceding five years after three decades of rapid increase. In 2004, adult per capita consumption was more than 26 per cent higher than it had been thirty years earlier. By 2015, one in five adults said they didn't drink alcohol at all, and it has been a decline in drinking among 16–24-year-olds that is mainly responsible for the change. Once-a-week bingeing has dropped slightly too.[18] In terms of alcohol consumption, Britain is roughly mid-table compared to other European countries, behind France, Germany and Spain.[19]

Paradoxically, however, rates of alcohol-related mortality have increased.[20] If you really want to see the grimmer side of drink, go and visit a liver unit in a modern British hospital.

Nobody would plan to be a member of this particular community but demand for beds is high. I'm shown around the unit at Southampton General Hospital by its head clinician, Dr Nick Sheron, one of the leading hepatologists in the country and a world authority on alcohol and liver disease. Dr Sheron talks with wry affection about his 'customers' as he walks me around the ward. I meet a lady in her fifties who has been connected up to tubes here for months, waiting for a transplant to replace her cirrhotic liver, tearfully regretting the years of heavy drinking that brought her here. One of the doctor's newest patients is in his mid-twenties, the youngest he's ever treated.

Dr Sheron has seen a huge increase in the number of patients presenting with serious liver disease in the last decade. For a quarter of those who arrive here, it is too late. Their liver damage is at such an advanced stage that they will die within a few months even though they have stopped drinking. For most, it's the sudden appearance of symptoms that first reveals that their livers are dangerously damaged. It could be a variceal bleed in the oesophagus or they might suddenly turn yellow from liver failure. One of the most shocking features of drink-induced liver disease is its symptomless development. In 2012 there were 8,367 alcohol-related deaths in the UK. Alcoholic liver disease accounted for 63 per cent of those, 18 per cent higher than the number of deaths in 2002.[21] 'You can look at liver mortality as a cipher for liver disease,' Dr Sheron explains to me. 'Over the last thirty years or so the mortality from most diseases has gone down, in many cases significantly. Smoking related disease, heart disease, you name it, the mortality rates have gone down. The mortality rates for liver disease as a whole have gone up five times since 1970 and were going up year on year by about nine per cent up until 2008. And practically all the increase has been in alcohol-related liver disease.'

Because 80 per cent of deaths from liver disease are alcohol related, it's a strong yardstick for gauging the effect of alcohol on a population. 'Europe is the highest drinking area of the world and has the highest level of mortality from liver disease, and there is a very tight correlation between population level consumption and liver disease mortality,' the doctor explains. France has seen its liver mortality drop substantially in recent years. In contrast, the two countries that have seen the biggest increase in liver mortality are the UK and Finland.

The statistics and harrowing personal stories of liver disease are not the only evidence that alcohol remains a serious public health problem in the UK. According to the Office for National Statistics, in 2011/12 there were more than a million alcohol-related hospital admissions in England alone and it is estimated that alcohol misuse costs the NHS in England around £3.5 billion every year.[22] Dr Sheron explains that alcohol contributes to many other health problems, but in ways that are harder to quantify than liver disease. For instance, alcohol is an addictive drug that causes dependency and has a spectrum of health problems associated with it. It contributes to diseases of the vascular system (such as high blood pressure, heart disease and stroke) and cancer. 'In Europe as a whole about ten per cent of cancers in males are alcohol related and three to four per cent of cancers in women are alcohol related. If a woman drinks on average a bottle of wine a week it puts her risk of breast cancer up by ten per cent. Because one in ten women get breast cancer the absolute risk is one per cent. But nobody ever has a diagnosis of alcohol-related breast cancer.' With most diseases the contribution of alcohol is 'dose-dependent'; in other words, the more that's drunk the greater the risk.

Then there are all the non-medical effects of drinking too much alcohol. These include disorder and damage, road traffic accidents and the 40 per cent of domestic violence cases in which drunkenness plays a part.

## A Political Price

It was this awareness of the damage heavy drinking does that focused the alcohol debate back onto price, a policy nettle politicians have always been wary of grasping, anxious not to penalise moderate drinkers or harm Britain's whisky, cider and beer industries. A shift in thinking was signalled by a hefty report from the Health Select Committee in January 2010. Its excoriating verdict was that successive government responses to England's alcohol problem ranged from the 'non-existent to the ineffectual', despite UK deaths from liver cirrhosis having increased five-fold over the last three decades while rates in France, Spain and Italy dropped significantly over the same period. It went on:

> Just as Government policy played a part in encouraging the gin craze, successive Government policies have played a part in encouraging the increase in alcohol consumption over the last 50 years. Currently over 10 million adults drink more than the recommended limits. These people drink 75% of all the alcohol consumed. 2.6 million adults drink more than twice the recommended limits.

The committee said increasing affordability of alcohol since the 1960s had been the 'major cause of the rise in consumption' and its key recommendation was to bring in a minimum unit price for alcohol, echoing the view of the then Chief Medical Officer for England, Sir Liam Donaldson.[23]

Select committees rattle off recommendations all the time, many of which are ignored by government, but this found a receptive audience within the coalition. For the first time since the First World War, ministers gave consideration to a significant intervention in the alcohol market. The targets were not pub opening hours or licensing rules, but shop shelves of cheap vodka, super-strength cider and extra strong lager. Most alcohol is consumed at home, and the heaviest drinkers, the ones that are doing the most damage to themselves, buy cheap booze from supermarkets. In March 2012, the government published its new Alcohol Strategy, which was built around a commitment to bring in a minimum unit price for alcohol. The Prime Minister's foreword to the strategy said the policy would reduce binge drinking and cut crime:

> For the first time it will be illegal for shops to sell alcohol for less than this set price per unit. We are consulting on the actual price, but if it is 40p that could mean 50,000 fewer crimes each year and 900 fewer alcohol-related deaths a year by the end of the decade. This isn't about stopping responsible drinking, adding burdens on business or some new kind of stealth tax – it's about fast, immediate action where universal change is needed. And let's be clear. This will not hurt pubs. A pint is around two units. If the minimum price is 40p a unit, it won't affect the price of a pint in a pub.

The announcement was applauded by health professionals and by groups such as Alcohol Concern. It also aligned England with Scotland, where a minimum price of 50p per unit had been introduced by the Scottish parliament in May 2012, to the fury of the country's whisky distilleries. A legal challenge from the Scottish Whisky Association in the European courts meant the policy had still not been implemented by the end of 2015.

The coalition government's embrace of minimum pricing did not last long enough to be tested in the courts. Following a consultation on the government's plans, its final alcohol policy was unveiled in July 2013. Despite David Cameron's proclaimed belief in the benefits of minimum pricing the year before, the idea was ditched. The reason? A lack of conclusive evidence that it would make any difference, said the government. A craven capitulation to the drinks industry, cried public health groups.

It was known the policy had its opponents in the Cabinet, notably the former Health Secretary Andrew Lansley. He had argued against minimum pricing when he was at the Department of Health and continued to do so after he was reshuffled to be Leader of the House of Commons in 2012.

When we meet in early 2015, I ask Andrew Lansley why minimum pricing should not at least be given a try. 'Giving it a try involves establishing an extremely unwelcome precedent in public policy making. Trying to control the price of commodities in the marketplace? We don't want to be in that position. That is not what Conservatives do,' he tells me sharply. He claims a minimum unit price would have to be 50p or 55p for it to make any difference, an amount which would shift hundreds of millions of pounds from the pockets of customers to retailers. 'There's no justification for that,' the former Health Secretary says. 'There was no evidence it would work. It would have been a large-scale measure to intervene in the market at a time there's a cost of living issue for people. It was going to be very unpopular. It's not good politics at all.'[24]

The Conservative Party's chief election strategist, Lynton Crosby, advised David Cameron to 'get the barnacles off the boat'. In other words, to abandon any extraneous and distracting policies that might make the Conservative Party's voyage towards polling day unhelpfully choppy. Minimum pricing was considered to be exactly such a policy, so overboard it went.

Drinks companies such as Diageo strongly oppose minimum pricing, arguing that it will have no impact on consumption among heavy drinkers and could damage the companies' exports if the idea is picked up by other countries. Andrew Lansley is convinced the voluntary cooperation between the industry, government and medical professionals would shatter if minimum pricing was imposed. In 2011 the Department of Health launched a 'Responsibility Deal' with the industry, which includes commitments to more informative bottle labelling and a pledge to remove one billion units of alcohol from the UK market by December 2015. 'We're working with the drinks industry so people can still enjoy alcohol while mitigating the risk,' concludes Lansley.

'That's complete bollocks!' Dr Nick Sheron shouts, as he clicks through his graphs on alcohol price, consumption, strength and harm several weeks later. The doctor is despairing at the government's opposition to minimum pricing. Dr Sheron points out that in 2008 Labour introduced an alcohol duty escalator (which automatically raised prices at 2 per cent above inflation); George Osborne abolished it in his 2014 Budget, to loud cheers from brewers, West Country cider makers, whisky distillers and the press. Politicians have always known there are few votes in raising the price of alcohol. But Dr Sheron is convinced a minimum unit price will make his ward less busy: 'My patients are buying the cheap booze. Irrespective of their income they are not drinking Chateau Lafite. And therefore when you look at the impact of a minimum unit price it's really concentrated at these harmful drinkers. Changes in price have a dramatic impact on the really heavy drinking end of the scale because they're already spending a large proportion of their income on alcohol. There's been a wealth of studies showing the connection between population level consumption and liver mortality as a cipher for other alcohol-related diseases. There's an equally clear connection between the price of alcohol and consumption of alcohol. If alcohol becomes three times more expensive my patients have no choice but to reduce their consumption.' Dr Sheron reels off a list of other policies he'd like to see, including new restrictions on the social media marketing of alcohol to young people and a ban on alcohol brands' sponsorship of sport.[25]

In January 2016, while many people were trying to give up alcohol for what is now dubbed Dry January, new drinking guidelines were published by the government, the first full review of alcohol advice since 1995. Its conclusions were sobering for people who thought their three glasses of wine a night were good for their health. The government now says men and women should consume no more than fourteen units of alcohol a week, the equivalent of six pints of beer or seven glasses of wine. That's a reduction from the previous guidelines that set daily drinking limits of three to four units for men and two to three for women. The guidelines say women should not drink anything during pregnancy and recommends people have 'several' alcohol-free days a week. England's Chief Medical Officer, Dame Sally Davies, said: 'Drinking any level of alcohol regularly carries a health risk for anyone, but if men and women limit their intake to no more than fourteen units a week it keeps the risk of illness like cancer and liver disease low.' She said the guidance was intended to give people information so they can make informed decisions about their drinking.

There were predictable shrieks of 'nanny state' from some, and even David Cameron distanced himself from the recommendations, saying: 'This Tory isn't a nanny.' But guidance is just that. Cameron's government appears to have buried its flirtation with price setting, choosing instead to let people decide how they balance the harm alcohol does with the pleasure that it brings.

On my way out of his office, I ask Dr Sheron if he thinks Britain has a particular problem with drink. 'We're getting the worst of both worlds,' he says. 'As well as feast-drinking on Friday night to celebrate battles won during the week we're now drinking wine with meals. We've adopted Mediterranean habits as well. So we have a hybrid culture where it's OK to drink on a daily basis and it's also OK to go and get battered at the weekend.'

Travelling back to London on the train, I watch men in suits swigging from cans of Stella on their post-work wind-down. At the local supermarket the shelves closest to the door are piled high with bottles of discounted wine that cost less than a couple of pizzas. At the weekend, my local high street will again be a raucous, booze-drenched mess by midnight. Drink has a presence in our lives that would have horrified those priggish temperance campaigners in the nineteenth century. But the freedom to drink freely has been a prized part of British life for centuries, providing politicians with an enduring dilemma. How should the state help dependent drinkers? Is it their duty to reduce consumption? How should alcohol be taxed? Where is the balance between an industry's right to sell a legally available commodity and a state's responsibility to minimise harm to its citizens? When it comes to drink, politicians have plenty of personal experience, as previous chapters have shown. The policy questions, though, remain as thorny as they have ever been, despite the accumulating evidence on the problems alcohol brings in its wake.

# EPILOGUE

## Last Orders?

It is tempting to assume that politicians themselves will soon mothball their ministerial drinks cabinets and shut the parliamentary bars for good. The days when a Chancellor of the Exchequer would enjoy a three-course lunch and a bottle of Margaux before delivering a Budget speech in the Commons are unlikely to return. The pace of the job is now too unrelenting, the scrutiny too great. At some point soon, Charles Barry's leaking, scaffolding-supported Palace of Westminster is going to need an epic renovation that will take many years and cost billions of pounds. No other workplace in Britain currently has as many places to buy and drink alcohol on site and when the builders move in it is hard to imagine them surviving. In the Britain of Dry Januaries, increasingly dire warnings of the harm done by drink, as well as public intolerance of taxpayer money being lavished on politicians, a refit of the bars is unlikely. Instead, there will be more juice bars and mindfulness zones, where politicians and the people who orbit them can extinguish their stress through meditation rather than alcohol. In California, corporate contacts are made at yoga sessions. In a not too distant future, political relationships and deals from Westminster to Washington may well be fused in a downward-facing dog.

This will be celebrated by those who believe centuries of political drinking have blinded politicians to the damage wreaked by alcohol. Instead, health-conscious policy makers will bear down on drinking with a clear head. But what will be lost? Before John Bellamy set up his pie and booze snack bar within the Palace of Westminster in the 1770s, politicians relied on the nearby alehouses and taverns. There were two pretty rough pubs known as Hell and Purgatory next to Westminster Hall and a third tavern called Heaven on what is now Abingdon Street.[1] If all the politicians who had drunk heavily and happily through history were to meet up in the Heaven tavern, the place would be heaving. Robert Walpole would be passing round the punch bowl, Roy Jenkins the claret; FDR would be knocking back the martinis while Winston Churchill soaked up the whisky and soda. Clubbable drinkers all and formidable characters of wit, charm and intelligence who were sustained, not harmed, by their alcohol intake. People who ran the country while almost certainly far over the limit to drive a car. But there would also be a quite a few political customers staggering between the other two bars, trapped in dependency and remorse, their careers ruined, their lives cut short by drink.

Only those who have experienced alcoholism know how desperate this drinking hell can be. Sifting through centuries of political drinking, there are plenty of star politicians who have been broken by alcohol, from Pitt the Younger to Charles Kennedy. The author and academic John Sutherland wrote about his own survival of alcoholism in his book *Last Drink to LA*:

Only some celestial audit could work out whether the fleeting happiness of inebriation is balanced by the terminal wretchedness of alcohol addiction. Good deal, bad deal? One would need a gigantic Benthamite pleasure-pain calculus: all those 'happy hours' on one pan; a seething mass of blood, broken bones, irritable bowels, foul breath and morning hangovers in the other.[2]

Political leaders, of course, have to place that calculation in the context of immense decision-making responsibilities. In the case of Richard Nixon, drink seems to have marred his judgment more than it helped at moments of crisis. Would his predecessor in the White House, Lyndon Johnson, have been more alert to the dangers of escalating war in Vietnam if he had not been so partial to a Scotch and soda? Possibly. But it was the same Johnson who had the foresight to pass the Civil Rights Act in 1964. Politicians' legacy is a ledger of success and failure, and that's the same whether they were heavy drinkers or not. A political reputation can be damaged quickly if drinking is thought excessive, as Herbert Asquith discovered at the start of the First World War. And looming over any audit of drink's role in decision making is always Churchill. His gargantuan consumption and wartime victory over the teetotal Adolf Hitler can always be played as a trump card.

Alcohol is not essential to the practice of politics. Some activities are clearly better done drunk – karaoke for instance. It is hard to argue that politicians perform more wisely or effectively after a few drinks. We prefer our plumbers and our surgeons to be sober, and we might expect no less from our legislators. But this story of political imbibing is crowded with characters who seem to have benefited from alcohol's power to relax and unwind. And for many years the demise of the lubricating role of alcohol in public life has been predicted and lamented. Writing in 1872 and looking back from the comparatively sober years of late-Victorian England, John Timbs regretted the new abstinence:

> Whether the power of conversation has declined or not we certainly fear that the power of drinking has; and the imagination dwells with melancholy fondness on that state of society in which great men were not forbidden to be good fellows, which we fancy, whether rightly or wrongly, must have been so superior to ours, in which wit and eloquence succumb to statistics, and claret has given place to coffee.[3]

This mournful nostalgia was misplaced. Political drinking continued to flourish, not least because of the pleasure drink delivered. Few have written more acutely and fondly about drink than Kingsley Amis, no stranger to a glass himself. Writing in the early 1970s Amis said, 'a team of American investigators concluded recently that, without the underpinning provided by alcohol and the relaxation it affords, Western civilisation would have collapsed irretrievably at about the time of the First World War. Not only is drink here to stay; the moral seems to be that when it goes, we go too.'[4]

Political life without alcohol would no doubt be duller. If we demand complete sobriety from politicians, they will be distanced even further from the people they represent. We are now in an age where leading politicians drink expensive wines and champagne in the cosseted privacy of a party conference hotel room or a Davos chalet, but are afraid to parade their pleasures for fear of public excoriation. The confidence of Boris Johnson and Nigel Farage to celebrate their enjoyment of drink is now rare among politicians. When it comes to sex, alcohol and other personal procliv- ities, we increasingly expect politicians to behave better than the rest of us (including newspaper editors). Such hypocrisy is absurd. Drink has been an essential balm and presence in the lives of politicians for centuries and, just like most of their voters, will continue to be.

But politicians have certainly sobered up. They now want to be seen jogging, cycling and working out, not sitting in bars. The long boozy lunches have gone and the mineral water has arrived. The drink-fuelled raucousness of late- night sittings in the Commons is now remembered only by the old-timers. The arrival of more women has broken the drinking culture of a gentleman's club. There are still examples of drunken excess, but they are increasingly rare.

Politics is now more professional, which for many is a cause for regret, and there are complaints that today's politi- cians are more blandly uniform than their predecessors, that the big beasts who used to prowl the political veldt are extinct. For some the decline of political drinking is a measure of this change, draining politics of much of its colour and character. For others it makes politics more serious and more inclusive. Drink has played a significant role in the politics of the past, but plays a diminished role in the present. Having sobered up themselves, politicians now have to help the rest of us do the same.

# ACKNOWLEDGMENTS

This book has fermented over a number of years and many people contributed to its publication. My agent, Charlie Brotherstone at Ed Victor Limited, along with Ed himself, have been tremendous champions of the project and I am very grateful to them both. They picked up a half-written book and believed it should be finished, finding it a perfect home with Duckworth Overlook. As a first time author I was very fortunate to be working with Peter Mayer, who was convinced there was a book in the subject over a memorably convivial lunch. Nikki Griffiths at Duckworth edited the text with great skill and sense, sharpening the story and providing invaluable guidance along the way. I am also indebted to Steve Gove for copy-editing the manuscript meticulously and to Malcolm Balen at the BBC. Any inaccuracies or errors are of course mine.

The book would not have happened at all if my friend, the writer and editor Sean Magee, had not suggested to me years ago that drink and politics might make a good read. At the time he said it was the perfect subject for a young man, which I was when the research first began. Sean has kept a close eye on the project over the years and thrown many bones for me to chase. I am also very grateful to my good friends Jonny Dymond and Nathaniel Hansen for reading early drafts of the manuscript and making many perceptive suggestions on how it could be better. In particular I would like to thank my father, Tony Wright. He has always provided me with shrewd insight and perspective into how politics is done and how it should be written about. He improved the book considerably and I am hugely grateful to him and to my mother for that and very much more.

A large cast of politicians and journalists generously gave me their time and drinking tales during my research. Their candour and insight is much appreciated. In particular I would like to thank Alastair Campbell, Joe Haines, Lord Lipsey, Lord Armstrong, Bernard Ingham, Colin Brown, Michael Brown, David Davis MP, Michael Skelton, Paul Flynn MP, Sadie Smith, Lord Grocott, Ian Hernon, Chris Moncrieff, Lord Strathclyde, Lord Owen, Harriet Harman MP, Lord Campbell of Pittenweem, Eric Joyce, Keith Simpson MP, Michael White, Nick Clegg MP, Boris Johnson MP, Lord Dobbs, Lord Donoughue, Damian McBride, Charlie Whelan, Harry Cole, Peter Oborne, Kevin Maguire, Jon Sopel, Baroness Williams, Tom Watson MP, Ian Lavery MP, Kevan Jones MP, Donald Richie, Haley Barbour, Jack Straw, Geoff Meade, Nigel Farage MEP, Will Walden and Andrew Lansley. Dr Nick Sheron at University Hospital Southampton generously gave me several hours of his expertise on alcohol, a subject I knew little about (through a medical lens) at the beginning. A number of politicians and political journalists provided valuable tips and stories off the record too. The London Library has been a goldmine for political memoirs and long-forgotten books on politics and drink. It has been a perfect sanctuary to research and write. I'm also grateful to the Library of Congress in Washington D.C. and Dr Paul

## Acknowledgments

Seaward at the tremendous History of Parliament Trust. Thank you to Mary Greenham for her unflagging encouragement for this project and much else besides.

Many friends and colleagues have chivvied me along, pepped me up and offered precious advice during the writing of this book. I would especially like to record my gratitude to Timothy Phillips, Professor Anthony Bale, Paul Ready, Treeva Fenwick, Ross Hawkins, Melody Drummond Hansen, Suzy McKeever, Ben Flatman, Dr Yasmin Khan, James Landale, Manveen Rana, Rebecca Keating, Nick Robinson, Dr Eliza Filby, Laura Kuenssberg, James Naughtie, Michael Crick, Becky Milligan, Gordon Corera, Callum May, Alex von Tunzelmann and Dr Lawrence Goldman, who taught me to think like a historian many years ago. I would have done nothing without all the love, support and encouragement of my parents. Along with my wonderful brothers Tim and Sam I am very lucky. And I can finally thank my wife, Poppy Mitchell-Rose, who endured my endless Saturdays in the library with great patience, good humour and love. Always a wise, kind counsel, throughout this odyssey in alcohol she has been my tonic.

# NOTES

## Introduction

1. Kathryn Tempest, *Cicero: Politics and Persuasion in Ancient Rome* (London: Continuum, 2011), p. 192.
2. *Memoirs of Babur*, trans. Annette Susannah Beveridge, Volume II (1921), p. 648.
3. William James, *The Varieties of Religious Experience: A Study in Human Nature* (London: Longmans, Green and Co., 1903), p. 387.

## Chapter 1: Government under the Influence

1. Fergus Linnane, *Drinking for England* (London: JR Books 2008), p. 46.
2. Evelyn Lord, *The Hell-Fire Clubs – Sex, Satanism and Secret Societies* (New Haven and London: Yale University Press, 2008), p. 101.
3. Linnane, *Drinking for England*, p. 48.
4. Donald McCormick, *The Hell-Fire Club* (Jarrolds, 1958), p. 76.
5. Horace Walpole, *Memoirs of the Reign of George III, Volume I* (1894), p. 198.
6. L.G. Mitchell, *Charles James Fox* (Oxford: OUP, 1992), p. 96.
7. *Life and Letters of Sir Gilbert Elliot, Volume I* (London: Longmans, Green and Co., 1874), p. 189.
8. Quoted in Linnane, *Drinking for England*, p. 90.
9. Oscar Sherwin, *Uncorking Old Sherry, The Life and Times of Richard Brinsley Sheridan* (Vision, 1960), p. 16.

10. George Otto Trevelyan, *The Early History of Charles James Fox* (London: Longmans, Green and Co., 1881), p. 95.
11. Jon Lawrence, *Electing Our Masters: The Hustings in British Politics from Hogarth to Blair* (Oxford: OUP, 2009), p. 15.
12. Harriette Wilson, *Memoirs* (London: Peter Davies, 1929), pp. 480–1.
13. Charles Dickens, *The Pickwick Papers, Volume One* (London: Chapman & Hall, 1861), p. 169.
14. Ibid., p. 183.
15. Lawrence, *Electing Our Masters*, p. 93.
16. J.B. Priestley, *Postscripts* (London: Heinemann, 1940), p. 27.
17. Alan Bullock, *The Life and Times of Ernest Bevin, Volume 3* (London: Heinemann, 1983), p. 288.
18. *Spectator*, 1 March 1957.
19. Richard Crossman, *The Backbench Diaries* (London: Hamish Hamilton, 1981), p. 631. Entry for 22 November 1957.
20. *Guardian*, 18 March 2000.
21. Anthony Howard, *Crossman: The Pursuit of Power* (London: Jonathan Cape, 1990), p. 207.
22. Anthony Crosland, *The Future of Socialism* (London: Jonathan Cape, 1956) which has the heading 'Liberty and Gaiety in Private Life; The Need for a Reaction Against the Fabian Tradition'.
23. Quoted in Susan Crosland, *Tony Crosland* (London: Jonathan Cape, 1982), p. 58.
24. Quoted in Kevin Jeffreys, *Anthony Crosland* (London: Richard Cohen Books, 1999), p. 51.
25. Alan Watkins, *Brief Lives* (London: Hamish Hamilton, 1982), p. 33.
26. Lord Lipsey interviewed by Ben Wright, December 2011.
27. Quoted in Jeffreys, *Anthony Crosland*, p. 93.
28. Joe Haines interviewed by Ben Wright, June 2011.
29. Roy Jenkins, *A Life at the Centre* (London: Macmillan, 1991), p. 225.
30. Alastair Campbell, *Diaries, Volume 1: Prelude to Power 1994–97* (London: Hutchinson, 2010), p. 112.
31. Sir Menzies Campbell interviewed by Ben Wright, December 2011.
32. Jenkins, *A Life at the Centre*, p. 245.
33. David Cannadine, in *Roy Jenkins: A Retrospective*, ed. Andrew Adonis and Keith Thomas (Oxford: OUP, 2004), p. 271.

34. Alan Watkins, in *Roy Jenkins: A Retrospective*, p. 33.
35. Lord Armstrong interviewed by Ben Wright, June 2011.
36. Peter Hennessy, *The Hidden Wiring* (London: Victor Gollancz, 1995), p. 173.
37. Andy Beckett, *When the Lights Went Out* (London: Faber and Faber, 2009), p. 165.
38. Lord Armstrong interviewed by Ben Wright, June 2011.
39. Ibid.
40. Lord Lipsey interviewed by Ben Wright, December 2011.
41. Quoted in Peter Paterson, *Tired and Emotional: The Life of George Brown* (London: Chatto & Windus, 1993), p. 151.
42. Richard Crossman, *Backbench Diaries*, ed. Janet Morgan (London: Hamish Hamilton and Jonathan Cape, 1981), p. 1041.
43. *The Observer*, 8 December 1963.
44. Letters quoted in Patterson, *Tired and Emotional*, p. 159.
45. Lord Armstrong interviewed by Ben Wright, June 2011.
46. Geoffrey Goodman interviewed by Ben Wright, December 2011.
47. Paterson, *Tired and Emotional*, p. 214.
48. Ibid., p. 196.
49. Ibid., p. 216.
50. Denis Healey interviewed on *The Westminster Hour*, BBC Radio 4, 7 April 2002.
51. *Daily Mirror*, 4 October 1967, p. 1.
52. George Brown interview on BBC, 4 October 1967.
53. Joe Haines interviewed by Ben Wright, June 2011.
54. *The Times*, 4 March 1976, p. 15.
55. Bernard Ingham interviewed by Ben Wright, December 2011.
56. Lord Armstrong interviewed by Ben Wright, June 2011.
57. *The Times*, 10 June 1993.
58. Ion Trewin, *Alan Clark: The Biography* (London: Weidenfeld & Nicholson, 2009), p. 245.
59. Alan Clark, *Diaries: In Power 1983–1992* (London: Phoenix, 1993), p. 30.
60. Ibid.
61. Ibid., p. 31.
62. Matthew Parris, *Chance Witness: An Outsider's Life in Politics* (London: Viking, 2002), p. 297.
63. Trewin, *Alan Clark: The Biography*, p. 268.

**64.** Ibid.
**65.** Ibid., p. 269.
**66.** Tony Blair, *A Journey* (London: Hutchinson, 2010), p. 37.
**67.** Ibid., p. 38.

## Chapter 2: Parliament: Drinks on the House?

1. Julian Critchley, *Westminster Blues* (London: Elm Tree, 1985), p. 79.
2. *The House of Commons Refreshment factsheet G19*, p. 2.
3. Nathaniel Hawthorne, *The English Notebooks 1853–1856*, ed. Thomas Woodson and Bill Ellis (Columbus: Ohio State University Press, 1997), p. 487.
4. Charles T. King, *The Asquith Parliament (1906–09)* (Hutchinson and Co., 1910), p. 82.
5. Ibid., p. 92.
6. Julian Critchley, *Palace of Varieties* (London: John Murray, 1989), p. 33.
7. Quoted in the *Daily Telegraph*, 20 April 2015.
8. A.P. Herbert, *Independent Member* (London: Methuen, 1950), p. 38.
9. Bernard Levin, *The Times*, 9 April 1981.
10. 'Catering Services: Costs to the House of Commons 2014–15'. Document available at www.parliament.uk
11. 'Alcohol spending – 2014'. Document available at www.parliament.uk
12. 'Alcoholic drinks – stock (2014)'. Document available at www.parliament.uk
13. 'Alcoholic drinks – 2013'. Document available at www.parliament.uk
14. *Manchester Guardian*, 16 June 1947. Cited in *Double Measures: The Guardian Book of Drinking*, ed. Richard Nelson (London: Guardian Books), p. 128.
15. Colin Brown interviewed by Ben Wright, January 2012.
16. Michael Brown interviewed by Ben Wright, November 2011.
17. Quoted in John Campbell, *Nye Bevan and the Mirage of British Socialism* (London: Weidenfeld & Nicholson, 1987), p. 64.

18. Michael Brown interviewed by Ben Wright, November 2011.
19. David Davis MP interviewed by Ben Wright, December 2012.
20. Critchley, *Westminster Blues*, p. 29.
21. *First Report into Catering and Retail Services in the House of Commons*, 10 May 2011.
22. *House of Commons Information Office: The House of Commons Refreshment Department, Factsheet G19*, October 2010.
23. Chris Moncrieff interviewed by Ben Wright, April 2011.
24. Michael Skelton interviewed by Ben Wright, November 2011.
25. Chris Moncrieff interviewed by Ben Wright, April 2011.
26. Paul Flynn MP interviewed by Ben Wright, October 2011.
27. Lord Grocott interviewed by Ben Wright, December 2011.
28. Simon Hoggart, *New Humanist*, Vol. 118, Issue 1, 2003.
29. Geoffrey Goodman interviewed by Ben Wright, December 2011.
30. Chris Moncrieff interviewed by Ben Wright, April 2011.
31. Paul Seaward, 'The House of Commons since 1949', in *A Short History of Parliament*, ed. Clyve Jones (Woodbridge: The Boydell Press, 2009), p. 290.
32. Lord Lipsey interviewed by Ben Wright, December 2011.
33. Simon Hoggart, *New Humanist*, 2003.
34. Margaret Thatcher, *The Downing Street Years* (London: HarperCollins, 1993), p. 3.
35. Matthew Parris, *Chance Witness: An Outsider's Life in Politics* (London: Viking, 2002), p. 237.
36. Lord Norton blog, 7 July 2009.
37. Ian Aitken, *New Statesman*, 4 December 1998.
38. Ian Hernon, recollections of Annie's Bar written to Ben Wright, October 2015.
39. Chris Moncrieff interviewed by Ben Wright, April 2011.
40. Ian Hernon, written recollections of Annie's Bar.
41. Chris Moncrieff interviewed by Ben Wright, April 2011.
42. Colin Brown interviewed by Ben Wright, January 2012.
43. Chris Moncrieff interviewed by Ben Wright, April 2011.
44. Andrew Marr, *My Trade* (London: Macmillan, 2004), p. 122.
45. *The Herald*, 10 May 2015.
46. Michael Boch, *Jeremy Thorpe* (London: Abacus, 2014), p. 154.
47. Michael Skelton interviewed by Ben Wright, November 2011.
48. Sadie Smith interviewed by Ben Wright, December 2012.

Lord Strathclyde interviewed by Ben Wright, February 2015.

Samuel Pepys, *Diary, Volume 2* (London: J.M. Dent and Sons, 1924), p. 154.

. Anthony Trollope, *The Way We Live Now, Volume 2* (Oxford: OUP, 1982), p. 318.

. Michael MacDonagh, *Parliament: Its Romance, Its Comedy, Its Pathos* (P.S. King & Son, 1902), p. 119.

3. An 1829 article for the *New Monthly Magazine*, reprinted in R.L. Sheil, *Sketches, Legal and Political*, ed. M.W. Savage (1855), pp. 183–6.

4. Philip Salmon, 'The House of Commons, 1801–1911', in *A Short History of Parliament*, p. 259.

55. Quoted in *The Literary Companion to Parliament*, ed. Christopher Silvester (London: Sinclair-Stevenson, 1998), p. 472.

56. Roy Jenkins, *Churchill* (London: Macmillan, 2001), p. 582.

57. Fenner Brockway, *Inside the Left* (London: George Allen & Unwin, 1942), p. 221.

58. Ibid., p. 222.

59. Henry Fairlie, *The Life of Politics* (London: Methuen, 1968), p. 39.

60. Quoted by Matthew Laban in *Total Politics*, April 2013.

61. Frank Johnson, *Out of Order* (London: Robson Books, 1982), p. 58.

62. Lord Owen interviewed by Ben Wright, June 2011.

63. Ibid.

64. Michael Brown interviewed by Ben Wright, November 2011.

65. Ibid.

66. *The Independent*, 2 April 1988.

67. John Prescott with Hunter Davies, *Prezza: My Story – Pulling No Punches* (London: Headline Review, 2008), p. 108.

68. John Biffen, *Inside Parliament* (London: Andre Deutsch, 1996), p. 147.

69. *The Times*, 3 May 2004.

## Chapter 3: Drying Out

1. Harriet Harman MP interviewed by Ben Wright, September 2015.

2. *Sunday Times*, 11 February 2007.

3. Jeremy Paxman, *The Political Animal* (London: Michael Joseph, 2002), p. 239.
4. W.S. Gilbert, *Iolanthe*, Act II (Chappell & Co., 1882), p. 24.
5. Jenkins, *A Life at the Centre*, p. 618.
6. *The Times*, 29 August 2006.
7. Menzies Campbell, *My Autobiography* (London: Hodder & Stoughton, 2008), p. 205.
8. Ibid., p. 215.
9. Sir Menzies Campbell interviewed by Ben Wright, December 2011.
10. *Guardian*, 2 June 2015.
11. *Mail on Sunday*, 11 July 2010.
12. BBC News Online, 11 July 2010.
13. Paul Flynn MP interviewed by Ben Wright, November 2011.
14. Eric Joyce interviewed by Ben Wright, December 2012.
15. Parris, *Chance Witness*, pp. 251–2.
16. Anonymous MP interviewed by Ben Wright, January 2015.
17. *Daily Telegraph*, 5 October 2011.
18. Sir Menzies Campbell interviewed by Ben Wright, December 2011.
19. Michael White interviewed by Ben Wright, December 2011.
20. Harriet Harman MP interviewed by Ben Wright, September 2015.
21. Ibid.
22. *The Financial Times*, 30 June 2016.
23. Lord Lipsey interviewed by Ben Wright, December 2011.
24. Nick Clegg MP interviewed by Ben Wright, November 2015.
25. Boris Johnson MP interviewed by Ben Wright, November 2015.

## Chapter 4: Prime Ministers: Tipplers at Number 10

1. Harold Macmillan, *Diaries, Volume 2, Prime Minister and After 1957–1966*, ed. Peter Catterall (London: Macmillan, 2011), p. 466.
2. J.H. Plumb, 'Sir Robert Walpole's Wine', in *Men and Places* (The Cresset Press, 1963), p. 147.
3. Ibid., p. 148.

4. William Hague, *William Pitt the Younger* (London: HarperCollins, 2004), p. 26.
5. Ibid., p. 221.
6. Charles Ludington, "'Claret is the liquor for boys, port for men": How Port Became the "Englishman's Wine", 1750s to 1800', *Journal of British Studies*, Vol. 48, No. 2 (April 2009).
7. Lord Rosebery, *Pitt* (Macmillan and Co., 1891), p. 267.
8. Hague, *William Pitt the Younger*, p. 308.
9. Michael J. Turner, *Pitt the Younger: A Life* (Hambledon and London: Continuum, 2003), p. 144.
10. Ibid., p. 272.
11. Quoted in Hague, *William Pitt the Younger*, p. 535.
12. Ibid., p. 576.
13. Quoted in *The Prime Ministers: Stories and anecdotes from Number 10*, ed. William Douglas Home (London: W.H. Allen, 1987), p. 74.
14. Stephen Koss, *Asquith* (London: Allen Lane, 1976), p. 16.
15. H.C.G. Matthew, *Oxford Dictionary of National Biography*.
16. Quoted by Alan Watkins, *Independent on Sunday*, 28 March 2004.
17. Quoted in Koss, *Asquith*, p. 139.
18. Colin Clifford, *The Asquiths* (London: John Murray, 2002), pp. 192–3.
19. R.B. McCallum, *Asquith* (Duckworth, 1936), p. 34.
20. W.S. Churchill, 'H.H. Asquith', in *Great Contemporaries* (Thornton Butterworth, 1937), p. 137.
21. Quoted in Koss, *Asquith*, p. 187.
22. Roy Jenkins, *Asquith* (London and Glasgow: Collins, 1964), p. 412.
23. Quoted in Koss, *Asquith*, p. 210.
24. *The Times*, 1 March 1915.
25. Jenkins, *Churchill*, p. 268.
26. Cita Stelzer, *Dinner with Churchill* (London: Short Books, 2011), p. xiv.
27. Quentin Reynolds, *By Quentin Reynolds* (London: Heinemann, 1964), p. 205.
28. *The Oxford Dictionary of Phrase, Saying and Quotation*, ed. Elizabeth Knowles (Oxford: OUP, 1997), p. 228.

29. Stelzer, *Dinner with Churchill*, p. 182.
30. Jenkins, *Churchill*, p. 466.
31. General Sir Ian Jacob, *Action this Day: Working with Churchill* (London: Macmillan, 1968), p. 183.
32. Stelzer, *Dinner with Churchill*, p. 182.
33. Norman McGowan, *My Years with Churchill* (London: Souvenir Press, 1968), p. 88.
34. Jenkins, *Churchill*, p. 356.
35. Sir John Colville, *Fringes of Power* (London: Hodder & Stoughton, 1985), p. 510.
36. National Archives, FO 1093/247.
37. Sir Alexander Cadogan, *Diaries*, ed. David Dilks (London: Cassell, 1971), p. 707.
38. Stelzer, *Dinner with Churchill*, p. 121.
39. Michael Dobbs interviewed by Ben Wright, December 2011.
40. David Owen, *Sickness and Power* (London: Methuen, 2008), p. 40.
41. Martin Gilbert, *In Search of Churchill* (London: HarperCollins, 1995), p. 209.
42. Stelzer, *Dinner with Churchill*, p. 181.
43. Ibid., p. 184.
44. Ibid., p. 186.
45. Violet Bonham Carter, *Daring to Hope* (London: Weidenfeld & Nicolson, 2000), p. 137.
46. *Daily Express* interview, 8 November 1962. Quoted in Ben Pimlott, *Harold Wilson* (London: HarperCollins, 1992), p. 267.
47. Pimlott, *Harold Wilson*, p. 266.
48. Quoted in Philip Ziegler, *Wilson* (London: Weidenfeld & Nicholson, 1993), p. 166.
49. Ibid.
50. Anthony Shrimsley, *The First Hundred Days of Harold Wilson* (London: Weidenfeld & Nicolson, 1965), p. 32.
51. Joe Haines interviewed by Ben Wright, June 2011.
52. Blair, *A Journey*, p. 109.
53. Ziegler, *Wilson*, p. 470.
54. Lord Donoughue interviewed by Ben Wright, October 2011.
55. Bernard Donoughue, *Downing Street Diary. With Harold Wilson in Number 10* (London: Jonathan Cape, 2005), p. 152.

56. Joe Haines interviewed by Ben Wright, June 2011.
57. Ziegler. *Wilson*, p. 471.
58. Michael White interviewed by Ben Wright, December 2011.
59. Lord Donoughue interviewed by Ben Wright, October 2011.
60. Joe Haines interviewed by Ben Wright, June 2011.
61. Lord Armstrong interviewed by Ben Wright, June 2011.
62. Bernard Ingham interviewed by Ben Wright, December 2011.
63. *Daily Mail*, 30 January 2010.
64. Nicholas Henderson, *Mandarin: The Diaries of an Ambassador 1969–1982* (London: Weidenfeld & Nicolson, 1995).
65. Michael Brown interviewed by Ben Wright, November 2011.
66. Quoted in Brenda Maddox, *Maggie: The First Lady* (London: Hodder & Stoughton, 2003), p. 140.
67. Ibid., p. 152.
68. Lord Armstrong interviewed by Ben Wright, June 2011.
69. Carol Thatcher, *Below the Parapet: The Biography of Denis Thatcher* (London: HarperCollins, 1996), p. 139.
70. Bernard Ingham interviewed by Ben Wright, December 2011.
71. Michael Dobbs interviewed by Ben Wright, December 2011.
72. Thatcher, *Below the Parapet*, p. 127.
73. Ibid., p. 148.
74. Ibid.
75. Chris Moncrieff interviewed by Ben Wright, April 2011.
76. Blair, *A Journey*, p. 621.
77. Ibid., p. 622.
78. Alastair Campbell interviewed by Ben Wright, February 2012.
79. Blair, *A Journey*, p. 622.
80. Damian McBride interviewed by Ben Wright, September 2015.
81. Ibid.
82. Ibid.
83. Conversation between David Cameron and Ben Wright, December 2013.
84. David Cameron on the *Andrew Marr Show*, BBC, 10 January 2016.
85. Max Chambers interview in the *Evening Standard*, 1 December 2016.

## Chapter 5: Pubs, Clubs and Parties

1. Nigel Farage interviewed by Ben Wright, September 2015.
2. Damian McBride, *Power Trip: A Decade of Policy, Plots and Spin* (London: Biteback Publishing, 2013), p. 50.
3. Damian McBride interviewed by Ben Wright, September 2015.
4. Charlie Whelan interviewed by Ben Wright, April 2013.
5. Ibid.
6. Harry Cole interviewed by Ben Wright, September 2014.
7. Damian McBride interviewed by Ben Wright, September 2015.
8. Alan Watkins in *Roy Jenkins: A Retrospective*, p. 34. Watkins describes a lunch with Roy Jenkins at L'Epicure in 1959. On this occasion Jenkins ordered an avocado pear to start, at the time a rather exotic dish. Jenkins sent it back saying it had seen better days.
9. Edward Pierce, *The Lost Leaders* (London: Little, Brown, 1997), p. 128.
10. Peter Oborne interviewed by Ben Wright, July 2014.
11. Kevin Maguire interviewed by Ben Wright, October 2013.
12. Peter Oborne interviewed by Ben Wright, July 2014.
13. Michael White interviewed by Ben Wright, December 2011.
14. Marr, *My Trade*, p. 179.
15. Jon Sopel interviewed by Ben Wright, August 2014.
16. Ibid.
17. Peter Oborne interviewed by Ben Wright, July 2014.
18. Kenneth Clarke speaking to BBC Radio 4's *Today* programme, 4 January 2014.
19. Sir Menzies Campbell speaking to BBC Radio 4's *Today* programme, 4 January 2014.
20. Baroness Williams interviewed by Ben Wright, October 2013.
21. Tom Watson MP interviewed by Ben Wright, October 2013.
22. Kevin Maguire interviewed by Ben Wright, October 2013.
23. Harriet Harman MP interviewed by Ben Wright, September 2015.
24. Peter Oborne interviewed by Ben Wright, July 2014.
25. Jonathan Rose, *The Intellectual Life of the British Working Classes* (New Haven and London: Yale University Press, 2001), p. 79.
26. Ian Lavery MP interviewed by Ben Wright, February 2015.
27. Kevan Jones MP interviewed by Ben Wright, February 2015.

28. Rob Phillips, *Alcohol: A History* (Chapel Hill: The University of North Carolina Press, 2014), p. 92.
29. BBC News, 27 June 2010.
30. *Daily Telegraph*, 23 July 2010.
31. Ian Lavery MP interviewed by Ben Wright, February 2015.
32. Oliver Heath writing on the LSE blog, 11 February 2015.
33. *Brooks's: A Social History*, ed. Philip Ziegler and Desmond Seward (London: Constable, 1991), p. 45.
34. Amy Milne-Smith, *London Clubland: A Cultural History of Gender and Class in Late Victorian Britain* (New York: Palgrave Macmillan, 2011), p. 94.
35. *Brooks's: A Social History,* p. 77.
36. Sir Charles Petrie and Alistair Cooke, *The Carlton Club 1832–2007* (London: The Carlton Club, 2007), p. 234.
37. Ibid., p. 189.
38. Barry Phelps, *Power and the Party: A History of the Carlton Club 1832–1982* (London; Macmillan, 1983), p. 78.
39. Petrie and Cooke, *The Carlton Club 1832–2007*, p. 209.
40. Phelps, *Power and the Party*, p. 79.
41. Lord Strathclyde interviewed by Ben Wright, February 2015.
42. Jeremy Paxman, *The Political Animal: An Anatomy* (Harmondsworth: Penguin, 2003), p. 146.
43. Critchley, *Westminster Blues*, p. 89.
44. 'Can UK political parties be saved from extinction?', BBC News Online, 19 August 2011.
45. Lord Donoughue interviewed by Ben Wright, October 2011.
46. Damian McBride interviewed by Ben Wright, September 2015.
47. Lord Strathclyde interviewed by Ben Wright, February 2015.

## Chapter 6: Cocktails and Congress: Political Drinking in the United States

1. Kristen D. Burton, '"A Toast to Your Health": Getting Drunk in Colonial America', The Appendix, 25 February 2013.
2. W.J. Rorabaugh, *The Alcoholic Republic: An American Tradition* (New York: Oxford University Press, 1979), p. 21.
3. Ibid., p. 34.

4. Ibid., p. 20.
5. Daniel Okrent, *Last Call: The Rise and Fall of Prohibition* (New York: Scribner, 2010), p. 47.
6. Rorabaugh, *The Alcoholic Republic*, p. 154.
7. Sharon V. Salinger, *Taverns and Drinking in Early America* (Baltimore: The Johns Hopkins University Press, 2002), p. 3.
8. John Quincy Adams, *Diary, 1794–1845*, ed. Allan Nevins (New York: Charles Scribner's Sons, 1951), p. 47.
9. Thomas Jefferson to John F. Oliveira Fernandes, 16 December 1815, Founders Online, National Archives.
10. *A Benjamin Franklin Reader*, ed. and annotated by Walter Isaacson (New York: Simon & Schuster, 2003), p. 108.
11. *Oxford Companion to Beer*, ed. Garrett Oliver (Oxford: OUP, 2012), p. 111.
12. Printed in the *Claremont Review of Books*, Vol. II, No. 3 (Spring 2002).
13. Rorabaugh, *The Alcoholic Republic*, p. 41.
14. William S. McFeely, *Grant* (New York: W.W. Norton & Co., 1981), p. 55.
15. Geoffrey Perret, *Ulysses S. Grant: Soldier and President* (New York: Random House, 1997), p. 262.
16. Rick Beard, 'General Grant Takes a Spill', quoted in the *New York Times*, 4 September 2013.
17. *Oxford Dictionary of Political Quotations*, ed. Anthony Jay (Oxford: OUP, 2001), p. 331.
18. Okrent, *Last Call*, p. 130.
19. Ibid., p. 129.
20. Quoted in Garrett Peck, *Prohibition in Washington D.C.* (Charleston, South Carolina: The History Press, 2011), p. 122.
21. Quoted in Peck, *Prohibition in Washington D.C.*, p. 125.
22. Quoted ibid., p. 96.
23. George Rothwell Brown, *Washington: A Not Too Serious History* (Norman Publ. Co., 1930).
24. Donald Trump interviewed by Harvey Levin for 'OBJECTified: Donald Trump', broadcast on the Fox News Channel, 18 November 2016.
25. Edward M. Kennedy, *True Compass* (London: Little, Brown, 2009), p. 360.

26. Samuel I. Rosenman, *Working with Roosevelt* (London: Rupert Hart-Davis, 1952), p. 147.
27. Robert H. Jackson, *That Man: An Insider's Portrait of Franklin D. Roosevelt* (Oxford: OUP, 2003), p. 137.
28. Elliott Roosevelt, *As He Saw It* (New York: Duell, Sloan & Pearce, 1946), pp. 34, 68, 99, 119, 183, 186.
29. Elliott Roosevelt and James Brough, *A Rendezvous with Destiny: The Roosevelts of the White House* (London: W.H. Allen, 1977), p. 306.
30. Robert A. Caro, *Master of the Senate* (New York: Alfred A. Knopf, 2002), p. 336.
31. Ibid., p. 653.
32. Ibid.
33. Joseph A. Califano Jr, *The Triumph and Tragedy of Lyndon Johnson* (New York: Simon & Schuster, 1991), p. 21.
34. Don Fulsom, *Nixon's Darkest Secrets* (New York: St Martin's Press, 2012), p. 187.
35. Ibid., p. 195.
36. John Ehrlichman, *Witness to Power: The Nixon Years* (New York: Simon & Schuster, 1982).
37. An interview Nixon gave to Theodore White in January 1969. Quoted in Anthony Summers, *The Arrogance of Power* (London: Viking, 2000), p. 316.
38. H.R. Haldeman and Joseph DiMona, *The Ends of Power* (New York: Times Books, 1978), p. 45.
39. Henry Kissinger, *Years of Renewal* (London: Weidenfeld & Nicolson, 1999), p. 55.
40. Ibid.
41. Walter Isaacson, *Kissinger* (London: Faber & Faber, 1992), p. 263.
42. Summers, *The Arrogance of Power*, p. 372.
43. Quoted ibid., p. 462.
44. Bob Woodward and Carl Bernstein, *The Final Days* (London: Secker & Warburg, 1976), p. 395.
45. Mark Leibovich, *This Town* (New York: Blue Rider Press, 2013), p. 46.
46. Tip O'Neill, *Man of the House* (New York: St Martin's Press, 1987), p. 148.

47. Donald Ritchie interviewed by Ben Wright, January 2013.
48. Haley Barbour interviewed by Ben Wright, June 2013.
49. Reprinted in *The Clarion Ledger*, Jackson, Mississippi, 24 February 1996, p. 3B.

## Chapter 7: From Canberra to the Kremlin

1. *Guardian*, 4 October 2009.
2. Bob Hawke, *The Hawke Memoirs* (London: Heinemann, 1994), p. 28.
3. *Time*, 24 March 2009.
4. Transcript of Australian Broadcasting Corporation obituary, 20 May 2002.
5. Barry Gustafson, *His Way: A Biography of Robert Muldoon* (Auckland University Press, 2002), p. 372.
6. Ibid., p. 375.
7. William Pokhlebkin, *A History of Vodka* (Verso, 1992), p. 86.
8. *New Yorker*, 16 December 2002.
9. Patricia Herlihy, *The Alcoholic Empire* (Oxford: OUP, 2002), p. 5.
10. Jasper Ridley, *Tito* (London: Constable, 1994), p. 328.
11. Jack Fishman and J. Bernard Hutton, *The Private Life of Josif Stalin* (London: W.H. Allen, 1962), p. 117.
12. Simon Sebag Montefiore, *Stalin: The Court of the Red Tsar* (New York: Vintage,, 2005), p. 313.
13. Ibid., p. 478.
14. Ibid., p. 520.
15. Ibid., p. 531.
16. Herlihy, *The Alcoholic Empire*, p. 160.
17. Mikhail Gorbachev quoted in the *New Yorker*, 16 December 2002.
18. Timothy J. Colton, *Yeltsin: A Life* (New York: Basic Books, 2008), p. 310.
19. Taylor Branch, *The Clinton Tapes: Wrestling History with the President* (New York: Simon & Schuster, 2009), p. 198.
20. Max Hastings, *Editor: An Inside Story of Newspapers* (London: Macmillan, 2002), p. 205.

21. Colton, *Yeltsin: A Life*, p. 313.
22. Quoted in *Diplomat* magazine, July 2012.
23. *Foreign Policy Magazine*, 4 March 2013.
24. Roosevelt, *As He Saw It*, p. 187.
25. Edward R. Stettinius Jr, *Roosevelt and the Russians: The Yalta Conference* (New York: Doubleday and Co., 1949), p. 111.
26. Michael Dobbs, *Six Months in 1945* (London: Hutchinson, 2012), p. 74.
27. Margaret MacMillan, 'Don't Drink the Mao-Tai', *Washingtonian Magazine*, 1 February 2007.
28. Richard Holbrooke, *To End a War* (London: Random House, 1998), p. 114.
29. Roger Cohen, *The Unquiet American: Richard Holbrooke in the World*, ed. Samantha Power and Derek H. Chollet (Public Affairs, 2011), p. 164.
30. *The Guardian*, 12 December 2010.
31. Jack Straw interviewed by Ben Wright, December 2012.
32. Paul Flynn, *The Unusual Suspect* (London: Biteback, 2010), pp. 246–7.
33. Harold Nicolson, 'Diplomacy Then and Now', *Foreign Affairs*, October 1961.
34. Nigel Farage interviewed by Ben Wright, September 2015.
35. John Campbell, *Roy Jenkins: A Well-Rounded Life* (London: Jonathan Cape, 2014), p. 517.
36. Geoff Meade interviewed by Ben Wright, September 2015.
37. Reuters, 1 July 2014.
38. Jean-Claude Juncker speaking to German TV channel ZDF, quoted in *Luxemburger Wort*, 4 February 2014.

## Chapter 8: Time, Gentlemen!

1. James Nicholls, *The Politics of Alcohol* (Manchester: Manchester University Press, 2009), p. 11.
2. Mark Spivak, *Iconic Spirits: An Intoxicating History* (Lyons Press).
3. Nicholls, *The Politics of Alcohol*, p. 36.
4. Ibid., p. 37.

5. Ibid., p. 37.
6. Jenny Uglow, *Hogarth: A Life and a World* (London: Faber & Faber, 1997), p. 494.
7. Charles Dickens, *Sketches by Boz* (London: Chapman & Hall, 1839), p. 198.
8. Nicholls, *The Politics of Alcohol*, p. 92.
9. Ibid., p. 111.
10. Ibid., p. 119.
11. The Law Commission, *Legal Curiosities: Fact or Fable?*, March 2013.
12. Luci Gosling, 'Trouble Brewing: Asquith's Licensing Bill', *History Today*, Vol. 58, No. 3 (March 2008).
13. Quoted in the *Publican*, 15 December 2008.
14. *Olympic Britain: Social and Economic change since the 1908 and 1948 London Games*, House of Commons Library.
15. Phillips, *Alcohol: A History*, p. 288.
16. Nicholls, *The Politics of Alcohol*, p. 207.
17. Ibid., p. 226.
18. National Statistics Authority, 2015 alcohol use figures.
19. Organisation for Economic Co-operation and Development (OECD) Health Data 2012.
20. Nicholls, *The Politics of Alcohol*, p. 254.
21. Office for National Statistics, *Alcohol-related Deaths in the United Kingdom, Registered in 2012*, 19 February 2014.
22. Office for National Statistics, *Adult Drinking Habits in Great Britain 2013*.
23. House of Commons Health Select Committee, *Alcohol Report*, 8 January 2010.
24. Andrew Lansley interviewed by Ben Wright, December 2014.
25. Dr Nick Sheron interviewed by Ben Wright, February 2015.

## Epilogue: Last Orders?

1. Chris Bryant: *Parliament: The Biography, Volume 2: Reform* (London: Black Swan, 2015), p. 306.
2. John Sutherland, *Last Drink to LA* (London: Short Books, 2001), p. 34.

# Notes

3. John Timbs, *Clubs and Club Life in London* (Chatto & Windus, 1872), p. 19.
4. Kingsley Amis, *Everyday Drinking* (London: Bloomsbury, 2008), p. 3.

# INDEX

# Index

# Index

354

# Index

# Index

Also published by Duckwo

## THE SENECANS

PETER STOTHARD

'Margaret Thatcher and Emperor Nero, two courts across two thou
sand years. A brilliant, haunting work from
a modern master of memoir'
Mary Beard

'An artful blend of fact and fiction... poetically written,
supremely stylish'
*Guardian*

A year after the death of Margaret Thatcher, a young woman arrives
to ask Peter Stothard, former Editor of *The Times*, some sharp
questions about his memories of the Thatcher era. During her
interview the offices from where he long observed British politics
are being flattened by wrecking balls. Forgotten stories return.
From the destruction of a collapsing newspaper plant emerge vivid
portraits of the Senecans: the Hollywood screen-writer who wrote
her speeches, the socialite former socialist who comforted her with
flattery, the comic political columnist whom she admired but rarely
read and the multi-millionaire film-producer whom she consulted
but never acknowledged.

The Senecans took their name from their taste for the work of Lucius
Annaeus Seneca, a philosopher, courtier and acquirer of massive
wealth from the age of the Emperor Nero. Blending memoir with
ancient and modern politics in the manner of his acclaimed diaries,
*On the Spartacus Road* and *Alexandria*, Stothard sheds a sideways
light on recent history. In finally identifying his interviewer he also
answers questions about his own literary and political journey.

Hardback, ISBN 9780715651377
£20

## ANGELA MERKEL

### MATTHEW QVORTRUP

...ds sometimes like an Icelandic saga... a complex life, full of little and greater mysteries'
*The Times*

'Affectionate and detailed... reveals a leader of real inter-personal skill and no small personal courage'
*Herald*

Expanded and updated to include recent events – notably Brexit and Donald Trump's election to the US Presidency – Matthew Qvortrup's definitive and riveting Angela Merkel is essential reading for anyone interested in current affairs, the fate of Europe, or simply the story of a truly remarkable woman.

In 2015 *Time* named Angela Merkel their 'Person of the Year', and there is little doubt that the woman who has been in control of the European Union and successfully negotiated with Vladimir Putin is widely regarded as the most crucial and formidable fixture in contemporary politics. Based on more than 12 years of in-depth research, Angela Merkel tells the story of the political titan's astonishing rise from obscurity to become the most influential leader in Europe today. It follows the German Chancellor's journey to prominence and power from a bleak childhood in East Germany, and offers an unprecedented insight into her inimitable personality and perspective, explaining how her unique qualities have made Merkel perhaps the most respected political figure on the world stage today.

Paperback, ISBN 9780715651827
£12.99

## BUFFET: THE BIOGRA

ROGER LOWENSTEIN

'Other books have been written about Warren Buffett a
his investment strategy... this is the one to read'
Bill Gates

Starting from scratch, simply by picking stocks and companies
for investment, Warren Buffett amassed an astonishing fortune –
a net worth of $64 billion and counting. His awesome investment
record has made him a cult figure popularly known for his seeming
contradictions: a billionaire with a modest lifestyle, a phenomenally
successful investor who eschews the revolving-door trading
of modern Wall Street, a brilliant dealmaker who cultivates a
homespun aura.

Journalist Roger Lowenstein draws on three years of unprecedented
access to Buffett's family, friends and colleagues to provide this
definitive inside account of the life and career of this American
original. He explains Buffett's investment strategy – a long-
term philosophy grounded in buying stock in companies that
are undervalued on the market and hanging on until their worth
invariably surfaces – and shows how it is a reflection of the character
of the man himself. In a brand new afterword, in the wake of the
news that Buffett has decided to give the bulk of his fortune to
the Bill and Melinda Gates foundation, Lowenstein reflects on the
largest charitable donation in American history.

Paperback, ISBN 9780715638309
£12.99